THE INTERNATIONAL CRIMINAL COURT AND NATIONAL JURISDICTIONS

This book has been published with a financial contribution from the Department of Legal Sciences of the University of Trento and the Italian Ministry of the University and Scientific Research, in the framework of the interuniversity research COFIN 2004 – The International Criminal Court and the Relationship with National Jurisdictions: Complementarity and Cooperation.

The International Criminal Court and National Jurisdictions

Edited by

MAURO POLITI and FEDERICA GIOIA

Routledge
Taylor & Francis Group
LONDON AND NEW YORK

First published 2008 by Ashgate Publishing

2 Park Square, Milton Park, Abingdon, Oxon OX14 4RN
711 Third Avenue, New York, NY 10017, USA

Routledge is an imprint of the Taylor & Francis Group, an informa business

First issued in paperback 2016

British Library Cataloguing in Publication Data
The International Criminal Court and national jurisdictions
1. International Criminal Court – Congresses 2. Criminal jurisdiction – International cooperation – Congresses
3. Criminal procedure (International law) – Congresses
I. Politi, Mauro II. Gioia, Federica
345'.01

Library of Congress Cataloging-in-Publication Data
The International Criminal Court and national jurisdictions / by Mauro Politi and Federica Gioia (editors).
p. cm.
Includes index.
ISBN 978-0-7546-7436-8
1. International Criminal Court--Congresses. 2. Criminal jurisdiction--International cooperation--Congresses. 3. Criminal procedure (International law)--Congresses. I. Politi, Mauro. II. Gioia, Federica.

KZ6310.I57795 2008
345'.01--dc22

2008003562

ISBN 978-0-7546-7436-8 (hbk)
ISBN 978-1-138-25419-0 (pbk)

Contents

PART III RECENT DEVELOPMENTS ON INTERNATIONAL COOPERATION AND NATIONAL IMPLEMENTATION

PART IV ROUND TABLE THE ICC RELATIONSHIP WITH NATIONAL JURISDICTIONS: WHAT FUTURE?

Editors' Preface

There may be some debate as to when a recurrent event ceases to be a series of independent events and becomes a tradition. Some may incline to deem it a matter of quantity, others may think it rather a matter of quality. Be that as it may, it is our view that the international colloquia organized by the Faculty of Law of the University of Trento on issues of international criminal law may be rightfully considered as a tradition, irrespective of the approach chosen. Following the successful events taking place in 1999 and 2001, respectively devoted to the 'The Rome Statute of the International Criminal Court – A Challenge to Impunity'[1] and 'The International Criminal Court and the Crime of Aggression',[2] also resulting in the publication of proceedings, this volume collects the contributions presented at or upon the occasion of the Colloquium on 'The International Criminal Court and National Jurisdictions', held in Trento on 4 and 5 May 2007 within the context of a research project financed by the Italian Ministry of University and Scientific Research. Like the two preceding events, the Colloquium saw the participation of a significant number of those who are regarded as leading experts on issues of international criminal law in general and the International Criminal Court in particular. The opening remarks by Philippe Kirsch, President of the ICC, and Ivo Maria Braguglia, Head of the Legal Department of the Italian Ministry of Foreign Affairs, offered a precious insight respectively into the activities of the Court and the role of a State Party in establishing and sustaining the latter. Unlike its predecessors, this latter gathering was also able to benefit from the knowledge of the first steps by the now fully operational International Criminal Court. Hence the 'first assessment' of complementarity presented by Pierre-Marie Dupuy, William Schabas and Giorgio Gaja under the chair of Mauro Politi. Luigi Ferrari Bravo and Fausto Pocar skilfully chaired panels respectively addressing issues going to the heart of the substantive and procedural law of the International Criminal Court, some of which had so far failed to reach the limelight (with contributions by Phani Livada, Edoardo Greppi and Federica Gioia), and recent developments in cooperation, many of which were unexpected (with contributions by Hans-Peter Kaul, Annalisa Ciampi and Håkan Friman and interventions by Maria Chiara Malaguti and Teresa Moschetta). The threads of the debate were all borne in mind by the participants in the round table which closed the event. Roberto Toscano, Fausto Pocar, Håkan Friman and Francesco Francioni, under the direction of Theodor Meron, provided perspectives and thoughts which aptly complemented the discussion. The overall high level of the contributions triggered a lively debate among all participants, in particular following the round table.

---

1 Politi, M. and Nesi, G. (eds) (2001), *The Rome Statute of the International Criminal Court – A Challenge to Impunity* (Aldershot: Ashgate).

2 Politi, M. and Nesi, G. (eds) (2004), 'The International Criminal Court and the Crime of Aggression' (Aldershot: Ashgate).

It is therefore with great pleasure that we present this volume, which contains the proceedings of the Trento Colloquium. Both the Colloquium and the publication were made possible by the support of the Italian Ministry of University and Scientific Research, the Autonomous Province of Trento and the University of Trento, which hosted the meeting. We also wish to express our special thanks to the Director of the Department of Legal Sciences, Luca Nogler, the Law School and its Dean, Roberto Toniatti. Furthermore, we are very grateful for the assistance offered throughout the editing process by Marco Pertile, researcher at the University of Trento and Sévrine Knuchel, research assistant at the International Criminal Court. Last but not least, our gratitude goes to all personnel of the Department of Legal Sciences (in particular, Ornella Bernardi, Carla Boninsegna and Stefano Talassi) for their extraordinary efforts in organizing the Colloquium.

We trust the volume will be a valuable contribution to the ongoing debate on international criminal law and the role of the International Criminal Court.

Mauro Politi – Federica Gioia
The Hague, September 2007

Message (wired) by H.E. Giorgio Napolitano, President of the Republic of Italy[1]

'The international Colloquium organised by the Department of Legal Sciences of the Law Faculty of Trento (Dipartimento di Scienze Giuridiche della Facoltà di Giurisprudenza di Trento) on "The International Criminal Court and its relationship with national jurisdictions", also in the light of its highly respected contributors and participants, marks a significant landmark in the context of the ongoing studies on the mission and objectives of the ICC as a permanent international jurisdictional body, the establishment of which (pursuant to the Rome Statute adopted on 17 July 1998) was worthily promoted and supported by Italy.'

'The very existence of this institution witnesses the increasing engagement of the international community in ensuring and enhancing respect for and effective protection of fundamental human rights, in which the dignity of all human beings is mirrored. Brought into existence with a view in particular to punishing crimes against humanity, the Court is called upon to play a critical role in the establishment of a full-fledged international legal order. Analysing the various issues which have arisen in the last few years will allow a first assessment of the achievements of the ICC, as well as of its relationship with national jurisdictions within the context of the overall development of the various systems of criminal justice, and will result in highlighting new challenging proposals which may lead to further developments in the future.'

'I wish you, Professor Politi, as well as all the participants, a very successful colloquium.'

Rome, 4 May 2007
Giorgio Napolitano
President of the Republic of Italy

1 Translated from the Italian by the editors.

Message (wired) by Mr. Giovanni Conso, President of the Rome Conference[1]

'Whilst unfortunately unable to participate in the important international colloquium taking place in Trento on the International Criminal Court, an institution which is so dear to our hearts, I would nevertheless like to send to all of you, and especially to its great President Philippe Kirsch, my warmest regards and my best wishes.'

Rome, 4 May 2007
Giovanni Conso

1 Translated from the Italian by the editors.

Message by Prof. Daria de Pretis, Acting Dean of the University of Trento[1]

I would like to express my greetings and welcome to all of the participants in this colloquium organized by our colleague Mauro Politi, full Professor in this University, currently serving as a judge of the International Criminal Court, with the assistance and support of other colleagues, namely Professors Antonino Alí and Alessandro Fodella and Dr. Marco Pertile, whom I would like to thank also on behalf of the Faculty.

I would like to highlight first of all that this initiative was strongly supported by the Faculty of Law, the Department of Legal Sciences and the University of Trento as a whole. The international dimension is and has always been crucial for our University, given its particular interest in issues of international law, human rights and humanitarian law, all of which feature prominently in the programme of this colloquium.

Equally crucial is the interest of the Faculty of Law in international law, comparative law and transnational law. Ever since its establishment, the Faculty has always offered courses in comparative law in an amount almost double that otherwise common in traditional curricula. We also boast a masters programme in Transnational European Law, a doctoral school and a school of international studies, to which various faculties, including the Faculty of Law, contribute. The Faculty of Law also offers a masters programme and has its own school of international studies.

All these initiatives and programmes share a common goal: to educate young lawyers, scholars and legal operators to be proficient in this new global dimension of the legal order and therefore able to address global legal issues such as the protection of human rights and the establishment of international legal institutions, all of which are at the heart of this colloquium. It is therefore my great pleasure to send you the greetings and wishes of the Faculty, of the Department and the University as a whole.

I wish you a successful debate and a nice day in Trento.

1 Translated from the Italian by the editors.

Chapter 1

Introductory Remarks

Philippe Kirsch

Thank you very much Judge Politi for your generous introduction. I would also like to thank both you and the University of Trento for taking the initiative to organize this excellent colloquium and for giving me the opportunity to speak with you today.

The theme of this colloquium – the International Criminal Court and national jurisdictions – is at the very heart of the International Criminal Court (ICC). It encompasses such fundamental elements as the principle of complementarity, the implementation of national legislation and the cooperation of States with the Court. In my introductory remarks, I would like to place these issues within a broader framework of the relationship between the ICC and States, as reflected in the establishment of the Court and the Court's activities to date. I will also offer an outlook for the future of the Court in the light of this relationship.

1. Establishment of the Court

I think it is fair to say that no international court has ever been established with more careful attention to its relationship to States than the ICC. There are two explanations for this focus.

The first reason stems from the fact that the ICC was created by an international treaty. This distinguishes the ICC from its predecessors such as the Nuremberg and Tokyo tribunals or the *ad hoc* tribunals for the Former Yugoslavia and Rwanda. The former were established by the victorious powers after World War II, the latter by the Security Council. This led to criticism that the tribunals were imposed on States. In setting up the ICC, States were particularly concerned with ensuring the Court's legitimacy. They considered a number of possibilities and concluded that setting up the ICC through a widely supported international treaty would provide it with maximum legitimacy.

This method of creation, however, meant that the ICC would need the active support of States, something which would not necessarily be automatic. Ratification of the Rome Statute imposes significant obligations on States Parties, including acceptance of the Court's jurisdiction over their nationals and territories, cooperation with requests from the Court and ensuring appropriate domestic legislation. To be a viable and successful institution, the Court therefore needed a Statute which would meet two objectives of States. The Court had to be robust enough to achieve States' desire for a strong institution capable of effectively addressing the most serious crimes of concern to the international community as a whole. At the same time, the Statute had to accommodate certain concerns, including the view that the Court should not interfere with matters considered by States to be their own domestic affairs.

The second reason for the careful attention given to the relationship between the ICC and States follows from the purposes underlying the creation of the Court. The ICC was not intended to supplant or substitute for national legal systems. The primary responsibility to prosecute and punish crimes belongs to States. The ICC was set up to address situations where national courts could not or would not act. That is something the ICC shares with any other international criminal court or tribunal, irrespective of the different circumstances of their creation. There is, however, an important difference between the ICC and these other institutions. Previous tribunals were established after the fact to respond to defined situations where the failures of national systems were clear. In contrast, the ICC was created to address future situations which could not be defined in advance. States therefore took great care in setting the judicial principles which would delineate the respective responsibilities of the ICC and national courts.

From this combination of factors – the creation of the ICC by treaty and the specific role assigned to it *vis-à-vis* national jurisdictions – certain basic features of the Court flow naturally.

First, the ICC's jurisdiction is a court of clearly limited jurisdiction. Its subject matter jurisdiction is limited to the most serious crimes of concern to the international community as a whole. The investigation and prosecution of other crimes is left to the sole responsibility of national courts.

The personal and territorial jurisdiction of the Court is also limited. The ICC does not have universal jurisdiction. Outside of a Security Council referral, for the ICC to exercise jurisdiction, the State of nationality of the accused or the State where the crime occurred must accept the Court's jurisdiction – either by becoming a State Party or by filing a separate declaration of acceptance. It should be noted here that the Statute's drafters did not accommodate all States' concerns indiscriminately. States rejected a proposal which would require the consent of the State of the accused's nationality in all cases. They did so because historically agents of the State themselves often were complicit in or even directing the crimes later referred to international tribunals. We saw this with Nazi Germany, Cambodia, the Former Yugoslavia and Rwanda. Conditioning the ICC's jurisdiction on the acceptance of the leadership of such States would have frustrated the Court's ability to end impunity.

Second, the ICC is complementary to national jurisdictions. This principle again reflects the deference given to national systems. The ICC is a court of last resort. It can only act where States are unwilling or unable genuinely to investigate or prosecute offences. The key word here is 'genuinely'. Not every national proceeding will satisfy the principle of complementarity. Proceedings must be genuine and cannot be undertaken solely to shield a person from justice. In any case, this determination will be made by the judges of the ICC objectively and in accordance with the Rome Statute. Interpreting the requirements of genuine willingness and ability may well be one of the issues confronted by the judges over the coming years.

In addition to these principles, the ICC was established as part of a system in which it works together with States to fulfil its mandate. Any judicial system necessarily rests on two pillars – the courts and the mechanisms of enforcement such as the police. In national systems, the two pillars are intertwined. Courts rely automatically on the enforcement powers of the State. With the ICC, States chose to separate the two pillars. The ICC is a strong judicial pillar, but the means of enforcement have been reserved to the States. The Court requires the cooperation of States, for example in the arrest and surrender of persons or in permitting access to their territories. In order to mitigate the Court's lack of enforcement powers, States included provisions on cooperation in the Statute. In joining the ICC, States Parties agree and become obliged to provide cooperation to the Court.

2. The Court's Activities to Date

I would like to turn now to the Court's activities to date and how these activities reflect the different aspects of the relationship between the Court and States to which I have referred so far.

I would start not with any of the situations formally referred to the Court, but with the over 2500 communications alleging crimes which have been received by the Prosecutor. Most of these communications come from private sources. All of the communications are examined by the Office of the Prosecutor in accordance with the Statute. The vast majority have been found to be outside the Court's limited jurisdiction on one or more grounds including the nature of the alleged crimes, the time of their commission or the lack of personal or territorial jurisdiction. In at least one situation not pursued by the Prosecutor, he has stated that national proceedings were also being conducted. Without speaking on the merits of any particular communication, this process reflects the Court's limited jurisdiction and the application of the principle of complementarity in the Court's analyses.

The Prosecutor has not yet requested the Pre-Trial Chambers to authorize any investigations under his *proprio motu* powers on the basis of any such communications. He is currently investigating three situations formally referred to the Court – Uganda, the Democratic Republic of Congo and Darfur, Sudan. A fourth situation referred to the Court – in the Central African Republic – is under analysis as the Prosecutor seeks to determine if there is a reasonable basis to proceed with an investigation. Here, I would make a preliminary observation which I understand will be discussed further in the course of this colloquium. At the time of the Statute's drafting, it was widely expected that States would refer situations occurring in other States to the Court or that the Prosecutor would have to open investigations *proprio motu*. What has happened is that States have referred situations on their own territories to the Court on the grounds that their national jurisdictions are either unwilling or unable to address the situations. As a result, the situations before the Court may present different issues than were previously envisaged.

Turning now to particular situations, in the situation in Uganda, the Court has issued warrants of arrest, which remain outstanding. This case illustrates the absolute necessity of cooperation for the work of the ICC. It is up to States or international organizations to execute these warrants. Without cooperation in arrests, there can be no trials.

The situation in Uganda has also given rise to public discussion about the roles of the ICC and other actors in relation to peace negotiations. It is not for me to enter into this public discussion. I would only note that the ICC was founded on the international community's shared conviction that justice is an indispensable part of a sustainable peace. More important for our purposes today, I would recall that the ICC has a clear judicial mandate set out in its Statute which it is bound to follow. There are other tools available to the international community to deal with such situations, but it is not up to the Court to use those tools.

In the situation of the Democratic Republic of Congo, we have witnessed the first surrender by a national jurisdiction of a person to the Court. This surrender involved interaction between the ICC and the national judicial authorities as well as cooperation of other States. The situation in the DRC has also highlighted the difficulties posed by circumstances in the field. The challenges of security and of logistics are numerous. In such circumstances, the cooperation of States and international organizations such as the UN peacekeeping mission is critical.

The situation in Darfur, Sudan, presents another set of challenges. Sudan is not a State Party. This situation has been referred to the Court by the Security Council. Arrest warrants were issued in this situation last week. As investigations and judicial activities continue, one can expect that questions of complementarity and of cooperation may arise.

From just this brief overview of the Court's activities, many of the features which derive from the relationship and the division of responsibility between the Court and States are evident in practice. Even before an investigation can be opened, a potential situation must be analysed in the light of the limited jurisdiction of the court and the principle of complementarity. As a situation proceeds through investigation and possibly judicial proceedings, these issues of jurisdiction and complementarity continue to exist. Meanwhile, the importance of cooperation in all areas – from arrests to security and logistics – becomes only more and more clear as the Court's activities progress.

3. An Outlook for the Future

I would like to turn now to an outlook for the future. It goes without saying that it will be imperative for the Court, and it is the responsibility of the Court, to continue to establish its own credibility through fair and efficient proceedings. In the context of this colloquium, however, I will focus on those factors that are directly linked to the relationship between the ICC and States as I have described it. From this perspective, there are at least three conditions which are essential to the success of the Court and to the success of the interrelated system of international and national criminal justice more broadly.

First, because the ICC is a court of last resort, national systems need to be able to function effectively to the maximum extent possible. National courts will continue to have the primary responsibility for responding to serious international crimes. Their abilities to investigate, prosecute and punish international crimes must therefore be reinforced. Ideally, national courts will try all crimes within the Court's jurisdiction.

Even where the ICC acts, it will only ever be able to handle a small number of cases. National prosecutions will be essential to avoiding an impunity gap. Many States – both Parties and non-parties – have used the adoption of the Rome Statute as an opportunity to review and upgrade their domestic legislation over genocide, crimes against humanity and war crimes. Strengthening national capacities will further States' abilities to deal with crimes themselves.

Second, the number of ratifications of the Rome Statute must continue to increase. The 104 ratifications of the Rome Statute since 1998 represent a remarkable pace for any treaty, let alone one establishing an international organization and imposing substantial obligations on States Parties. Yet, universality remains an important goal for two reasons. On the one hand, the Court's legitimacy is strengthened by broad acceptance of the Statute, cutting across all regions and all legal systems. On the other hand, the Court's jurisdiction normally extends only as far as the nationals and territories of its States Parties. Its ability to end impunity globally is enhanced with each ratification.

Third, States (and by extension international organizations) must provide sufficient cooperation to meet the needs of the Court. This cooperation must adapt to changing circumstances and reflect the current needs of the Court. At the Rome Conference, most people probably imagined the ICC would operate under easier circumstances than is actually the case. There may have been an unstated assumption that international criminal justice follows a certain trajectory: a conflict erupts, crimes are committed, the conflict ends, readily available evidence is collected, alleged perpetrators are arrested, and because the national system cannot or will not act effectively an international court steps in – in other words a scenario like Nuremberg or Tokyo. The first years of the ICC's activities have shown that it functions in very different circumstances. The ICC operates in situations of ongoing conflict where crimes continue to be committed. Investigations are taking place in very diverse countries, often in remote and difficult-to-access regions.

The difficult conditions in which the Court operates present significant challenges in terms of evidence collection, security of staff, victims and witnesses and logistics. These circumstances make ensuring adequate support all the more important. On the face of it, obtaining cooperation is not a problem of principle. The commitment of States Parties to cooperation is real and has been regularly and increasingly reiterated. The challenge, and one of the most immediate tasks for the Court and for States Parties, will be to translate the commitment of States Parties to the Court into practical cooperation. Of course, the nature of the situations in which the Court operates complicates issues of cooperation. States may be unable not only to conduct trials, but also to take specific initiatives in the judicial process – for example, to arrest persons, to protect witnesses, or to enforce sentences. Where the relevant territorial State is unwilling or unable to act, the responsibility for cooperation is diffused among the different members of the international community.

Having said that, there is also at least one significant positive consequence from operating in such situations – namely, the potential exists for the Court to have a deterrent effect in the short term on ongoing crimes. At the time of the Court's creation, it was largely expected that the deterrent effect would be gradual, building over time after multiple trials. This is reflected in the language of the preamble to the Rome Statute which refers to the Court putting an end to impunity and thus contributing to the prevention of crimes. We see today, however, that the impact of the Court may be more immediate.

4. Conclusion

We still are at a very early stage in the development of the permanent ICC. The system established in Rome is only beginning to be understood. We will continue to learn much more about this system through both the Court's jurisprudence and the development of cooperation in practice.

Colloquia such as this one, with its clear focus on the relationship between the ICC and national jurisdictions, have an important role in furthering our understanding of how the different parts of this system can work together most effectively. I wish you a highly successful and informative two days.

Thank you.

Chapter 2

Italy and the International Criminal Court

Ivo Maria Braguglia

First of all, I would like to thank you for your invitation, which I really appreciate. This initiative comes after research carried out by the two universities of Trento and Salento (previously, University of Lecce) within a combined project on 'ICC: judicial cooperation and domestic implementation in the light of the Statute of Rome and national and international practice'. Professor Mauro Politi, who, as you know, is one of the Court's judges, coordinated the project. This research has two targets: one is to determine the content and functioning of the complementarity principle as contained in the Rome Statute in the light of the continuous development of international criminal law; the second is evaluating how the system of international cooperation provided by the Statute is effective when considering the laws on international cooperation issued by States Parties.

These two issues, complementarity and cooperation – which we will discuss during today's sessions – are crucial to the functioning of the International Criminal Court (ICC). The first years of the Court's activity demonstrate that point. This is why it is extremely important that scholars, academics, professionals and experts in general in international law have gathered here to share their views on these matters. And that is also why I am here – to represent the Italian Ministry of Foreign Affairs: Italy has indeed supported the Court since the very beginning.

1. Italy and the Rome Statute: Steps taken at the National Level

It is about our country's support for the functioning and the several activities of the ICC that I would like to speak. I will not dwell on the issue of the role played by our country in the adoption of the Rome Statute, which took place on 17 July 1998.

Italy is the fifth largest contributor to the ICC's budget. This year we have provided it with approximately 11 million Euros.

Italy signed the Rome Statute on 18 July 1998, that is the day after its adoption. It was among the first countries to ratify the Statute by means of Law No. 232 of 1999 and the subsequent filing of the ratification instrument on 26 July 1999. It was thus one of 60 countries whose ratification allowed the Statute to enter into force on 1 July 2002. Today 104 countries abide by the Statute.

At that particular time, Italy wanted to apply the Statute immediately within its system in order to show its strong support for implementation. That is why, just after adoption, the Italian Parliament, on the initiative of the Government, decided to proceed immediately with ratification, without simultaneously adopting the relevant rules of implementation, which would have required a longer elaboration and thus delayed the ratification process.

The procedure for the adoption of the Italian implementing legislation has still to be concluded; nevertheless, the Minister of Justice has recently declared that the implementation of the Statute is one of the current Government's priorities.

Therefore, we may say that Italian politicians are working on the matter, even though nothing has yet been officially presented during this parliamentary session. The Ministry of Justice alone is currently involved in the proceedings, unlike previous legislatures when several ministerial commissions (including one established by the Ministry of Foreign Affairs) were involved in the drafting of the law of implementation.

Besides procedure, the draft legislation currently under elaboration differs from previous efforts as it only focuses on cooperation issues with the ICC and does not provide for any substantive criminal rules. At an earlier stage of the preparation of the law, one of the hypotheses taken into account consisted in implementing the Rome Statute and, at the same time, starting to revise the Italian criminal system with regard to war crimes and crimes against humanity. Other States have adopted this solution, which, by the way, is not imposed by the Rome Statute: States Parties are not asked to introduce the crimes provided by articles 6-8 within their legal systems. The Statute, nevertheless, favours a solution by which the States Parties (and not only them but any State in general) do implement these articles as well, in the light of the principle of complementarity, which qualifies ICC jurisdiction. This is actually one of the most significant implications of this principle, which characterizes the relationship between the ICC and national courts. I am sure that my colleagues will deal with this issue in the following speeches.

To tell the truth, one of the reasons why the proceedings related to the Italian legislation on cooperation have been protracted for so long is the wish to take advantage of this opportunity to start revising the substantive Italian rules, especially those related to the war crimes, in view of what was established in the Rome Statute. Yet, it seems that now the proceedings will be focused especially on the procedural rules in order to specify the cooperation that the Italian judicial powers are going to provide to the Court, similar to what was done with regard to the International Criminal Tribunal for the Former Yugoslavia and the International Criminal Tribunal for Rwanda. All that being considered, we might expect that Italy will soon adopt an implementation act (besides, the Italian legal system already provides for some substantive rules with regard to international crimes, including war crimes).

This said, I would now like to say a few words about Italy and its role in the process of ratification and implementation of the Rome Statute in other States Parties.

2. Italy and the European Union

Everybody knows that the European Union (EU) has always supported both the establishment of the Court and the adoption of the Statute. As an actual example of this cooperative spirit, on 10 April 2006 the Council issued a Decision on a cooperation agreement between the ICC and the EU.[1]

More generally, the EU acknowledges that the principles set by the Rome Statute and those that regulate its functioning are fully in line with the Union's principles and objectives. This is stated in the preamble of a series of common positions on the ICC, which have been adopted by the Council according to article 15 of the Treaty on European Union related to common foreign and security policy.

These common positions state that the establishment of the ICC is an essential means to promote the observance of the international humanitarian law and human rights, thus contributing to freedom, security, justice and the rule of law, as well as contributing to peace and the strengthening of international security, in accordance with the purposes and principles of the Charter of United Nations.

The first of these common positions was adopted on 11 June 2001 upon a proposal by Italy, during the Swedish chairmanship, in order to favour the adoption of the Statute and the functioning of the Court.[2]

Article 2 of this Position states that both the Union and the Member States shall raise 'the issue of the widest possible ratification, acceptance, approval or accession to the Rome Statute and the implementation of the Statute in negotiations or political dialogues with third States, groups of States or relevant regional organisations, whenever appropriate.'

On 15 May 2002, a special Action Plan was drafted in order to comply with these commitments;[3] previously, on 28 February 2002, the European Parliament had approved a related resolution on the Court.[4] Amongst several implementations of such measures, a special mention should be made of the EU-Japan Action Plan, which was adopted in 2001.[5] The subsequent common positions of 20 June 2002[6] and 16 June 2003[7] confirmed those commitments. They acknowledged that all the Member States of the European Union had ratified the Rome Statute and intend to support the effective functioning of the Court and promote a universal assistance to it, encouraging as many States as possible to join the Rome Statute. Therefore, both the Union and the Member States confirmed their commitment to promote, during

1 Council Decision of 10 April 2006 concerning the conclusion of the Agreement between the International Criminal Court and the European Union on cooperation and assistance, OJ L 115, 28.4.2006, 49.

2 Council Common Position of 11 June 2001 on the International Criminal Court, OJ L 155, 12.6.01, 19.

3 Action Plan to follow-up on the Common Position on the International Criminal Court (available at http://register.consilium.europa.eu/pdf/en/02/st09/09019en2.pdf accessed 12 September 2007).

4 European Parliament Resolution on entry into force of the Statute of the International Criminal Court, OJ C 293 E, 28.11.2002, 88.

5 The EU-Japan action plan is available at http://ec.europa.eu/external_relations/japan/summit_12_01/actionplan.pdf accessed 12 September 2007.

6 Council Common Position of 20 June 2002 amending Common Position 2001/443/CFSP on the International Criminal Court, OJ L 164, 22.6.02, 1.

7 Council Common Position 2003/443/CFSP of 16 June 2003 on the International Criminal Court, OJ L 150 18.06.2003, 67.

negotiations or political dialogues with third States, groups of States or relevant regional organizations, the ratification and implementation of the Rome Statute as widely as possible; moreover, both the Union and the Member States affirmed their commitment to contribute to the worldwide ratification and implementation of the Statute also with other means, such as the adoption of initiatives that promote the awareness of values, principles and rules of the Statute.

3. Italy and the Proceedings of the Fifth Session of the Assembly of States Parties

The proceedings that took place in New York, from 28 January to 1 February 2007, during the Fifth Session of the Assembly of States Parties are worth a separate mention; a number of legal experts from the Italian Delegation at the United Nations and the Legal Service of the Ministry of Foreign Affairs took part in this session.

This was almost entirely devoted to the *Special Working Group on the Crime of Aggression*. As you know, the Group has been working for years on the definition of 'aggression', as well as on the conditions under which the Court shall exercise jurisdiction with respect to this crime according to article 5(2) of the Statute.

The best improvements achieved were those related to the definition of the crime of aggression. Nowadays the leadership nature of the crime of aggression is commonly agreed, that is the idea that only those holding an effective position of control or otherwise able to influence the main political choices of a State are personally responsible for the act of aggression, also under criminal law.

On the other hand, procedural aspects remain controversial. The relationship between the initiation of an investigation by the ICC on the crime of aggression and a possible action by the Security Council is one of the most debated issues, as it touches upon the basic relationship between the powers entrusted to the Security Council in the determination of the existence of an act of aggression and the exercise of the Court's jurisdiction.

We are probably close to reaching a solution on the first of such issues. With regard to the second – the role of the Security Council – negotiations are being blocked by the permanent members, their position being that only when the Security Council acknowledges the existence of an act of aggression by a State can the Court proceed to ascertain the individual responsibilities for the relevant crime. On the contrary, the majority of the States – including Italy – want to preserve the independence of the Court from the Security Council's decisions. When the latter, being a political entity, is not able to decide whether an act is to be considered as an aggression, the Court has to be free to autonomously proceed. Moreover, the right of the defence to dispute, during the proceedings, the existence of all the facts ascribed to the defendant, also when the crime is an act of aggression, has to be preserved. Both the principle of the independence of the judge and the defence's rights are included in the United Nations International Covenant on Civil and Political Rights and in the European Convention on Human Rights. All the States that are members to these two international acts have to comply with these principles.

It is to be hoped that the negotiations on the crime of aggression – which will continue with an informal procedure in the Princeton meeting, from 11 to 14 June

2007 – might be concluded within 2008, 12 months before the beginning of the first Conference of the Revision of the Rome Statute, which will take place in 2009–10.

4. Italy and the Security Council

To conclude, I would like to talk briefly about Italy's – at least potential – role as a non-permanent member of the Security Council, starting from 15 January 2008.

It is certainly possible that the Council will intervene to support the cooperation between States and the ICC. It is apparent that both the investigations and the trials in front of the Court are only possible when both the States involved (either in the investigations or in the trials) and the other States Parties decide to cooperate with the Court.

If we think how strongly Italy has always supported the Court, it is to be expected (and it is indeed my firm belief) that Italy will also support future initiatives to be taken by the Security Council with a view to enhancing the effective functioning of the Court.

PART I
Complementarity: A First Assessment

Chair: Mauro Politi

I simply wish to make a few remarks to introduce the session. I intend to be extremely brief, since we have a full agenda ahead of us and we are all eager to listen to the presentations that will follow.

The members of this panel are in fact more than just well-known experts in international criminal justice. They are amongst the leading scholars on the ICC. I wish to thank them again for having accepted the invitation of the University of Trento, and to thank all of you for being here, in some cases for the second or third time after the meetings of 1999 and 2001.

In 1999, in the immediate aftermath of the Rome Conference, we discussed in Trento a great number of general issues, including complementarity. The main purpose at that time was to understand this relatively new concept, how the division of labour between the ICC and national jurisdictions was intended to work, and what had been the basic trade-off between national sovereignty and the fight against impunity.

At the 2001 meeting, complementarity was rather an ancillary question within the subject of the crime of aggression. The focus was (and still remains within the special Working Group of the Assembly of States Parties) on the definition of aggression and on the relationship between the Court and the Security Council.

This Colloquium comes six years later. Meanwhile, many events have taken place, the most important being that the ICC is now an operational reality. Today, those who decide to embark on a study of the Court's case-law are confronted with an extensive body of decisions and orders by the Pre-Trial Chambers and the Appeals Chamber. The first trial is about to start. Many parts of the Statute and of the Rules have been tested, interpreted, applied by the Court's jurisprudence. For example, the provisions on arrest warrants and requests for arrests and surrender; those on disclosure of evidence and on the standards for confirmation of charges; on protection and participation of victims; on interim release and challenge to jurisdiction; on the characterisation of a conflict. Comments also have switched from being based on hypothetical scenarios to relying on concrete elements and, of course, the Court's findings. It is only natural that these comments include concern and criticism. We are here in Trento once more to express our views, to have a debate, to learn from each other.

Now, where are we on complementarity? This is the basic question that we may wish to address. The title of the session speaks of a 'first assessment' and this reflects somehow the fact that the ICC practice provides only a limited number of elements specifically related to complementarity and admissibility under the Rome Statute. Essentially, we are talking about a few decisions of the Pre-Trial Chambers in connection with the arrest warrants, the latest of these decisions having been issued just a few days ago by Pre-Trial Chamber I in the situation and cases concerning Darfur.

But, as we know, there are some broader issues that may also have an impact on the complementarity regime of the ICC: for example, complementarity and universal jurisdiction, the practice of self-referrals, which has characterized so much of the current activity of the Court, the questions linked to referrals by the Security

Council. In particular, the issues raised by the mechanism that have triggered so far the jurisdiction of the Court, conveying a certain idea of the instances in which the ICC should be the proper forum for prosecuting and punishing the most heinous crimes *in lieu* of national courts.

The intent is then to look at the Court's initial steps in this perspective, to see how significant these steps are in shaping the role of the Court within the system of the international criminal justice, perhaps to revisit the philosophy of the relationship between national and international criminal jurisdictions in the light of the experience of the ICC.

Now, following these short notes, it will be extremely interesting to hear at the outset the presentation by Pierre-Marie Dupuy, who will speak about complementarity and general international law. I am sure that he will give us a solid theoretical grounding and a comprehensive perspective for our discussion.

We will then listen to Bill Schabas and his 'uncomplimentary' remarks on complementarity in practice, which I'm afraid will show no signs of indulgence towards what the Court has achieved or not achieved in these years. He also kindly agreed to touch on the question of complementarity and peace processes, which was originally the subject of a separate presentation by Kai Ambos, who unfortunately cannot be with us today. This is another subject of crucial importance, since it involves what is often described as the 'dilemma' between peace and justice.

Finally, Giorgio Gaja will discuss admissibility in relation to self-referrals. The issues that he will address seem, once again, to fit perfectly the idea of starting this Colloquium with an overview of the main problems raised by the initial practice of the Court. Undoubtedly, self-referrals is one of them and is among those mostly debated by scholars in recent times, both as a matter of legal policy and as a matter of law.

Chapter 3

Principe de Complémentarité et Droit International Général

Pierre-Marie Dupuy

En écho a son préambule, l'article premier du Statut de Rome déclare que la Cour Pénale Internationale (CPI) est 'complémentaire des juridictions criminelles nationales'. L'article 17 traitera ensuite des cas d'irrecevabilité d'une affaire par la Cour dont le premier est le cas dans lequel 'l'affaire fait l'objet d'une enquête ou de poursuites de la part d'un Etat ayant compétence en l'espèce...'. Ainsi, contrairement aux deux tribunaux *ad hoc* respectivement chargés de juger les crimes internationaux commis dans l'ex-Yougoslavie et au Rwanda, la Cour Pénale Internationale n'a pas priorité sur les tribunaux nationaux pour juger les auteurs des crimes énoncés aux articles 5 à 8. L'Etat sur le territoire duquel le comportement en cause s'est produit ou celui dont la personne accusée du crime est un national auront prévalence sur la Cour s'ils décident de poursuivre eux-mêmes les personnes soupçonnées de crime(s).

Non sans analogie structurelle avec le principe substantiel de subsidiarité en droit communautaire européen, le principe de complémentarité, a fait très tôt l'objet de commentaires abondants de la part de la doctrine. On y a vu en particulier l'une des marques déterminantes de la nouveauté du droit international pénal défini dans le cadre du Statut.[1] Nul ne songe à nier l'importance de ce principe. Il a de multiples justifications, à la fois théoriques et pratiques. Il permet notamment d'éviter l'encombrement de la Cour et de faire jouer à celle-ci le rôle d'un incitateur à la vigilance judiciaire de la part des Etats parties. Il place ces derniers devant leurs responsabilités face à la commission des crimes de génocide, contre l'humanité, crimes de guerre et d'agression.

Pour contribuer à saisir l'apport de ce principe statutaire, défini dans le corps de la *lex specialis* que constitue la convention adoptée le 17 juillet 1998, il convient cependant de le resituer par rapport au droit international général. Comme les récents travaux de la Commission du droit international le confirment,[2] et ainsi qu'on a eu

1 Voir par exemple Holmes, J. T. (2002), 'Complementarity, National Courts versus the ICC', in Cassese, A., Gaeta, P. and Jones, J.R.W.D. (eds), *The Rome Statute of the International Criminal Court: A Commentary* (Oxford: Oxford University Press), pp. 667 et ss.

2 Conclusions du *Groupe d'études sur la fragmentation du droit international: difficultés de la diversification et de l'expansion du droit international*, *Annuaire de la Commission du Droit International,* 2006, Vol. 2. Pour un commentaire, voir notamment Conforti, B. (2007), 'Unité et fragmentation du droit international: glissez mortels, n'appuyez pas!', in *Revue Générale de Droit International Public*, 5-18.

l'occasion d'y insister dans un autre ouvrage,[3] le droit international général et le droit international spécial entretiennent eux-mêmes des rapports de complémentarité. Aucun régime spécial n'est 'suffisant à lui-même' et ce serait une vue de l'esprit ou une faiblesse de considérer le droit international pénal déterminé par le Statut de Rome comme un système juridique clos sur lui-même, sans rapport avec le reste du droit international. La responsabilité internationale des individus pour commission des crimes internationaux n'a pas été créée par le Statut. Il a seulement contribué à en déterminer les contours. Il lui a donné un cadre organique et normatif aussi précis qu'il est possible, autre façon de dire que ce cadre est également et inévitablement lacunaire, quoique aient pu en penser certains des négociateurs de la Convention constitutive de la CPI.

A ce titre, l'application du Statut demande et demandera qu'on se réfère souvent au droit international général, notamment (mais pas seulement) pour en interpréter les dispositions. Le Statut demeure ainsi intégré dans l'ordre juridique international.

C'est si vrai que l'article 21, relatif au droit applicable, s'il donne comme il est normal la priorité à l'application par la Cour du Statut lui-même, mentionne aussitôt à la suite non seulement les 'autres traités applicables' mais aussi, paragraphe 1er alineé b, les 'principes et règles du droit international, y compris les principes établis du droit international des conflits armés'.

Le droit international pénal, dont le Statut de Rome constitue le fleuron central, c'est aussi du droit international, et plus précisément du droit international *public.*[4] Ainsi, la question de la comparaison des rapports du principe de complémentarité dans le cadre du Statut et en droit international général se justifie-t-elle pleinement. Elle permet de mesurer le degré d'originalité du principe en droit international pénal. C'est lui qui constitue l'objet de cette brève étude. A cet égard, on se permettra trois séries d'observations portant respectivement sur la banalité relative du principe de complémentarité, sur deux de ses implications notables et, enfin, sur la question de ses rapports avec la compétence universelle, en relation avec la CPI.

1. Banalité relative de la complémentarité par le respect initial des compétences souveraines

Cette observation sera plus longue que les autres et mérite qu'on y distingue successivement les aspects touchant à la répartition des compétences puis à la structure normative.

---

3 Dupuy, P.M. (2002), 'L'unité de l'ordre juridique international', Cours général de droit international public, *Recueils des cours de l'Académie de droit international de La Haye,* Vol. 297, notamment pp. 428-460.

4 Même s'il établit des normes substantielles (primaires) empruntées ou inspirées des droit pénaux internes comparés. Le droit international pénal, en d'autres termes, n'est pas du droit pénal international. La place qu'y tient le droit coutumier international est déterminante. Elle est même prépondérante dans le cadre du droit applicable par les deux tribunaux *ad hoc* institués par le Conseil de sécurité.

1.a. Rationalité de la distribution des compétences

On a déjà signalé les dispositions principales du Statut dans lesquelles il figure. La priorité donnée au juge pénal de l'Etat partie, qu'il s'agisse de l'Etat 'territorial' (par référence au lieu de commission du crime) ou de l'Etat de 'nationalité active' (par référence à celle de l'individu poursuivi) s'explique par une idée simple: dans la poursuite des 'crimes internationaux' énoncés à l'article 6, c'est normalement à l'un ou l'autre de ces Etats (du moins lorsqu'ils sont distincts) de 'faire le travail' lui-même[5] parce qu'il est directement concerné. C'est lui aussi, et d'abord l'Etat territorial, le mieux à même d'instruire le procès de l'individu poursuivi, notamment parce que la réunion des preuves devrait lui poser moins de problèmes qu'aux autres.

La poursuite devant les juridictions pénales nationales des auteurs de crimes commis sur le territoire pénal national n'est ainsi que la confirmation du caractère en principe général et exclusif des compétences de l'Etat souverain sur son territoire. Elle se prolonge au plan normatif par le principe général de la territorialité de la loi pénale. Il n'est donc, en soi, nullement surprenant que le Statut de Rome, désireux de respecter la situation de droit commun, reconnaisse la priorité de compétence de l'Etat territorial.

Le fait qu'il y joigne, au même plan, la compétence de l'Etat de nationalité ne saurait pas davantage surprendre. En effet, le Statut permet, dans les cas où il y aurait dissociation de fait entre la territorialité du crime et la nationalité de la personne poursuivie pour sa commission, de rendre complémentaires le jeu de la compétence territoriale et celui de la compétence personnelle. L'innovation est cependant limitée, la compétence personnelle venant classiquement au secours de la compétence territoriale dans ce genre de cas, si l'on oublie pour un temps les situations dans lesquelles l'une et l'autre risquent d'entrer en conflit.[6]

La *ratio legis* du système plus que du principe de complémentarité, déjà évoquée, est énoncée dès le Préambule, lorsqu'il affirme que les Etats parties sont 'déterminés à mettre un terme à l'impunité des auteurs de ces crimes et à concourir ainsi à la prévention de nouveaux crimes'. Il ne faut par conséquent laisser subsister de lacunes dans l'organisation et la répartition des compétences judiciaires pour poursuivre les crimes concernés. Les criminels ne doivent pas échapper aux poursuites, au plan interne, d'abord, et, à défaut, au plan international.

C'est également dans le Préambule que l'on peut trouver l'énonciation du 'devoir de chaque Etat de soumettre à sa juridiction criminelle les responsables de crimes

5 La comparaison avec l'article 5 de la Convention pour la prévention et la répression du crime de génocide s'impose ici spontanément. Cet article prévoit lui aussi la compétence des tribunaux pénaux de l'Etat territorial. Il énonce aussi, par anticipation, la compétence d'une 'cour criminelle internationale' 'qui sera compétente à l'égard de celles de parties contractantes qui en auront reconnu la juridiction'. On voit ainsi que dans la Convention de 1948, le rapport entre compétence nationale et compétence de la Cour internationale est alternatif, non pas hiérarchique. A la lettre, il n'y a donc pas énonciation d'un principe de complémentarité à l'article 6 de la Convention sur le génocide.

6 Le Statut prévoit à son article 20 le respect du principe général de droit pénal *non bis in idem*.

internationaux'. Du *devoir*, énoncé en préambule à l'*obligation* juridique stricte d'exercer cette compétence il y a, certes, une nuance. Le texte du Statut ne comprend pas l'énoncé d'une telle obligation. Cependant, une interprétation dynamique de ses termes, tenant compte de la disposition précitée du Préambule, permettrait de parvenir à cette conclusion.

Toujours est-il que c'est, finalement très classiquement, par référence à ce devoir collectif de mettre un terme à l'impunité des auteurs des crimes de droit international que s'organise l'exercice d'une compétence reconnue par le droit international général aux Etats dépositaires des compétences territoriale et personnelle. Son jeu prioritaire par rapport à l'exercice de la compétence de la Cour se comprend comme le *maintien préférentiel du régime général ou de droit commun sur le régime spécial permettant l'intervention de la Cour*. Un tel choix est compréhensible parce que réaliste; les négociateurs du Statut ont voulu innover au minimum. Cela remet à sa place, réduite, l'innovation apportée par le Statut.

1.b. Structure normative

Si l'on élargit la perspective, on se rendra compte qu'est très classique le genre de situations dans lesquelles le droit international ne fait intervenir ses normes ou ses institutions juridiques qu' 'en dernier recours' sinon 'en désespoir de cause', c'est-à-dire à titre seulement supplétif, lorsque la mise en œuvre des règles et l'intervention des organes existant en droit interne n'ont pas ou mal fonctionné. Ceci est notamment vérifié dans le cas d'invocation de la protection diplomatique. L'*épuisement des voies de recours interne* par l'individu étranger se considérant victime d'une violation du droit est un préalable à la sollicitation de son Etat de nationalité par le même individu. Comme le soulignait Roberto Ago en qualité de rapporteur spécial devant la Commission du Droit International, la responsabilité internationale de l'Etat n'apparaîtra que si, ayant accompli un acte illicite au regard du droit international, il n'a pas, dans son ordre interne, rétabli l'étranger concerné dans ses droits reconnus internationalement.[7] Comme l'a du reste précisé la jurisprudence, notamment celle de la Cour Internationale de Justice dans l'affaire ELSI,[8] il serait inéquitable de réclamer de la personne victime un épuisement effectif des voies de recours internes si celles-ci s'avèrent inefficaces ou inexistantes.

On ne peut, à ce stade, qu'être frappé par la ressemblance structurelle existant alors entre les conditions de mise en jeu de la protection diplomatique, l'une des institutions juridiques les plus classiques du droit international général, et celles établies dans le Statut pour permettre le déclenchement d'une procédure devant la Cour pénale internationale. Consultons pour le vérifier l'article 17 du Statut.

Son paragraphe premier énonce les cas dans lesquels la Cour doit s'effacer, c'est-à-dire déclarer une affaire à elle soumise irrecevable. Il en va ainsi si ladite affaire

---

7 Voir Dupuy, P.M. (2003), 'Quarante ans de codification du droit de la responsabilité internationale des Etats', in *Revue Générale de Droit International Public,* 305.

8 Cour Internationale de Justice, Affaire *Elettronica Sicula S.P.A. (ELSI),* (Etats-Unis d'Amérique c. Italie), Arrêt du 20 Juillet 1989, *C.I.J. Recueil 1989,* p. 15, paragraphes 59-63, http://www.icj-cij.org/docket/files/76/6706.pdf (accès 5 Septembre 2007).

'a fait l'objet d'une enquête de la part d'un Etat ayant compétence en l'espèce', ou bien 'a déjà été jugée pour le comportement faisant l'objet de la plainte', ou 'n'est pas suffisamment grave pour que la Cour y donne suite'.

Cependant, l'alinéa b) de ce même paragraphe fait déjà l'énoncé d'un cas manifestant la carence de l'Etat compétent pour poursuivre. Il s'agit du 'manque de volonté ou de l'incapacité de l'Etat de mener à bien des poursuites'. Le paragraphe 2 de l'article 17 donne les critères en fonction desquels la Cour pourra déterminer l'existence de ce 'manque de volonté'. Il s'agit du dessein manifeste 'de soustraire la personne concernée à sa responsabilité pénale pour les crimes relevant de la compétence de la Cour'; ou d'un 'retard injustifié' démentant 'l'intention de traduire en justice la personne concernée'; ou d'une conduite manifestant le manque d'indépendance ou d'impartialité des juges.

Pour ce qui est de l''incapacité' de l'Etat concerné, le paragraphe 3 évoque en particulier 'l'effondrement de la totalité ou d'une partie substantielle de son propre appareil judiciaire'.

Ainsi retrouve-t-on dans le texte conventionnel la même structure, le même enchaînement logique que dans l'institution coutumière classique de l'épuisement des voies de recours interne. *L'interne tient l'international en l'état* ; en d'autres termes, il a barre sur lui, et ce dernier ne se substitue au jeu des institutions nationales que si celles-ci sont déficientes. Principe de bonne économie, en quelque sorte. Il y a ainsi une hiérarchie fonctionnelle entre droit international et droit interne. Le second est mis au service du premier, par l'intermédiaire de ses normes et de ses organes, en l'occurrence judiciaires, pour réaliser de la façon la plus efficace possible le respect de la norme posée au plan international.

De même que l'épuisement des voies de recours interne offre la possibilité pour l'Etat de rétablir un ordonnancement juridique conforme à ses obligations internationales en amont de l'invocation et de la mise en jeu de sa responsabilité internationale, de même la réalisation de la règle posée dans le Statut (il faut poursuivre et condamner tous les auteurs de crimes internationaux) doit être tentée devant les juridictions internes de l'Etat compétent ou, à défaut, mais seulement à défaut, par la Cour Pénale Internationale.

Le principe de complémentarité doit être ainsi pris pour ce qu'il est: un dispositif emprunté au droit international général mais réaménagé conventionnellement pour garantir la réalisation effective de la règle de poursuite judiciaire posée internationalement. Il s'agit d'une règle de collaboration fonctionnelle entre les ordres juridiques, interne et international. Le premier se voit instrumentalisé par le second pour la garantie du respect de la légalité définie par ce dernier. Ceci évoque bien sûr le schéma dont Georges Scelle s'était fait le théoricien dans les années trente du vingtième siècle. Il lui avait donné le nom de *dédoublement fonctionnel.*[9] L'Etat prête à l'international, dépourvu d'institutions efficaces, le secours de ses règles et de

9 Pour un exposé de la théorie voir notamment Scelle, G. (1932), *Précis de droit des Gens, Principes et systématique*, Vol I., pp. 43, 54-6, 217 et (1934) *Précis de droit des Gens, Principes et systématique*, Vol. II, pp. 10, 319, 450. Pour un exposé commenté de la théorie, voir Thierry, H. (1990), 'The Thought of Georges Scelles' et Cassese, A. (1990), 'Remarks on Scelles's Theory of "Role Splitting" (dédoublement fonctionnel) in International Law', both

ses organes internes pour la réalisation de la légalité collective. Ici, cependant, l'ordre juridique international étant désormais pourvu d'une cour pénale, du moins entre les Etats ayant ratifié son Statut, si le dédoublement n'est plus une nécessité, il reste un moyen de l'application du droit international, privilégié par la complémentarité. On verra plus loin qu'en revanche, l'invocation pure et dure du dédoublement fonctionnel demeure envisageable en dehors du champ d'application du Statut, notamment à propos des cas de compétence universelle. La complémentarité concilie primat de la souveraineté et recherche fonctionnelle de l'efficacité internationale.

2. Effets induits par la complémentarité

Deux effets induits par l'application du principe de complémentarité méritent ici d'être notés.

a. Le premier est purement normatif. Si l'on veut que les Etats, territorial ou de nationalité active, poursuivent en priorité les auteurs de crimes internationaux, une condition normative paraît nécessaire pour garantir l'harmonie d'application de ce nouveau droit international pénal conventionnel; celle d'après laquelle tous les Etats parties auront mis leur droit interne en accord avec les définitions que le Statut donne de chacun des crimes internationaux. En pratique, nombreux sont d'ailleurs les Etats qui ont déjà pris les dispositions législatives nécessaires dans leur ordre interne, même s'il subsiste encore de trop nombreux cas de carence législative à déplorer chez nombre d'Etats parties au Statut. Ainsi, à l'articulation organique entre ordre interne et ordre international définie dans les articles 17 à 20 correspond logiquement une harmonisation normative. Elle est parfois contestée en doctrine mais sera néanmoins imposée par les nécessités de la complémentarité.
b. Une seconde implication résulte non pas de la pratique effective du Statut, encore trop récente, mais de la lecture que l'on peut faire de ses dispositions pertinentes. Elles sont à nouveau à trouver à l'article 17. Tout se passe (ou pourrait se passer) en effet comme si ce dernier, en prévoyant les causes d'irrecevabilité des affaires soumises à la Cour définissait *à contrario* les déviances ou carences dont le constat par la Cour se traduirait par une conséquence, celle de sa substitution à l'Etat prioritairement compétent.

L'articulation entre les ordres interne et international établie par le principe de complémentarité jouerait alors comme à l'instar d'une sanction. A l'Etat territorial ou de nationalité active d'effectuer en priorité la poursuite du criminel. A défaut, soit que cet Etat ait manifesté sa mauvaise volonté, ses organes leur manque d'indépendance ou leur incapacité technique à rendre la justice pénale, la CPI pourra prendre la place du juge interne. De ce point de vue, on doit constater une originalité du régime conventionnel par rapport au droit commun.

---

in *European Journal of International Law,* 1:1/2 http://www.ejil.org/journal/Vol1/No1/index.html (accès 5 Septembre 2007).

3. Principe de complémentarité et compétence universelle

La comparaison du droit international général et du Statut en relation avec le principe de complémentarité incite à évoquer une dernière série de questions: celle des rapports entre la compétence universelle pour la poursuite des *core crimes* et l'ordre dans lequel ledit principe organise l'intervention respective du juge national et de la CPI.

Si l'on met ici à part le cas des crimes énoncés dans les quatre conventions de Genève de 1949, une première interrogation, à certains égards plus encore d'actualité qu'il y a quelques années, consiste à savoir si et dans quelle mesure cette compétence universelle existe à l'égard des 'crimes les plus graves qui touchent l'ensemble de la communauté internationale.'[10] L'expérience des refontes successives de la loi belge inciterait à penser que la compétence universelle générale, insubordonnée à quelque lien que ce soit entre l'Etat poursuivant et l'individu poursuivi, a désormais vécu. Il faudrait qu'existe au moins un lien de nationalité passive (celle des victimes) avec l'Etat poursuivant ou quelque type de relation entre le territoire de l'Etat se déclarant compétent et la personne qu'il poursuit. Ce lien pourra être au moins constitué par la présence, même momentanée, de la personne poursuivie sur le territoire de l'Etat poursuivant, base invoquée par la France dans l'affaire l'opposant actuellement à la République du Congo.[11]

De plus, on s'acheminerait en doctrine, conformément à ce que suggère le professeur Antonio Cassese, vers un conditionnement de cette compétence par un ordre de préséances qui n'est pas sans faire penser à un décalque du principe de complémentarité, comme s'il était tiré du Statut pour inspirer le droit international général. En effet, l'éminente auteur propose que la compétence universelle ne puisse (ou ne devrait pouvoir) s'exercer que si l'Etat territorial et l'Etat de nationalité active n'ont pas préalablement exercé leur propre compétence de poursuite pénale.[12] Cette opinion demanderait à être confirmée par une pratique suffisamment dense, ce qui ne semble pas être encore le cas. Toutefois, il existe déjà quelques décisions judiciaires ainsi que des législations nationales allant dans ce sens.[13]

Toujours est-il que la question se pose de savoir comment situer l'intervention éventuelle de la Cour Pénale Internationale par rapport à l'exercice de la compétence universelle. Ainsi, Damien Vandermeersch, le vice-président du Tribunal de première instance de Bruxelles ayant instruit plusieurs affaires fondées sur l'invocation de la compétence universelle, déclarait-il: 'Nous déplorons à cet égard que la primauté n'ait pas été reconnue pour la Cour Pénale Internationale qui sera amenée à

---

10 Terminologie usitée à l'article 5 du Statut.

11 L'auteur du présent article est conseil de la France dans la dite affaire.

12 Cassese, A. (2003), 'Is the Bell Tolling for Universality? A Plan for a Sensible Notion of Universal Jurisdiction', in *Journal of International Criminal Justice,* 1:3, 589-95.

13 Voir l'arrêt de la Cour suprême espagnole dans l'affaire *Guatemala,* décisions du 25 février 2003 et du 26 septembre 2005. Voir aussi, toujours en Espagne, la Ley Organica 18/2003 sur la coopération avec la CPI. Voir Vandermeersch, D. (2004), 'The ICC Statute and Belgian Law', in *Journal of International Criminal Justice*, 2:1, 145.

fonctionner sur le principe de complémentarité par rapport à l'action des juridictions nationales'.[14]

A propos de la même question, le Bureau du Procureur de la CPI a publié en février 2006 un '*Policy Paper*'.[15] Il y exprimait le point de vue, paradoxal seulement en apparence, selon lequel une manifestation du succès de la nouvelle Cour serait donné par le nombre aussi peu élevé que possible des affaires dont elle serait finalement saisie. Cette situation manifesterait en effet que, dans la grande majorité des cas, les poursuites pénales contre les auteurs de crimes auraient été déjà exercées en amont, soit par l'Etat territorial ou national compétent, soit, par le biais de la compétence universelle, par un autre Etat; le rôle du Procureur serait alors plutôt de promouvoir les procès au niveau interne avec des garanties telles qu'elles n'entraînent pas le dessaisissement des tribunaux de l'Etat concerné au bénéfice de la CPI.

Concernant l'ordre des priorités d'intervention, on a alors pu évoquer l'application d'une 'complémentarité inversée' ('*reversed complementarity*') selon laquelle la CPI pourrait se saisir de l'affaire en cas de défaut de l'Etat territorial ou de l'Etat de nationalité active mais en ayant barre sur l'Etat prétendant à l'exercice de la compétence universelle, celui-ci n'intervenant qu'en cas d'abstention de la Cour. Dans une situation de ce dernier type, on trouverait alors une hypothèse de *dédoublement fonctionnel* de type scellien puisque l'Etat faisant agir ses tribunaux sur la base de la compétence universelle le ferait pour palier la carence de la CPI.

4. Conclusion

En définitive, le principe de complémentarité nous ramène à la considération de l'une des questions les plus classiques du droit international: celle des rapports entre les ordres juridiques, celui de l'Etat et celui qu'il partage avec les autres Etats. La priorité accordée à l'intervention de l'Etat territorial ou de nationalité active s'inscrit dans la logique du respect traditionnel des compétences souveraines. Elle pourrait encore s'accommoder d'une vision dualiste du rapport entre les ordres. En revanche, l'articulation poussée qu'elle organise au sein du Statut entre droit interne et juge pénal international traduit une inspiration nettement moniste. La primauté du but à atteindre est inscrite dans l'ordre international. Il s'agit de ne pas laisser les crimes de génocide, les crimes contre l'humanité, les crimes de guerre ainsi que le crime d'agression impunis.

Subordonnés à cette fin, les ordres juridiques internes doivent prêter le concours de leurs normes et de leurs organes à sa réalisation. A défaut de l'assumer, ils laisseront la place à l'action internationale, qu'elle émane de l'organisation internationale intitulée 'Cour Pénale Internationale' ou d'un autre Etat, agissant quant à lui dans le cadre de la compétence universelle. Le principe de complémentarité s'inscrit ainsi à la fois dans la tradition et dans le renouveau du droit international public, dont fait partie intégrante le droit international pénal.

---

14 Cité par Vermeersch, D. (2001), 'La compétence universelle', in Cassese, A. et Delmas-Marty, M. (eds), *Juridictions nationales et crimes internationaux* (Paris: Presses Universitaires de France), pp. 589-611, à la p. 609, note 1.

15 Ce document interne n'a pas fait l'objet de publication sur le site de la CPI.

Chapter 4

Complementarity in Practice: Creative Solutions or a Trap for the Court?

William A. Schabas

In the solemn undertaking he made upon assuming office, on 16 June 2003, International Criminal Court Prosecutor Luis Moreno Ocampo said that 'as a consequence of complementarity', the number of cases before the Court should not be used as a measure of its efficiency. 'On the contrary', he insisted, 'the absence of trials before this Court, as a consequence of the regular functioning of national institutions, would be a major success'. Moreno Ocampo's remarks were very much in the spirit of the preamble of the Rome Statute, which recalls that 'it is the duty of every State to exercise its criminal jurisdiction over those responsible for international crimes', and which '[e]mphasiz[es] that the International Criminal Court established under this Statute shall be complementary to national criminal jurisdictions'.

'As a general rule, the policy of the Office of the Prosecutor will be to undertake investigations only where there is a clear case of failure to act by the State or States concerned' he wrote later.[1] Moreno Ocampo insisted:

> The principle of complementarity represents the express will of States Parties to create an institution that is global in scope while recognising the primary responsibility of States themselves to exercise criminal jurisdiction. The principle is also based on considerations of efficiency and effectiveness since States will generally have the best access to evidence and witnesses.[2]

Moreover, 'the system of complementarity is principally based on the recognition that the exercise of national criminal jurisdiction is not only a right but also a duty of States'.[3]

The concept of complementarity, as formulated by the Prosecutor, seemed to imply an antagonistic relationship between national justice and the International Court. Initiatives by the Prosecutor would be a sign that the national system had failed to do its duty. This was certainly in line with the focus during the negotiations leading to adoption of the Rome Statute. Yet from the beginning of the work of the International Criminal Court, there have been initiatives aimed at attracting cases for

1 'Paper on some policy issues before the Office of the Prosecutor', September 2003, 2 (available at http://www.icc-cpi.int/library/organs/otp/030905_Policy_Paper.pdf accessed 9 September 2007).

2 *Ibid.*, 4.

3 *Ibid.*, 5.

prosecution rather than insisting that States fulfil their obligations. They have been unthreatening to the States concerned, because they have targeted rebel groups rather than pro-government militias and others associated with the regimes concerned.

Even before Moreno Ocampo himself had taken office, the Office of the Prosecutor had commissioned an expert study on what it termed 'complementarity in practice'. Several prominent authorities on international criminal law, both academics and practitioners, participated in preparing a report, which appeared later that year.[4] Using terms like 'partnership', 'dialogue with States' and 'burden-sharing', it affirmed the desirability of a benign and constructive relationship between national justice systems and the International Criminal Court. The expert report emphasised forms of cooperation and assistance. Amongst other things, it contemplated what was labelled 'uncontested admissibility'. The document set out a rather novel construction of the scope of the duty of States to bring perpetrators to justice:

> Article 17 specifies the consequences for admissibility where a state is investigating or prosecuting, but does not expressly oblige states to act. However, paragraph 6 of the preamble refers to the "duty" of states to exercise criminal jurisdiction. While the preamble does not as such create legal obligations, the provisions of the Statute may be interpreted in the light of the preamble. The duty to "exercise criminal jurisdiction" should be read in a manner consistent with the customary obligation *aut dedere aut judicare*, and is therefore satisfied by extradition and surrender, since those are criminal proceedings that result in prosecution. However, as noted above, the reference to a duty also reflects the spirit of the Statute that states are intended to carry the main burden of investigating and prosecuting. This is necessary for the effective operation of the ICC. In the types of situations described here, to decline to exercise jurisdiction in favour of prosecution before the ICC is a step taken to enhance the delivery of effective justice, and is thus consistent with both the letter and the spirit of the Rome Statute and other international obligations with respect to core crimes. This is distinguishable from a failure to prosecute out of apathy or a desire to protect perpetrators, which may properly be criticized as inconsistent with the fight against impunity.[5]

The experts had developed a theory by which a State respected its obligation to prosecute by failing to prosecute.

The Prosecutor himself began to endorse this philosophy, by which the Court's operations might result from cooperation rather than antipathy:

> [T]here may be cases where inaction by States is the appropriate course of action. For example, the Court and a territorial State incapacitated by mass crimes may agree that a consensual division of labour is the most logical and effective approach. Groups bitterly divided by conflict may oppose prosecutions at each others' hands and yet agree to a prosecution by a Court perceived as neutral and impartial.[6]

This new theoretical paradigm set the Prosecutor on a quest whose consequence would be to bring the first situations and cases before the Court.

---

4 'Informal expert paper: The Principle of Complementarity in Practice' (available at http://www.icc-cpi.int/library/organs/otp/complementarity.pdf accessed on 30 August 2007).

5 *Ibid.*, 19, fn. 24.

6 'Paper on some policy issues before the Office of the Prosecutor', 5.

Although there had never been even the slightest suggestion, in the drafting history of the *Statute*, that a State might refer a case 'against itself', some early documents emerging from the Office of the Prosecutor had begun to hint at such a novel construction. In his September 2003 Policy Paper, the Prosecutor wrote:

> Where the Prosecutor receives a referral from the State in which a crime has been committed, the Prosecutor has the advantage of knowing that that State has the political will to provide his Office with all the cooperation within the country that it is required to give under the Statute. Because the State, of its own volition, has requested the exercise of the Court's jurisdiction, the Prosecutor can be confident that the national authorities will assist the investigation, will accord the privileges and immunities necessary for the investigation, and will be anxious to provide if possible and appropriate the necessary level of protection to investigators and witnesses.[7]

Along somewhat the same lines, an expert consultation held by the Office of the Prosecutor in late 2003 said that '[th]ere may also be situations where the Office of the Prosecutor (OTP) and the State concerned agree that a consensual division of labour is in the best interests of justice; for example, where a conflict-torn State is unable to carry out effective proceedings against persons most responsible'.[8] The expert paper did not expressly consider a State party referring a case 'against itself', but it did contemplate what it called 'uncontested admissibility': 'There may even be situations where the admissibility issue is further simplified, because the State in question is prepared to expressly acknowledge that it is not carrying out an investigation or prosecution'.[9]

Two scenarios were considered. In the first, the experts considered the case of a suspect who had fled to a third State: 'All interested parties may agree that the ICC has developed superior evidence, witnesses and expertise relating to that situation, making the ICC the more effective forum. Where the third State has not investigated, there is simply no obstacle to admissibility under article 17, and no need to label the State as "unwilling" or "unable" before it can co-operate with the Court by surrendering the suspect'.[10] The second scenario envisaged a State 'incapacitated by mass crimes' or alternatively 'groups bitterly divided by conflict' who feared prosecution at each other's hands but would 'agree to leadership prosecution by a Court seen as neutral and impartial. In such cases, declining to exercise primary jurisdiction in order to facilitate international jurisdiction is not a sign of apathy or lack of commitment.' The experts were evidently troubled by the suggestion that such 'uncontested admissibility' might imply that States were shirking their duty to prosecute, which is affirmed in the preamble to the Statute and which the experts recalled was also a requirement under customary international law. They wrote:

---

7 'Annex to the "Paper on some policy issues before the Office of the Prosecutor": Referrals and Communications', September 2003 (available at http://www.icc-cpi.int/library/organs/otp/policy_annex_final_210404.pdf accessed on 9 September 2007).

8 'Informal expert paper: The principle of complementarity in practice', 3.

9 *Ibid.*, 18; 20.

10 *Ibid.*, 19.

> In the types of situations described here, to decline to exercise jurisdiction in favour of prosecution before the ICC is a step taken to enhance the delivery of effective justice, and is thus consistent with both the letter and the spirit of the Rome Statute and other international obligations with respect to core crimes. This is distinguishable from a failure to prosecute out of apathy or a desire to protect perpetrators, which may properly be criticized as inconsistent with the fight against impunity.[11]

This paper will examine the legality and strategic value of the 'self-referrals', together with the related issue of whether prosecutions should focus on non-state or rebel groups. It will consider whether the Court should proceed, as it has done in the Lubanga case from the Democratic Republic of Congo, given that the accused person is also charged with serious international crimes (although not those with which he is charged in The Hague) in his own country's justice system. Finally, it will discuss the long-underestimated second prong of the admissibility determination, whether a case is of 'sufficient gravity to justify further action by the Court'.[12]

1. Soliciting 'Self-Referrals'

Within months of taking office, the Prosecutor began to solicit what soon became known as 'self-referrals' by States Parties to the Rome Statute. He approached certain States in the throes of internal conflict and encouraged them to refer 'the situation' to the Court, in accordance with article 14 of the Rome Statute. '[W]hile *proprio motu* power is a critical aspect of the Office's independence, the Prosecutor adopted the policy of inviting and welcoming voluntary referrals by territorial states as a first step in triggering the jurisdiction of the Court', he said.[13] Because the States concerned were parties to the Rome Statute, the Prosecutor could well have launched investigations using his *proprio motu* powers, in accordance with article 15, but he chose to proceed otherwise. It has since been held, by Pre-Trial Chamber I, that self-referral 'appears consistent with the ultimate purpose of the complementarity regime'.[14]

The Government of Uganda was the first. It referred the situation in northern Uganda to the International Criminal Court on 16 December 2003.[15] The letter of referral apparently made reference to the 'situation concerning the Lord's Resistance

---

11 *Ibid.*, 19, fn. 24.

12 Article 17(1)(d) ICC Statute.

13 Office of the Prosecutor, 'Report on the Activities Performed During the First Three Years (June 2003-June 2006)', 12 September 2006 (available at http://www.icc-cpi.int/library/organs/otp/OTP_3-year-report-20060914_English.pdf accessed 9 September 2007), 7.

14 Pre-Trial Chamber I, 'Decision on the Prosecutor's Application for a Warrant of Arrest' (ICC-01/04-01/06-8), 10 February 2006, paragraph 35.

15 For the background to the conflict, see: El Zeidy, M. (2005), 'The Ugandan Government Triggers the First Test of the Complementarity Principle: An Assessment of the First State's Party Referral to the ICC', in *International Criminal Law Review* 5:1, 83.

Army in northern and western Uganda'.[16] The press release issued by the Office of the Prosecutor at the time spoke of 'locating and arresting the LRA leadership', and made it quite clear that it was the rebel Lord's Resistance Army rather than the official Ugandan People's Defence Forces that were targeted,[17] although the Prosecutor later responded to Uganda indicating his interpretation that 'the scope of the referral encompasses all crimes committed in Northern Uganda in the context of the ongoing conflict involving the [Lord's Resistance Army]'.[18] On 29 January 2004, the Prosecutor made a public announcement of the referral. The Uganda referral resulted in issuance of five arrest warrants later in 2004, directed against leaders of the Lord's Resistance Army.[19] In authorising the arrest warrants, the Pre-Trial Chamber assigned to the case invoked a letter of 28 May 2004 from the Government of Uganda stating it had been 'unable to arrest ... persons who may bear the greatest responsibility' for the relevant crimes; that 'the ICC is the most appropriate and effective forum for the investigation and prosecution of those bearing the greatest responsibility' for those crimes; and that the Government of Uganda 'has not conducted and does not intend to conduct national proceedings in relation to the persons most responsible'.[20] Uganda was acknowledging that it had been 'unable' to arrest the individuals concerned, and seemed to be conceding that it was 'unwilling' to prosecute them. None of the suspects has been arrested or surrendered,[21] and there has been no real progress in prosecuting the case for two years. There have been no other arrest warrants applied for with respect to the situation in Uganda.

On 3 March 2004, the Democratic Republic of Congo (DRC) followed Uganda's example and referred the situation in the Ituri region to the Court. In its letter of referral, the DRC said that '*les autorités compétentes ne sont malheureusement pas en mesure de mener des enquêtes sur les crimes mentionnés ci-dessus ni d'engager*

---

16 Pre-Trial Chamber II, 'Decision to Convene a Status Conference on the Investigation in the Situation in Uganda in Relation to the Application of Article 53', (ICC-02/04-01/05-68), 2 December 2005, paragraph 3.

17 'President of Uganda refers situation concerning the Lord's Resistance Army (LRA) to the ICC', ICC-20040129-44-En (available at http://www.icc-cpi.int/press/pressreleases/16.html accessed 9 September 2007), 29 January 2004.

18 Pre-Trial Chamber II, 'Decision to Convene a Status Conference on the Investigation of the Situation in Uganda in Relation to the Application of Article 53' (ICC-02/04-01/05-68), 2 December 2005, paragraph 4. Note that he made no similar objection when the Security Council attempted to exclude certain individuals from the scope of the referral concerning Situation in Darfur: UN Doc. S/RES/1593 (2005), paragraph 6.

19 Pre-Trial Chamber II, 'Warrant of Arrest for Joseph Kony Issued on 8 July 2005 as Amended on 27 September 2005' (ICC-02/04-01/05-53), 27 September 2005; Pre-Trial Chamber II, 'Warrant of Arrest for Vincent Otti' (ICC-02/04-01/05-54), 8 July 2005; Pre-Trial Chamber II, 'Warrant of Arrest for Raska Lukwiya'(ICC-02/04-01/05-55), 8 July 2005 (proceedings terminated pursuant to ICC-02/04-01/05-248); Pre-Trial Chamber II, 'Warrant of Arrest for Okot Odhiambo'(ICC-02/04-01/05-56), 8 July 2005; Pre-Trial Chamber II, 'Warrant of Arrest for Dominic Ongwen'(ICC-02/04-01/05-57), 8 July 2005.

20 Pre-Trial Chamber II, 'Warrant of Arrest for Joseph Kony Issued on 8 July 2005 as Amended on 27 September 2005'(ICC-02/04-01/05-53), paragraph 37.

21 One of the arrest warrants has since been cancelled: Pre-Trial Chamber II, 'Decision to Terminate the Proceedings Against Raska Lukwiya' (ICC-02/04-01/05-248), 11 July 2007.

les poursuites nécessaires sans la participation de la Cour Pénale Internationale'. Like Uganda, Congo was in effect waiving admissibility although, unlike Uganda, without indicating whether this was because it was unwilling or because it was unable to proceed. In July 2003, the Prosecutor had indicated that the Ituri region of the DRC was his first priority. At the time, he had said it would be a likely target for the first exercise of his *proprio motu* powers, in accordance with article 15 of the Rome Statute.[22] But this became superfluous with the 'self-referral' by the Democratic Republic of Congo. Early in 2006, the Prosecutor identified an individual, Thomas Lubanga, who was already in custody in the Congo awaiting prosecution before national courts on charges of genocide and crimes against humanity. The Prosecutor obtained an arrest warrant against Lubanga for charges concerning enlistment of child soldiers, for which he was not charged in the Democratic Republic of Congo,[23] and the suspect was quickly brought to The Hague. Given that France has excluded itself from the jurisdiction of the Court with respect to war crimes, pursuant to article 124, it was ironic that Lubanga's transfer was effected by a French military airplane. Charges against Lubanga were confirmed in January 2007,[24] and preparations are now under way for his trial. There is no other indication of prosecutions resulting from the referral by the Democratic Republic of Congo.

Finally, on 21 December 2004, the Prosecutor received a 'self-referral' from the Central African Republic, which he communicated to the President of the Court the following day. The referral was announced publicly on 7 January 2005. On 25 May 2007, some 29 months after the referral, and not without prodding from both the government of the Central African Republic and the Pre-Trial Chamber assigned to the case,[25] the Prosecutor announced he had decided to initiate an investigation. He explained that the *Cour de Cassation*, the country's highest judicial body, had confirmed that the national justice system was unable to carry out the complex proceedings necessary to investigate and prosecute the alleged crimes, and that this was important in his own decision to proceed.[26]

Since December 2004, there have been no further referrals pursuant to article 14. Nor has there been any exercise of the Prosecutor's *proprio motu* powers, in accordance with article 15. The only other situation under consideration by the Court is that of Darfur, Sudan, which was referred to the Court by the Security Council in

22 'Communications Received by the Office of the Prosecutor of the ICC', pids.009.2003-EN (available at http://www.icc-cpi.int/library/press/mediaalert/16_july__english.pdf accessed 9 September 2007), 16 July 2003, 2–3.

23 Pre-Trial Chamber I, 'Decision on the Prosecutor's Application for a Warrant of Arrest'(ICC-01/04-01/06-8), 10 February 2006.

24 Pre-Trial Chamber I, 'Décision sur la confirmation des charges' (ICC-01/04-01/06-803), 29 January 2007.

25 Pre-Trial Chamber III, 'Decision Requesting Information on the Status of the Preliminary Examination of the Situation in the Central African Republic' (ICC-01/05-6), 30 November 2006.

26 'Prosecutor opens investigation in the Central African Republic', ICC-OTP-PR-20070522-220_EN (available at http://www.icc-cpi.int/press/pressreleases/248.html accessed 9 September 2007), 22 May 2007.

March 2005, in accordance with article 13.[27] Two arrest warrants with respect to the Situation in Darfur were issued by Pre-Trial Chamber I on 27 April 2007.[28]

2. Is Self-referral Authorised by the Rome Statute?

'Self-referral' flows from a creative interpretation of article 14 of the Rome Statute that was not seriously contemplated by the 1998 Diplomatic Conference and during the prior negotiations.[29] The 1994 draft statute submitted to the General Assembly by the International Law Commission included the concept of 'state-party referral', but described the source of the referral as a 'complainant state'.[30] A State Party could lodge a 'complaint'.[31] The court was authorized to exercise its jurisdiction with respect to genocide if a State Party to the Statute that was also a contracting party to the 1948 *Genocide Convention* took the initiative to 'lodge a complaint' that genocide had been committed.[32] In the case of aggression, war crimes and crimes against humanity, the court could proceed if a 'complaint' was lodged by the 'custodial state' (that is, the State which had 'custody of the suspect with respect to the crime') and by 'the State on the territory of which the act or omission in question occurred'.[33] The language makes it clear enough that what was contemplated was a 'complainant State' 'lodg[ing] a complaint' against *another* State.

The reference to 'complaint' continued through the early drafts, and was still being used in the so-called 'Zutphen draft'[34] and in the final draft adopted by the Preparatory Committee that formed the basis of negotiations at the Rome Conference.[35] The nomenclature, though not the substance, was changed in a 'discussion paper' issued by the Bureau of the Rome Conference on 6 July 1998.[36] The title 'Complaint' was changed to 'Referral of a situation by a State', and the triggering of the jurisdiction of the Court by either the Security Council or a State Party was described as 'referral'. Probably, the change in terminology was related to the fact that a complainant State was being prevented from submitting a specific case or crime to the Court. It could

27 UN Doc. S/RES/1593 (2005).

28 Pre-Trial Chamber I, 'Warrant of Arrest for Ahmad Harun'(ICC-02/05-01/07-2), 27 April 2007; Pre-Trial Chamber I, 'Warrant of Arrest for Ali Kushayb' (ICC-02/05-01/07-3), 27 April 2007.

29 See generally, Kress, C. (2004), '"Self-Referrals" and "Waivers of Complementarity"', in *Journal of International Criminal Justice* 2:4, 944, 946.

30 'Report of the International Law Commission on the Work of its Forty-Sixth Session, 2 May-22 July 1994', Chapter II, UN Doc. A/49/10, paragraph 25(5).

31 *Ibid.*

32 *Ibid.*, paragraph 21(1)(a).

33 *Ibid.*, paragraph 21(1)(b).

34 'Report of the Inter-Sessional Meeting From 19 to 30 January 1998 in Zutphen, The Netherlands', UN Doc. A/AC.249/1998/L.13, article 45[25], 85.

35 'Report of the Preparatory Committee on the Establishment of an International Criminal Court', 'Draft Statute for the International Criminal Court', UN Doc. A/CONF.183/2/Add.1, article 11, 35–36.

36 'Discussion Paper, Bureau, Part 2. Jurisdiction, Admissibility and Applicable Law', UN Doc. A/CONF.183/C.1/L.53, 16.

only refer a 'situation'. According to Philippe Kirsch, who chaired the Bureau at the Conference, 'the general approach of referring "situations" rather than "cases" seems a prudent one. This helps reduce the arguably unseemly prospect of States Parties referring complaints against specific individuals, which might create a perception of using the Court to "settle scores".'[37]

There is not a trace in the *travaux préparatoires* or in the various commentaries by participants in the drafting process to suggest that a State referring a case *against itself* was ever contemplated by this change in terminology. When the chair of the Committee of the whole, Philippe Kirsch, presented the Bureau draft for discussion, he did not draw the attention of delegates to the change from 'complaint' to 'referral', as he would have been expected to do were some important change being implied.[38] When the coordinator responsible for the Bureau draft, Erkki Kourula, introduced the debate, he said that '[a]rticle 11, entitled "Referral of a situation by a State", was a technical issue',[39] thereby confirming that a substantive modification was not intended. The change in terminology did not provoke a single comment, further confirming that the delegates to the Rome Conference considered 'referral' to be a synonym for 'complaint'.[40] The absence of any reference to self-referral in the main commentaries on the Rome Statute, which were generally authored by participants in the negotiations, further bolsters this observation.[41] In other words, the drafting history of article 14 of the Rome Statute leaves little doubt that what was considered was a 'complaint' by a State party against another State.

It has been suggested that something akin to 'self-referral' was actually considered during the drafting of the Rome Statute in the concept of 'waiver'. There is a reference in the report of the *ad hoc* committee, which met during 1995, to a scenario whereby a State might 'voluntarily decide to relinquish its jurisdiction in favour of the ICC'.[42] The Report notes that others said such an approach was inconsistent with the principle of complementarity, because the Court 'should in no way undermine the effectiveness of national justice systems and should only be resorted to in exceptional cases'.[43] That the discussion continued until the Rome Conference itself can be seen in the official records. For example, the draft provision on admissibility in the draft

---

37 Kirsch, P. and Robinson, D. (2002), 'Referral by States Parties', in Cassese, A., Gaeta, P. and Jones, J.R.W.D. (eds), *The Rome Statute of the International Criminal Court: A Commentary*, (Oxford: Oxford University Press), p. 623.

38 UN Doc. A/CONF.183/C.1/SR.25, paragraph 3.

39 UN Doc. A/CONF.183/C.1/SR.29, paragraph 6.

40 UN Doc. A/CONF.183/C.1/SR.29, paragraphs 11-187; UN Doc. A/CONF.183/C.1/SR.30, paragraphs 7–133; UN Doc. A/CONF.183/C.1/SR.31, paragraphs 1–44.

41 Kirsch, P. and Robinson, D. (2002), 'Referral by States Parties', in Cassese, A., Gaeta, P. and Jones, J.R.W.D. (eds), *The Rome Statute of the International Criminal Court: A Commentary*, (Oxford: Oxford University Press), pp. 619–25; Archesi, A. (1999), 'Referral of a situation by a State Party', in Triffterer, O. (ed.), *Commentary on the Rome Statute of the International Criminal Court, Observers' Notes, Article by Article* (Baden-Baden: Nomos), pp. 353–58.

42 'Report of the Ad Hoc Committee on the Establishment of an International Criminal Court', UN Doc. A/50/22, paragraph 47.

43 *Ibid.*

statute submitted by the Preparatory Committee contained a footnote: 'The present text of article 15 is without prejudice to the question of whether complementarity-related admissibility requirements of this article may be waived by the State or States concerned.'[44] No concrete proposal appears to have been presented in order to reflect the issue, however. What the record shows, then, is that the issue of waiver was present but that it was never of any significance in the drafting history. The final text of the relevant provisions, authorising the Court to declare a case inadmissible even when the parties do not raise the matter, confirms that waiver is not contemplated by the Statute.[45] The argument that the possibility of waiver in some way reinforces the concept of self-referral is therefore not a particularly strong one.

But even if waiver was a live issue, it should not be completely confounded with 'self-referral', of which there is no evidence in the *travaux préparatoires*. Referral is described in the Rome Statute as a 'precondition for the exercise of jurisdiction' and, more colloquially, as one of the instrument's three 'trigger mechanisms'. It defines how cases begin their journey to the docket of the Court. This is not the same thing as a State deciding not to argue whether or not it is willing and able to investigate or prosecute. A State may waive the debate about admissibility no matter how a case is triggered. In any event, evidence of discussion by the drafters about the possibility of waiver cannot support the argument that 'self-referral' is implicit, because the Rome Statute unequivocally rejects the idea that a State can waive admissibility. Article 19(1) of the Rome Statute states that '[t]he Court may, on its own motion, determine the admissibility of a case in accordance with article 17'. Thus, the Court can declare a case inadmissible even if the State itself remains silent, and this means there can be no 'waiver' of admissibility.

Certainly, there are examples of States triggering international justice with respect to crimes committed on their territory. The United Nations criminal tribunals for Rwanda, Sierra Leone and Lebanon have all been created as a result of initiatives from the States on whose territory the crimes were perpetrated, and before whose courts the offenders would normally be prosecuted.[46] Although Rwanda ultimately quarrelled about several issues in the configuration that the Security Council gave to the International Criminal Tribunal for Rwanda, it did not question the concept as a whole. It seems highly doubtful that the Tribunal would have been established in the absence of Rwandan support. As for the Special Court for Sierra Leone, it is a creature of treaty; the government's consent is a *sine qua non* of its existence. The Special Tribunal for Lebanon is being created at the request of the Prime Minister, but over the objections of a significant segment of the political forces in the country, including the President. Although it was hoped it would be established by treaty,

---

44 UN Doc. A/CONF.183/2, 27, fn. 43.

45 Article 19(1) Rome Statute.

46 'Letter Dated 28 September 1994 From the Permanent Representative of Rwanda to the United Nations Addressed to the President of the Security Council', UN Doc. S/1994/1115; 'Letter dated 9 August 2000 from the Permanent Representative of Sierra Leone to the United Nations addressed to the President of the Security Council', UN Doc. S/2000/786, annex; 'Letter Dated 13 December 2005 From the Prime Minister of Lebanon to the Secretary-General of the United Nations', UN Doc. S/2005/783, annex.

similar to the case in Sierra Leone, political obstacles forced the Security Council to proceed by resolution, acting pursuant to Chapter VII of the Charter of the United Nations.[47]

While these institutions show that international justice is not necessarily incompatible with a consensual relationship between the State of territorial jurisdiction and the international body, they do not directly answer the argument that such a paradigm was not what was contemplated when the Rome Statute was drafted. By ratifying or acceding to the Rome Statute, States do much the same thing that Rwanda, Sierra Leone and Lebanon did in consenting to the creation of the relevant institutions. Rwanda, Sierra Leone and Lebanon have no say in what cases actually come before the Court. But if the doctrine of 'self-referral' is accepted, it seems to indicate that States Parties to the Rome Statute have done more than simply consent to the exercise of jurisdiction, and that they have reserved the right to put specific situations before the Court for prosecution.

Obviously, 'self-referral' and waiver of admissibility are not entirely unrelated notions. In both cases, the State agrees to cooperate with international justice, rather than to resist it. But when a State is actively engaged in initiation of the process, there is potential for manipulation. In effect, the State quite predictably uses the international institution to pursue its enemies. When the Special Court for Sierra Leone was being established, President Kabba wrote to the United Nations asking that it unleash international justice against the Revolutionary United Front, just as President Museveni did against the Lord's Resistance Army when referring the 'situation in Uganda' to the International Criminal Court. Likewise, Rwanda intended for the *ad hoc* Tribunal to be aimed at the *génocidaires* of the previous regime, and not at atrocities committed by those now in power in the country. And the Lebanese Government expects the new Tribunal to attack its adversaries, in particular those aligned with Syria and perhaps Syria itself.

The argument that 'self-referral' is compatible with article 14 may not be supported by the drafting history of the Rome Statute. But legal instruments take on a life of their own, and creative interpretation of their provisions is usually desirable. Certainly, 'self-referral' is not explicitly prohibited by the text. Pre-Trial Chamber I, in *Lubanga*, said that in the Democratic Republic of Congo situation, self-referral 'appears consistent with the ultimate purpose of the complementarity regime'.[48] This is a somewhat different argument, of course, in that it attempts to harness 'self-referral' to the 'ultimate purpose of the complementarity regime' rather than what was intended by the Rome Conference. The Pre-Trial Chamber provided little to indicate what this 'ultimate purpose' actually was, aside from the rather

47 UN Doc. S/RES/1757 (2007).

48 Pre-Trial Chamber I, 'Decision on the Prosecutor's Application for a Warrant of Arrest', 10 February 2006(ICC-01/04-01/06-8), paragraph 35.

simplistic observation that 'the Court by no means replaces national jurisdictions, but is complementary to them'.[49]

The least one can say is that Pre-Trial Chamber I has not provided a very convincing explanation for the relationship between 'self-referral' and the 'ultimate purpose' of complementarity. In fact, from a purely logical standpoint, the opposite seems just as plausible, indeed perhaps more so. A State that refers a case to the International Criminal Court is indirectly answering one of the prongs of the complementarity text, namely, that it is 'willing' to prosecute, at least in the sense that it is willing to see the alleged perpetrators brought to justice. It may, on the other hand, find itself 'unable' to proceed because of a breakdown in its own justice system or possibly a serious legal impediment, such as an amnesty. In the two cases of State-encouraged international tribunals, those of Sierra Leone and Rwanda, the initiatives are explained by inability, not unwillingness. Sierra Leone was legally bound by an amnesty in the peace agreement; Rwanda's courts following the genocide were in a state of total disarray. Neither country was in a situation where it could undertake the prosecutions but chose not to do so. The materials relating to the Special Tribunal for Lebanon provide little in the way of explanation of the need of an international tribunal, aside from a perfunctory reference in a report from the Secretary General speaking of a 'shared assumption that a purely national tribunal would not be able to effectively fulfil the task of trying those accused of the crime'.[50]

3. Self-referral: Expedient or Trap?

With respect to the Uganda and Democratic Republic of Congo situations resulting from 'self-referral' now pending before the International Criminal Court, the issue is actually unwillingness, not inability. Uganda, in particular, has simply preferred to hand the prosecutions over to the Court. Its referral did not allege that the national courts were unable to prosecute. Everything would indicate, in fact, that Uganda has one of Africa's better criminal justice systems, and that its courts are more than able to prosecute the leaders of the Lord's Resistance Army.[51] With respect to the Democratic Republic of Congo, it may well have been unable to undertake prosecution when the self-referral was submitted to the Court, in early 2004. But in the *Lubanga* decision, the above-cited sentence of the Pre-Trial Chamber invoking the compatibility of complementarity with the self-referral is accompanied by another sentence explaining that this was the case *at the time* of the self-referral and that it was a result of inability, not unwillingness. The Pre-Trial Chamber went

---

49 *Ibid.*, citing the leading insider account on the drafting of article 17: John T. Holmes, J.T. (1999), 'The Principle of Complementarity', in Lee, R.S. (ed.), *The International Criminal Court: The Making of the Rome Statute – Issues, Negotiation, Results* (The Hague-London-Boston: Kluwer Law International), p. 41.

50 'Report of the Secretary-General pursuant to paragraph 6 of resolution 1644' (2005), S/2006/176, paragraph 5.

51 In June 2005, for example, the Constitutional Court of Uganda declared the country's capital punishment statute to be unconstitutional: *Susan Kigula and 416 Others v. Attorney General*, Constitutional Petition No. 6 of 2003, 5 June 2005.

on to note that the situation in the national justice system had evolved in the nearly two years since the self-referral, and that Congolese courts might well now be in a position to undertake prosecution.[52]

As for Central African Republic, perhaps less is known about this situation, and there has not yet been any meaningful judicial activity of the Court. It is curious, to say the least, that the Prosecutor would rely upon the decision of the *Cour de cassation* as authority for the inability of the country's judicial system to proceed with the prosecutions. After all, if the *Cour de cassation* is a source of reliable judicial determination, doesn't that tend to prove the opposite, that is, that the courts of the country are functional?

Uganda has offered the Prosecutor what has appeared to be a fairly simple prosecution on which to cut his teeth. He could be relatively sure of the cooperation of the Ugandan authorities in apprehending those who might be charged, something that was not so obvious in other possible targets of the Office of the Prosecutor, such as Colombia. That is because those he was investigating were the enemies of the Ugandan State. President Museveni was, in effect, asking the Prosecutor to help him investigate rebels within the country. After the referral, the Prosecutor promptly reminded the Ugandan Government that the referral could not be focussed in such a manner, and that he could not limit his investigation to only one side of the conflict. But in practice, this is what he has done. It is completely consistent with the self-referral strategy of the Office of the Prosecutor, of course, because the moment he seeks charges against pro-government forces, cooperation from the Government side is likely to become less obvious. Moreover, it would seem unlikely that any other States would then follow the Ugandan example, in the hopes that the Prosecutor's attention might be aimed at their own rebels. In other words, if the Prosecutor hopes that the self-referral approach will continue to interest States, it seems he must reassure them that in practice he is interested in the rebels, and not the government forces.

When the Ugandan arrest warrants were made public, the Prosecutor was sharply criticized by international non-governmental organisations for being one-sided.[53] He responded by attempting to explain that the rebel crimes were more serious than any committed by pro-government forces. Along with complementarity, the issue of 'gravity' is the other prong in the admissibility determination. We shall return to the debate about gravity later in this essay.

The motivation of the Government of Uganda in making the 'self-referral' was obvious enough. The Court amounted to a further source of pressure that Uganda could bring to bear on rebels whom it had been impossible to defeat on the battlefield. President Museveni must have calculated that the threat of prosecution might compel the leaders of the Lord's Resistance Army to negotiate a peaceful settlement to the two-decade long war. He is a shrewd and skilled operator, and on this point he judged

---

52 Pre-Trial Chamber I, 'Decision on the Prosecutor's Application for Warrant of Arrest, Article 58', (ICC-01/04-01/06-8), paragraph 36.

53 Amnesty International, 'Uganda: First ever arrest warrants by International Criminal Court – a first step towards addressing impunity', 14 October 2005, AI Index: AFR 59/008/2005; Human Rights Watch, 'ICC Takes Decisive Step for Justice in Uganda', 14 October 2005.

correctly. It is widely acknowledged that the threat of prosecution by the International Criminal Court has helped to bring the Lord's Resistance Army to the negotiating table. On a visit to the Court, the Ugandan Minister for Security, Amama Mbabazi, noted that the issuance of warrants had contributed to driving the Lord's Resistance Army leaders to the negotiating table. In September 2006, Jan Egeland, the United Nations Under-Secretary-General for Humanitarian Affairs and Emergency Relief, made similar observations in a briefing to the Security Council.[54] Speaking to the Assembly of States Parties in November 2006, Prosecutor Ocampo said:

> The Court's intervention has galvanized the activities of the states concerned. [...] Thanks to the unity of purpose of these states, the LRA has been forced to flee its safe haven in southern Sudan and has moved its headquarters to the DRC border. As a consequence, crimes allegedly committed by the LRA in Northern Uganda have drastically decreased. People are leaving the camps for displaced persons and the night commuter shelters which protected tens of thousands of children are now in the process of closing. The loss of their safe haven led the LRA commanders to engage in negotiations, resulting in a cessation of hostilities agreement in August 2006.[55]

In other words, issuance of the arrest warrants had contributed to conflict resolution in Northern Uganda. In May 2006, new efforts to mediate an end to the civil war gained momentum. Hostilities came to an end in August 2006.

The situation was somewhat reminiscent of the situation faced by Richard Goldstone, Prosecutor of the International Criminal Tribunal for the Former Yugoslavia, in July 1995. While the war in Bosnia and Herzegovina was still raging, he obtained indictments against Serb leaders Radovan Karadžić and Ratko Mladić. Goldstone was later chastised by United Nations Secretary-General Boutros Boutros-Ghali for failing to consult at a political level. He replied that as a prosecutor it was not his job to take political factors into account.[56] Nevertheless, the charges helped to isolate Karadžić and Mladić, and may well have contributed to the successful outcome of peace negotiations at Dayton later that same year.

But if the charges against the Lord's Resistance Army might have helped to provoke peace negotiations, they also soon proved to be a potential obstacle to their successful completion.[57] Jan Egeland reported to the Security Council that in meetings with internally displaced persons, civil society and the parties themselves, the 'International Criminal Court indictments were the number one subject of

---

54 UN Doc. S/PV.5525, 4.

55 'Opening Remarks, Luis Moreno Ocampo, Fifth Session of the Assembly of States Parties', 23 November 2006.

56 Goldstone, R. J. (2000), *For Humanity. Reflections of a War Crimes Investigator* (New Haven: Yale University Press), pp. 102–3.

57 This is discussed by Apuuli, K. P. (2004), 'The International Criminal Court (ICC) and the Lord's Resistance Army (LRA) Insurgency in Northern Uganda', in *Criminal Law Forum* 15:4, 408; Id., (2006), 'The ICC Arrest Warrants for the Lord's Resistance Army Leaders and Peace Prospects for Northern Uganda', in *Journal of International Criminal Justice* 4:1, 179; Ssenyonjo, M. (2005), 'Accountability of Non-State Actors in Uganda for War Crimes and Human Rights Violations: Between Amnesty and the International Criminal Court', in *Journal Conflict & Security Law* 10:3, 405.

discussion [...] All expressed a strong concern that if the indictments were not lifted, they could threaten the progress in these most promising talks ever for northern Uganda'.[58] The rebel leaders quite predictably insisted that the arrest warrants be withdrawn as a condition for the peace settlement. President Yoweri Museveni of Uganda, who had triggered the prosecutions two years earlier when he referred the situation in northern Uganda to the Court, asked the Prosecutor to withdraw the warrants. He promised those who had been charged that they would have immunity from arrest in Uganda.[59] Richard Goldstone remarked:

> It would be fatally damaging to the credibility of the international court if Museveni was allowed to get away with granting amnesty. I just don't accept that Museveni has the right to use the International Criminal Court like this.[60]

But what if failure to withdraw the charges eventually provoked a return to hostilities? In other words, instead of contributing to peace the International Criminal Court might actually prolong a conflict, with the result that hundreds of thousands of innocent victims could suffer. This was certainly not the intention of those who set up the institution.

If international justice is brought to bear on situations like that of northern Uganda because it can help to bring peace when there is conflict, then it should probably be prepared to stand down when criminal prosecution becomes an obstacle to peace. To the extent that the leaders of the Lord's Resistance Army came to the negotiating table *because* of the threat of prosecution, then their withdrawal would seem to be necessary in order to complete the process. Otherwise, the threat of criminal prosecution only does half the job, and the boast that the Court has helped to promote peace is ultimately a hollow one. On this point, however, there is great resistance, not from the Ugandan authorities but rather from the Prosecutor himself and the various players in the international criminal justice community who surround him. They argue that to attempt to withdraw the charges would betray the search for justice and discredit the Court.

This position seems too extreme. Those who argue that prosecution should not be sacrificed in a peace bargain should be prepared to answer for the alternative, which can never be ruled out, namely a return to conflict *because* of the inability of negotiators to be able to promise the rebel leaders that if they lay down their arms they will not be prosecuted. Are those who argue that the arrest warrants cannot be dropped as a matter of principle truly prepared for a resumption of hostilities, with all of the terrible human suffering that may involve?

The peace vs. justice conundrum was debated at length during the Rome Conference, but it was never resolved. This was because there was no consensus on the subject. South Africa's delegation, for example, regularly reminded the drafters of their country's national approach to post-conflict justice, which was predicated upon a renunciation of criminal prosecution for the crime against humanity of

---

58 UN Doc. S/PV.5525, 4.

59 McGreal, C., *African Search for Peace Throws Court into Crisis*, The Guardian, 9 January 2007.

60 *Ibid.*

apartheid, and an amnesty mechanism in the event of specific atrocities where the offender acknowledged the crimes committed. Some commentators have observed that the complementarity regime of the International Criminal Court would stand as an obstacle to a South African-style transition from a racist, authoritarian regime to a pluralist and democratic one. The matter is presented as if such an outcome is desirable, and a progressive development in the campaign against impunity. This is where the present author has to part company with those who prize accountability above peace. Probably no issue has so marked the development of human rights in the second half of the twentieth century as the struggle to end the *apartheid* regime of South Africa. Nelson Mandela and his associates managed to find a workable solution, enabling a transition without a bloodbath. It is one of the great miracles of our time. The suggestion that the South African solution is in some way a perverse development that needs to be corrected by article 17 of the Rome Statute is a suggestion that is hard to accept.

In fact, the 'international community' has accepted the South African model, as can be seen from State practice. Some contend that customary international law requires all States to prosecute all serious violations of international humanitarian law. It is argued that this message underpins the preamble and the *raison d'être* of the Rome Statute. Yet if this be the case, why have *no* States attempted to break the bargain Mandela made with de Klerk, and bring those responsible for the racist South African regime to justice for the crime against humanity of *apartheid*? Many States have legislation enabling them to exercise universal jurisdiction over crimes against humanity. Several of them are now pursuing this actively, pursuing those suspected of committing crimes against humanity in places like Rwanda, and Iraq, and Argentina. But nobody dares unravel the peace for justice bargain made by Nelson Mandela. The answer can only be that international practice actually acknowledges the validity of such pacts when they are genuine. If a compromise with justice is necessary in order to ensure peace, and it is guided by credible leaders like Nelson Mandela, this is accepted internationally. Precisely for this reason, those who drafted the Rome Statute left some constructive ambiguity in its provisions. They were torn between the apparent principled solution of admissibility whenever a State failed to prosecute serious crimes, and the pragmatic answer of leaving productive bargains like that of the South African transition alone. No language could be found to translate this, which is a matter more of policy than of law, into an unequivocal legal text.

In the Uganda situation, this problem, left unresolved at Rome, has come back to haunt the Court, and show that self-referral, far from being an expedient to provide a fledgling institution with some cases, is actually a trap. If a State refers a situation against itself, that is, against its rebels, in the context of a conflict, it is doing so with a result in mind. And that result may well involve, as it does in Uganda, withdrawing the threat of prosecution in exchange for something. Put another way, over the medium to long term, self-referral will only work if it can be followed by self-deferral. But there is great political opposition within the Court and among its strongest supporters to any suggestion that justice might be sacrificed at the altar of peace.

4. Encouraging States to Assume their Obligations

The preamble of the Rome Statute recalls that 'effective prosecution must be ensured by taking measures at the national level' and that 'it is the duty of every State to exercise its criminal jurisdiction over those responsible for international crimes'. Pronouncements of the Prosecutor indicating his commitment to these principles have already been cited earlier in this essay. In practice, however, the Prosecutor's actions seem inconsistent with his profession of faith in the importance of national justice.

In the situation in northern Uganda, for example, it has never been suggested that the Ugandan courts are unable to conduct prosecutions. Indeed, Uganda's courts are among the best in sub-Saharan Africa. Nothing in the Court's discussion of the five arrest warrants suggests that the matter has arisen. Rather, the Prosecutor and the Government of Uganda have simply decided it would be more convenient to hold trials in The Hague before the International Criminal Court. This is a case where the State that would normally exercise jurisdiction has indeed waived any contestation based upon complementarity, and where the Court has not, at least so far, shown any inclination to raise the matter of its own motion.

It seems preposterous to argue that Uganda is 'unable' to proceed against the Lord's Resistance Army leaders. Perhaps it might be said it is 'unable' in the sense that it cannot apprehend the accused, something that it alleged in its 'Letter on Jurisdiction' of 28 May 2004, but the same can be said of the International Criminal Court. As for whether Uganda is 'unwilling', article 17(2) of the Rome Statute provides a formula for assessing this:

> 2. In order to determine unwillingness in a particular case, the Court shall consider, having regard to the principles of due process recognized by international law, whether one or more of the following exist, as applicable:
> (a) The proceedings were or are being undertaken or the national decision was made for the purpose of shielding the person concerned from criminal responsibility for crimes within the jurisdiction of the Court referred to in article 5;
> (b) There has been an unjustified delay in the proceedings which in the circumstances is inconsistent with an intent to bring the person concerned to justice;
> (c) The proceedings were not or are not being conducted independently or impartially, and they were or are being conducted in a manner which, in the circumstances, is inconsistent with an intent to bring the person concerned to justice.

None of these factors seems applicable to Uganda at present. All that Uganda has said is that it 'has not conducted and does not intend to conduct national proceedings in relation to the persons most responsible'. The whole idea of 'unwillingness' was built around the concept of a State that did not want to see the offender brought to justice, and not the State that merely chose, in agreement with the Prosecutor of the International Criminal Court, to defer prosecution.

The situation in the Democratic Republic of Congo is closer to the classic paradigm of a state whose failing justice system renders it 'unable' to prosecute. Here, too, article 17 provides guidelines for determining inability:

> 3. In order to determine inability in a particular case, the Court shall consider whether, due to a total or substantial collapse or unavailability of its national judicial system, the State is unable to obtain the accused or the necessary evidence and testimony or otherwise unable to carry out its proceedings.

In the letter of referral to the Court, the Government of the Democratic Republic of Congo stated that the competent authorities were unfortunately unable to pursue investigations and to undertake prosecutions without the participation of the International Criminal Court.[61] In applying for the arrest warrant, the Office of the Prosecutor told the Court that since the referral, 'the Government of the DRC, being well aware of the investigations of the OTP, has not informed the OTP otherwise'.[62] But the Pre-Trial Chamber did not consider that these elements were adequate to dispose of the 'inability' question. In issuing the arrest warrant, it wrote:

> In the Chamber's view, when the President of the DRC sent the letter of referral to the Office of the Prosecutor on 3 March 2004, it appears that the DRC was indeed unable to undertake the investigation and prosecution of the crimes falling within the jurisdiction of the Court committed in the situation in the territory of DRC since 1 July 2002… However, for the purpose of the admissibility analysis of the case against Mr Thomas Lubanga Dyilo, the Chamber observes that since March 2004 the DRC national justice system has undergone certain changes, particularly in the region of Ituri where a *Tribunal de Grande Instance* has been re-opened in Bunia. This has resulted *inter alia* in the issuance of two warrants of arrest by the competent DRC authorities for Mr Thomas Lubanga Dyilo in March 2005 for several crimes, some possibly within the jurisdiction of the Court, committed in connection with military attacks from May 2003 onwards and during the so-called Ndoki incident in February 2005. Moreover, as a result of the DRC proceedings against Mr Thomas Lubanga Dyilo, he has been held in the *Centre Pénitentiaire et de Rééducation de Kinshasa* since 19 March 2005. Therefore, in the Chamber's view, the Prosecution's general statement that the DRC national judicial system continues to be unable in the sense of article 17(1)(a) to (c) and (3) of the Statute does not wholly correspond to the reality any longer.[63]

In other words, Pre-Trial Chamber I considered that the Congolese justice system was not suffering from 'a total or substantial collapse or unavailability of its national judicial system', to borrow the words of article 17.

The fact that Lubanga was in custody in Congo at the time the Prosecutor took an interest in him might suggest that the national justice system was actually working, and that the State was meeting its international obligations in terms of addressing impunity. There is, in fact, a passing reference to this when the Pre-Trial Chamber cited the Prosecutor's submission: Lubanga was being prosecuted in Congo for genocide and crimes against humanity! But the Democratic Republic of Congo had another problem, according to the Pre-Trial Chamber. Proceedings in Congo were

61 'Letter of Joseph Kabila to the Prosecutor', 3 March 2004.

62 Prosecutor's Application for Warrant of Arrest for Thomas Lubanga Dyilo, paragraph 186, quoted by Pre-Trial Chamber I, 'Decision on the Prosecutor's application for a warrant of arrest, Article 58' (ICC-01/04-01/06-8), 10 February 2006, fn. 24.

63 Pre-Trial Chamber I, 'Decision on the Prosecutor's application for a warrant of arrest, Article 58' (ICC-01/04-01/06-8), 10 February 2006, paragraphs 35–6.

not based upon the policy or practice of enlisting, conscripting and active use of children under the age of 15 in armed conflict.[64] As a result, wrote the Pre-Trial Chamber, 'the DRC cannot be considered to be acting in relation to the specific case before the Court…'[65] And therefore it held that the complementarity test was satisfied.

Commenting on the Lubanga arrest warrant in a press statement, Prosecutor Moreno Ocampo said '[f]orcing children to be killers jeopardises the future of mankind'.[66] But arguably, the justice system of the Democratic Republic of Congo was doing a *better* job than the Court itself, because it was addressing crimes of greater gravity. Certainly genocide and crimes against humanity might also be said to 'jeopardise the future of mankind'. There is no attempt within the Statute itself to rank crimes based on gravity, and it might be claimed, as judges have done at the International Criminal Tribunal for the Former Yugoslavia,[67] that there is no objective distinction between war crimes, crimes against humanity and genocide in terms of seriousness. They don't always act as if they believe this, however. It is common practice, in plea bargaining, to withdraw charges of genocide but maintain those of crimes against humanity, and it seems absurd that this would take place if the two crimes were objectively of equal gravity. With respect to the Rome Statute, it contains certain indicators suggesting a hierarchy in crimes. For example, article 124 allows States to opt out of jurisdiction over war crimes, but not crimes against humanity and genocide. Similarly, the Statute is more tolerant of the defences of superior orders[68] and defence of property[69] when only war crimes are involved. These are small signs in and of themselves, but they tend to confirm that there is indeed a hierarchy of crimes, and that war crimes follow genocide and crimes against humanity.

It would appear, then, that the International Criminal Court has removed Thomas Lubanga from jeopardy before the criminal tribunals of his own country for crimes that are more serious than those for which he is being prosecuted in The Hague. To be fair to the Prosecutor, his position was that the courts of the Democratic Republic of Congo were not prosecuting adequately. Although it rejected the Prosecutor's submission on this point, Pre-Trial Chamber I 'note[d] the Prosecution's allegations that the DRC authorities are not pursuing the investigations against Mr. Thomas Lubanga Dyilo'.[70] But perhaps the Prosecutor would agree that if the Congolese justice system is working, then it would be better for Lubanga to stand trial at home for genocide and crimes against humanity than to stand trial in The Hague for recruitment of child soldiers. As for Lubanga himself, he must be delighted to

64 *Ibid.*, paragraph 38.

65 *Ibid.*, paragraph 39.

66 'Statement by Luis Moreno-Ocampo, Press Conference in relation with the surrender to the Court of Mr. Thomas Lubanga Dyilo', 18 March 2006.

67 *Prosecutor* v. *Furundžija* (Case No. IT-95-17/1-A), Judgment, 21 July 2000, paragraph 247; *Prosecutor* v. *Tadić* (Case No. IT-94-1-A*bis*), Judgment in Sentencing Appeals, 26 January 2000, paragraph 69.

68 Article 33 Rome Statute.

69 Article 31(1)(c) Rome Statute.

70 Pre-Trial Chamber I, 'Decision on the Prosecutor's application for a warrant of arrest, Article 58' (ICC-01/04-01/06-8), 10 February 2006, paragraph 36, fn. 32.

find himself in The Hague facing prosecution for relatively less important offences concerning child soldiers rather than genocide and crimes against humanity.

Thus, in practice, neither the Uganda nor the Democratic Republic of Congo situations have been addressed by the Court in a manner aimed at best encouraging the national justice system to assume its duties under international law. Of the three situations pending, it is the Darfur referral by the Security Council that best demonstrates how the Court may effectively encourage national justice initiatives. In December 2006, the Prosecutor told the Security Council that he had requested an update from the Government of Sudan with respect to its national proceedings, and that he was told that 14 individuals had been arrested for violations of international humanitarian law and human rights abuses.[71] All of his bi-annual reports to the Council have included evidence that the threat of prosecution by the Court had prompted judicial initiatives with Sudan.[72] When the Prosecutor made his bi-annual report to the Security Council, in June 2006, Sudan took the floor:

> Our police and prosecutors are prosecuting the perpetrators of those crimes. The Prosecutor learned about a great many cases that have been decided and about charges and allegations that have been followed up since a special prosecutor was appointed to look into those cases in Darfur. Special courts have been established and have handed down many criminal sentences, including execution and life imprisonment. The Prosecutor also had the opportunity to better understand how best to deal with security and tribal problems and disputes. [...] The Government of the Sudan will continue its efforts to establish the rule of law and justice through the courts and other mechanisms set up in Darfur, to put an end to impunity and to hold accountable all those convicted of violations of human rights and international humanitarian law.[73]

Even if Sudan's efforts are inadequate, they are certainly more than any result the Court might claim with respect to Uganda or the Democratic Republic of Congo. All of this suggests that referral in the classic sense, that is, in the sense of a resolution of the Security Council or a 'complaint' by a third State, rather than so-called self-referral, better fulfils the underlying purpose of the Rome Statute than 'self-referral'.

5. The Numbers Game: The Gravity Threshold and Prosecutorial Discretion

Most of the early writing on the International Criminal Court tended to underestimate the role of 'gravity' in the determination of admissibility. There has been a tendency to conflate 'admissibility' with 'complementarity', as if they are one and the same. But after addressing the issues of inability and unwillingness, article 17(1)(d) says that the Court shall declare a case inadmissible when it 'is not of sufficient gravity to justify further action'. In *Lubanga*, Pre-Trial Chamber I insisted upon the question of 'gravity' in determining whether a case was admissible. In effect, it treated

71 UN Doc. S/PV.5589, 2.

72 UN Doc. S/PV.5450, 3-4; UN Doc. S/PV.5321, 3; UN Doc. S/PV.5589, 2; UN Doc. S/PV.5450, 5–6.

73 UN Doc. S/PV.5450, 5–6.

admissibility as a debate involving two dimensions, complementarity and gravity. Its discussion of gravity was interesting and original, introducing a novel criterion of 'social alarm' as a methodology for applying the concept.

'Gravity' had already figured in the Prosecutor's discussion of his priorities in selecting cases. As has already been mentioned, when the Uganda arrest warrants were made public, in October 2005, the Prosecutor was challenged by international non-governmental organisations for dealing with only one side in the conflict.[74] Answering his critics, in a speech to legal advisors of Ministries of Foreign Affairs, delivered in New York on 24 October 2005, the Prosecutor said:

> In Uganda, the criterion for selection of the first case was gravity. We analysed the gravity of all crimes in Northern Uganda committed by all groups – the LRA, the UPDF and other forces. Our investigations indicated that the crimes committed by the LRA were of dramatically higher gravity. We therefore started with an investigation of the LRA. At the same time, we have continued to collect information on allegations concerning all other groups, to determine whether other crimes meet the stringent thresholds of the Statute and our policy are met.[75]

A month later, in his address to the Assembly of States Parties, the Prosecutor stated:

> In Uganda, we examined information concerning all groups that had committed crimes in the region. We selected our first case based on gravity. Between July 2002 and June 2004, the Lord's Resistance Army (LRA) was allegedly responsible for at least 2200 killings and 3200 abductions in over 850 attacks. It was clear that we must start with the LRA.[76]

The Prosecutor returned to this quantitative approach in February 2006, when he issued a public letter explaining his decision not to proceed against British nationals for war crimes committed in Iraq. The Prosecutor explained that during his analysis of the situation in Iraq following the invasion by the United Kingdom and the United States,

> allegations came to light in the media concerning incidents of mistreatment of detainees and wilful killing of civilians. General allegations included brutality against persons upon capture and initial custody, causing death or serious injury. In addition, there were incidents in which civilians were killed during policing operations in the occupation phase. After analyzing all the available information, it was concluded that there was a reasonable basis to believe that crimes within the jurisdiction of the Court had been committed, namely

---

74 Amnesty International, 'Uganda: First ever arrest warrants by International Criminal Court – a first step towards addressing impunity', 14 October 2005, AI Index: AFR 59/008/2005; Human Rights Watch, 'ICC Takes Decisive Step for Justice in Uganda', 14 October 2005.

75 'Statement by Luis Moreno Ocampo Prosecutor of the International Criminal Court, Informal meeting of Legal Advisors of Ministries of Foreign Affairs', New York, 24 October 2005 (available at http://www.icc-cpi.int/library/organs/otp/speeches/LMO_20051024_English.pdf accessed 9 September 2007), 7.

76 Statement by Luis Moreno Ocampo Prosecutor of the International Criminal Court, Fourth Session of the Assembly of States Parties, 28 November – 3 December 2005, The Hague, 28 November 2005, 2.

> wilful killing and inhuman treatment. The information available at this time supports a reasonable basis for an estimated 4 to 12 victims of wilful killing and a limited number of victims of inhuman treatment, totalling in all less than 20 persons.[77]

The Prosecutor went on to consider the 'gravity' dimension of the admissibility determination:

> The Office considers various factors in assessing gravity. A key consideration is the number of victims of particularly serious crimes, such as wilful killing or rape. The number of potential victims of crimes within the jurisdiction of the Court in this situation – 4 to 12 victims of wilful killing and a limited number of victims of inhuman treatment – was of a different order than the number of victims found in other situations under investigation or analysis by the Office. It is worth bearing in mind that the OTP is currently investigating three situations involving long-running conflicts in Northern Uganda, the Democratic Republic of Congo and Darfur. Each of the three situations under investigation involves thousands of wilful killings as well as intentional and large-scale sexual violence and abductions. Collectively, they have resulted in the displacement of more than 5 million people. Other situations under analysis also feature hundreds or thousands of such crimes. Taking into account all the considerations, the situation did not appear to meet the required threshold of the Statute.[78]

Although his analysis did not hinge upon this point, the Prosecutor also pointed out that 'national proceedings had been initiated with respect to each of the relevant incidents',[79] thus answering the other prong of the admissibility assessment. It is worth noting, however, that even if British courts were proceeding on these complaints at the time of the Prosecutor's letter, they do not appear to have been effective and have not resulted in convictions.[80]

The Prosecutor's letter concerning Iraq was issued on 9 February 2006. A few weeks earlier, he had applied to Pre-Trial Chamber I for issuance of an arrest warrant in the *Lubanga* case, which involved conscription, enrolment and active use of child soldiers, but no charge involving murder of human beings. One implication seems to be that crimes such as child soldier recruitment that do not necessarily involve homicide are objectively more serious than those of wilful killing, to the extent that the numbers of victims are more substantial. At the very least, such an analysis seems simplistic.

But the fundamentally quantitative approach to gravity suggested by the Prosecutor in the Lord's Resistance Army arrest warrants and the Iraq situation also seems to neglect another important dimension of the crimes. Even assuming that the Ugandan People's Defence Forces have killed significantly fewer innocent civilians than the Lord's Resistance Army, is not the fact that the crimes are attributable to the State germane to the gravity of the case? After all, the only genuine problem of impunity

---

77 'Letter of Prosecutor dated 9 February 2006' (Iraq) (available at http://www.icc-cpi.int/library/organs/otp/OTP_letter_to_senders_re_Iraq_9_February_2006.pdf accessed 9 September 2007), 7–8.

78 *Ibid.*, 8–9.

79 *Ibid.*, 10.

80 Evans, M., *Case Collapses*, The Times, 15 February 2007.

with respect to the Lord's Resistance Army perpetrators has been the inability of the Ugandan authorities to apprehend them. With respect to the government forces, on the other hand, we are confronted with the classic impunity paradigm: individuals acting on behalf of a State that shelters them from its own courts. But in a domestic justice setting involving ordinary crime, would we countenance a national prosecutor who ignored clandestine police death squads on the grounds that gangsters were killing more people than the rogue officials? We need not totally dismiss the relevance of the relative numbers of victims in order to appreciate the need to consider other factors, such as the fact that crimes are committed by individuals acting on behalf of the State as contributing to the objective gravity of the crime.

A somewhat similar analysis might be applied to the situation in Iraq. Even if it is admitted that wilful killing attributable to British forces only concerns 15 or 20 victims, surely the fact that this results from an aggressive war that has resulted in the deaths of hundreds of thousands of Iraqi civilians is germane to the gravity determination. Even if aggression may not yet be prosecuted by the Court, article 5(1) of the Rome Statute declares it to be one of 'the most serious crimes of concern to the international community as a whole'. Moreover, the preamble to the Rome Statute reminds us that 'all States shall refrain from the threat or use of force against the territorial integrity or political independence of any State, or in any other manner inconsistent with the Purposes of the United Nations'. Is aggressive war not, at the very least, an aggravating factor of relevance to the assessment of gravity?

Pre-Trial Chamber I, in its discussion of gravity in the *Lubanga* case, did not dwell upon the number of victims. Rather, it took a more qualitative approach, in which it considered such issues as the position and leadership role of the accused, and the organizational involvement including participation of the State.[81] This was justified with reference to the deterrent effect of prosecution for serious international crimes: 'In the Chamber's opinion, only by concentrating on this type of individual can the deterrent effect of the activities of the Court be maximised because other senior leaders in similar circumstances will know that solely by doing what they can to prevent the systematic or large-scale commission of crimes within the jurisdiction of the Court can they be sure that they will not be prosecuted by the Court'.[82]

Obviously, there are significant differences between the approaches to gravity taken by the Prosecutor and the Pre-Trial Chamber. Theoretically, it is possible for the Court's judges to pronounce upon cases when the Prosecutor decides not to proceed. Article 53 of the Statute declares that when a situation or a case has been referred to the Court by a State Party or by the Security Council, a prosecutorial decision not to pursue the referral, on grounds of either complementarity or gravity, may be reviewed by the Pre-Trial Chamber. This review must be requested by the State Party or the Security Council, as the case may be. In any event, Uganda did not refer crimes committed by its own defence forces to the Court (although the Prosecutor said he would interpret the referral otherwise), and it is surely not going to challenge

81 Pre-Trial Chamber I, 'Decision on the Prosecutor's application for a warrant of arrest, Article 58' (ICC-01/04-01/06-8), 10 February 2006, paragraphs 51–3.

82 *Ibid.*, paragraph 54.

the Prosecutor should he conclude that crimes committed by government forces are not serious enough to warrant further action.

6. Conclusions

These are early days yet in the history of the International Criminal Court. It is applying and interpreting provisions for which there is little or no guidance in earlier case law. Moreover, it is navigating through waters that are full of daunting political challenges. When the International Criminal Tribunal for the Former Yugoslavia began operations in 1994 and 1995, it took on cases that would be deemed insufficiently serious according to standards of selection adopted when the institution was in a more mature phase. According to the Tribunal's first operational prosecutor, Richard Goldstone, the initial indictee Dragan Nikolić was not 'an appropriate first person for an indictment by the first international war crimes tribunal'. However, governments, the United Nations and international NGOs were impatient for prosecutions to begin, and as a result 'we had to get out an indictment quickly'.[83] Much the same can be said of Duško Tadić, an insignificant thug who serendipitously fell into the sights of the Tribunal when it was starved for cases. His name is destined to resonate through the case law for many years to come. Nor did the first prosecutors of the International Criminal Tribunal for the Former Yugoslavia attempt to tackle Slobodan Milošević, although he was an obvious suspect. Milošević wasn't charged with crimes committed in Croatia and Bosnia and Herzegovina until late 2001,[84] some eight and a half years after the establishment of the Tribunal, and nearly nine years after the United States Secretary of State had publicly identified him as a prime suspect for prosecution.[85] Perhaps in a decade we will look back on Lubanga and the Lord's Resistance Army prosecutions in much the same way as we view Nikolić and Tadić, and the failure to proceed against Museveni's loyal troops and the British soldiers in Iraq as we look at the Tribunal's long silence concerning Milošević.

It is not always easy to discern a logical thread in the decisions on targets of prosecution, either by the Prosecutor or the Pre-Trial Chambers. This results in the nagging suspicion that the decision not to proceed in Iraq, for example, may well have been influenced by political considerations. Uganda and the Democratic Republic of Congo are 'soft targets' for the Prosecutor; Britain is a hard one. Although a resistance to tackle the more difficult situations may be disappointing, it may also reflect a laudable caution in establishing priorities of a still fragile institution.

---

83 Goldstone, R.J. (2002), 'Prosecuting Rape as a War Crime', in *Case Western Reserve Journal of International Law* 34, 277, 281. Nikolić eventually pleaded guilty to the crime against humanity of persecution, and was sentenced to 23 years in prison: *Prosecutor* v. *Dragan Nikolić* (Case No. IT-94-2-S), Sentencing Judgment, 18 December 2003. The sentence was reduced to 20 years by the Appeals Chamber: *Prosecutor* v. *Dragan Nikolić* (Case No. IT-94-2-A), Judgment on Sentencing Appeal, 4 February 2005.

84 *Prosecutor* v. *Milošević* (Case No. IT-01-51-I), Indictment, 22 November 2001.

85 Sciolino, E., U.S. *Names Figures it Wants Charged with War Crimes*, New York Times, 17 December 1992, 1.

Implicit in self-referral is the idea that the Court operates in a benign and cooperative relationship with States. Rather than focus on crimes of State, which was surely the vision when the Court was being established, it has turned its attention to rebel groups. Not only is such a Court not particularly threatening to States, they will call upon its services in pursuit of their own domestic political agendas, as the Uganda situation indicates. In some sense, the fundamentally cooperative relationship between the Prosecutor and the Museveni regime is rather galling. Weeks after the arrest warrants were issued by the International Criminal Court against the enemies of the Ugandan Government, the International Court of Justice ruled that the very same regime was liable for serious violations of international humanitarian law committed in the territory of another State.[86] At the same time as the International Court of Justice is condemning Museveni and his regime, the International Criminal Court is cooperating with it. The international legal regime looks incoherent.

The situation that better suits the underlying philosophy of the Rome Statute is Darfur. Ironically, it may be the contribution of the United States, which acquiesced in referring Darfur to the Court, that helps to direct the institution's energies to the situations and cases for which it was truly designed. As the Court proceeds, the shortcomings in the earlier cases will probably become increasingly apparent, and they will be looked upon as flawed sophomoric experiments. From its beginnings, the Court has outperformed the expectations of even its keenest supporters. Problems that seem insurmountable eventually find a solution and, inexorably, the institution moves forward to new and greater challenges.

86 International Court of Justice, *Case Concerning Armed Activities on the Territory of the Congo (Democratic Republic of the Congo v. Uganda)*, Judgment 19 December 2005.

Chapter 5

Issues of Admissibility in Case of Self-referrals

Giorgio Gaja

1. Introduction

It is well known that, apart from Darfur, all the situations that have up to now been referred to the International Criminal Court (ICC) were submitted by the State on whose territory the alleged crimes within the Court's jurisdiction *ratione materiae* had taken place. They are therefore called self-referrals.[1] No question of jurisdiction *ratione personae* would arise when the referring State is a State Party and the alleged crimes were committed after the ICC Statute entered into force for the State concerned.

Under articles 13(1) and 14 of the ICC Statute a State Party – arguably, any State Party – may refer to the Court a 'situation in which one or more of such crimes appears to have been committed'. Self-referrals are thus valid triggering mechanisms for the exercise by the Court of its jurisdiction.[2]

Typically, self-referrals are unilateral acts of the referring State, although it is to be expected that the Prosecutor will have had a role in promoting them and also in defining the situation which is referred to the Court.

Various views have been expressed on the advantages and risks of self-referrals.[3] It is not my purpose to continue this debate here, but only to discuss how issues concerning admissibility under the Statute present themselves when a case relates to a situation that has been the object of a self-referral. However, the solution of some of the problems concerning admissibility is likely to affect the question of whether self-referrals are desirable.

---

1 Another form of self-referral, which is less likely to occur, is that of a State referring a situation only insofar as it involves crimes committed by its own nationals.

2 According to Olasolo, H. (2005), *The Triggering Procedure of the International Criminal Court* (Leiden/Boston: Martinus Nijhoff), pp. 169–70, self-referrals could possibly be considered as 'mere communications of the *notitia criminis*' under article 15(1)of the ICC Statute.

3 See Kress, C. (2004), '"Self-Referrals" and "Waivers of Complementarity"', in *Journal of International Criminal Justice* 2:4, 944–48; Gaeta, P. (2004), 'Is the Practice of "Self-Referrals" a Sound Start for the ICC?', in *Journal of International Criminal Justice* 2:4, 949–52; Arsanjani, M.H. and Reisman, W.M. (2005), 'The Law-in-Action of the International Criminal Court', in *American Journal of International Law* 99:2, 385 at 387–388.

I shall consider a basic scenario. I shall assume first that the investigation by the Prosecutor has been initiated on the basis of the self-referral: second, that no other State claims to exercise jurisdiction over the alleged crimes; third, that there is no Security Council resolution affecting the investigation or prosecution.

2. Self-referrals and Complementarity

It would be contradictory for a State to refer a situation to the Court on the one hand and, on the other, to assert its own jurisdiction over a crime relating to that situation in order to assert priority on the basis of the principle of complementarity.[4] A self-referral necessarily implies that the State accepts that all the cases relating to the referred situation that may give rise to investigation or prosecution of crimes covered by the Statute come within the purview of the exercise of the Court's jurisdiction. It is only with regard to those cases that the Court leaves to the investigation or prosecution of the referring State that the latter is entitled to exercise its jurisdiction.

Policy considerations confirm this solution. The use of the Prosecutor's investigative resources could otherwise be wasted. His activities would be frustrated by a move taken by the referring State, which would thus be in a position to influence the Prosecutor's investigations by threatening to put an end to them with regard to specific cases. The need to protect the Prosecutor's independence requires one to treat self-referrals as triggering mechanisms that give the necessary impulse to the exercise of the Court's jurisdiction and do that once and for good. They do not provide the referring State with an opportunity to interfere with investigations and prosecutions.

3. The Question of Whether a Self-referral May Be Withdrawn

Similar reasons militate against allowing a State to withdraw its referral. This would have the more general result of preventing the Prosecutor from continuing its activities with regard to the referred situation. Not even the alleged presence of a change of circumstances[5] should lead to a different conclusion.

4. The Assessment of the Referring State's Unwillingness or Inability

According to article 19 (2) of the ICC Statute, 'a State which has jurisdiction over a case' may challenge admissibility 'on the ground that it is investigating or prosecuting the case or has investigated or prosecuted'. This opportunity can no longer be available to the referring State with regard to all the cases relating to

---

4 El Zeidy, M.M. (2006), 'Critical Thoughts on Article 59 (2) of the ICC Statute', in *Journal of International Criminal Justice* 4:3, 448, at 463 notes that a self-referral implies 'a waiver of complementarity'.

5 For the possible relevance of 'exceptional circumstances', see Akhavan, P. (2005), 'The *Lord's Resistance Army* Case: Uganda's Submission of the First State Referral to the International Criminal Court', in *American Journal of International Law* 99:2, 403, at 415.

the referred situation which have not been left to the State's own investigation or prosecution.

Were the self-referring State the only entity concerned by the assessment of admissibility, this would be the end of the matter. However, the grounds of inadmissibility are not only designed to protect the interest of States that would have jurisdiction over the crimes.

Under article 19 of the Statute, challenges to admissibility may be raised also by 'an accused or a person for whom a warrant of arrest or a summons to appear has been issued under article 58'. Moreover, the Court may raise a question of admissibility on its own motion, as was done with regard to the arrest warrant concerning Lubanga.[6] Also the Prosecutor may seek a ruling on a question of admissibility.

Thus the Court may have to examine questions of admissibility of a case relating to a situation that was the object of a self-referral. But is there scope for the Court to consider whether the referring State 'is unwilling or unable genuinely to carry out the investigation or prosecution' (article 17 (1)(a))? Or, when an investigation has occurred, whether there is 'unwillingness or inability of the State genuinely to prosecute' (article 17 (1)(b))?

In the *Lubanga* case Pre-Trial Chamber I noted that 'the self-referral or statement by the government of a State that it is unable to investigate or prosecute is not binding on the Court'.[7] While the existence of a self-referral does not dispose of the issue of inability, it conveys that, in the referring State's view, the exercise of the Court's jurisdiction would be justified for all the crimes related to the situation. Thus, if one takes the view that the self-referring State is nevertheless able to investigate or prosecute, one would have to conclude that the same State is in any case unwilling to do so.

Objectively, the ability of the referring State to carry out an investigation or prosecution with regard to the case may or may not be there. Also willingness on the part of that State may or may not be there. The self-referring State may be willing to investigate, but be conscious of its own inability to do so effectively. Even the fact of referring a situation to the Court may be seen as a positive step towards investigation, in line with the statement in the preamble of the Statute that 'the most serious crimes of concern to the international community must not go unpunished'. Be that as it may, once the referring State has vested the Court with the function to exercise its jurisdiction over the alleged crimes relating to the referred situation, the issue of unwillingness or inability with regard to that State should no longer be relevant.[8]

6 See Pre-Trial Chamber I, 'Decision on the Prosecutor's application for a warrant of arrest, article 58', 10 February 2006, as amended by and annexed to Pre-Trial Chamber I, 'Decision concerning Pre-Trial Chamber's I decision of 10 February 2006 and the incorporation of documents into the record of the case against Mr Thomas Lubanga Dyilo' (ICC-01/04-01/06-8), 24 February 2006, paragraph 17.

7 *Ibid*., footnote 26.

8 According to El Zeidy, M.M. (2005), 'The Ugandan Government Triggers the First Test of the Complementarity Principle: An Assessment of the First State's Party Referral to the ICC', in *International Criminal Law Review* 5:1, 83, at 103, 'the case should be admissible by implication', but this only if 'no action has taken place at all from the outset'.

When a State refers a situation to the Court, it is to be expected that it will only investigate or prosecute cases that the Court would have left to that State. Should the referring State take initiatives that contradict its own referral, for the reasons stated above, this should not affect the exercise of the Court's jurisdiction. With regard to the *Lubanga* case, Pre-Trial Chamber I considered that the ground for inadmissibility was not present because there were no national proceedings concerning 'both the person and the conduct which is the subject of the case before the Court'.[9] However, even if those proceedings had taken place, the conclusion should have been that they would not have affected the admissibility of the case once the situation had been referred.

5. The Gravity of the Crime

Admissibility could be challenged also on the ground of the insufficient gravity of the crime. According to article 18, the accused or the person for whom a warrant of arrest or a summons to appear has been issued may challenge admissibility on this ground. Also the Court may raise this issue on its own motion as Pre-Trial Chamber I did in the *Lubanga* case.[10] The fact that the case originates in a self-referral is clearly immaterial for this ground of inadmissibility.

6. Conclusions

The conclusions to be drawn are relatively simple. Self-referring States cannot affect the admissibility of cases relating to the referred situation. Moreover, the Court should not review the inability or unwillingness of the self-referring State, but only the gravity of the crime. These conclusions may make the option of a self-referral less attractive for a State. However, they preserve the independence of the Court in the exercise of its functions. Self-referrals cannot be distorted so as to provide a form of cooperation which would at the end of the day leave investigation and prosecution in the hands of the State where the alleged crimes occurred.

---

9 See Pre-Trial Chamber I, 'Decision on the Prosecutor's application for a warrant of arrest, article 58', 10 February 2006, as amended by and annexed to Pre-Trial Chamber I, 'Decision concerning Pre-Trial Chamber I's decision of 10 February 2006 and the incorporation of documents into the record of the case against Mr Thomas Lubanga Dyilo' (ICC-01/04-01/06-8), 24 February 2006, paragraph 37.

10 *Ibid.*, paragraphs 62–74.

PART II
Substantive and Procedural Aspects of Complementarity

Chair: Luigi Ferrari Bravo[1]

Well, I think we are ready to start. English has indeed become a universal language, contrary to my expectations (I tried to balance English and French when serving as President of the European Court of Human Rights, until a French delegate started speaking English; at that point I gave up, telling myself it was impossible for me to continue to protect it); however, although I can understand English, I prefer to speak Italian.

The forthcoming panel, which I have been asked to chair, complements what has been said at the end of this morning, namely what Professor Gaja said as a way of introduction to this debate on 'substantive and procedural aspects of complementarity'.

These are very important issues, in particular now when we have to admit that ratification of the Statute by Italy looks very much like a fake one, given the persisting absence of those provisions which would allow such ratification to become operational. I sincerely wish that these provisions will be put in place soon. God forbid that a suspect criminal investigated by the international justice seeks refuge in Italy and benefits from legal assistance by one of our lawyers (as you know, Italy is home to many good lawyers). That would result in the Italian Government cutting one of its poorest figures ever in history… let us hope this will not happen.

That said, I have the pleasure of giving the floor to Mrs Phani Livada, who is an old friend of mine, and who will speak on complementarity and Security Council referrals, if I said it correctly. I'll give you the floor.

1 Translated from the Italian by the editors.

Chapter 6

The Principle of Complementarity and Security Council Referrals

Phani Dascalopoulou-Livada

The principle of complementarity is a fundamental idea which permeates the Statute of the International Criminal Court (ICC) for reasons which can be considered practical, legal, and even philosophical. Practical because complementarity is an intelligent way to keep away the bulk of cases which might reach the ICC if that principle did not exist while, at the same time, the Court is keeping all the cards in its favour, since where the State is objectively unable to deal with or is not virtuous in its intentions towards a case or cases, the ICC will take it or them in its own hands. It should not, furthermore, be forgotten that the Statute is a conventional text, an international treaty which has been negotiated by States, and in that legal context, complementarity was a common denominator which some may consider lower than desirable but on which everyone, or as many as possible, could agree at the time. From a philosophical perspective, on the other hand, the existence of complementarity is justified by the need to assert the primacy of national jurisdiction on a subject so deeply identified with national sovereignty as criminal justice is.

Let us now turn to the question of referrals of 'situations' by the Security Council to the ICC, in accordance with article 13(b) of the Statute. The first thing to observe is that the Security Council may, in accordance with the above-mentioned provision, order that a situation within which the commission of crimes falling within the jurisdiction of the ICC is highly probable, be brought before the ICC even if the State concerned is not a party to the ICC Statute. This possibility seems to be anchored in the Chapter VII of the UN Charter powers of the Security Council and more particularly its powers to take action with respect to threats to the peace, breaches of the peace and acts of aggression.[1] [2]

The Security Council already made use of that possibility when it set up the *ad hoc* tribunals for the crimes committed in the Former Yugoslavia and in Rwanda by resolutions taken on the basis of Chapter VII of the UN Charter.[3] At the time of the

1 Article 39 of the UN Charter.

2 See Prezas, I. (2006), 'La justice pénale internationale à l'épreuve du maintient de la paix: à propos de la relation entre la Cour pénale internationale et le Conseil de sécurité', in *Revue belge de droit international* 1, 57–98.

3 UNSC Resolutions 808(1993) and 827(1993) for the International Tribunal for the Former Yugoslavia and UNSC Resolution 955(1994) for the International Tribunal for Rwanda.

adoption of these resolutions, there had been some doubts expressed as to whether the maintenance of peace and security should be connected with the rendering of justice. These doubts may persist from a theoretical point of view but, things having progressed in international life along those lines, it is perhaps beside the point to dwell on that now.

The next question to be asked, once there has been a Security Council referral in accordance with article 13(b), is whether complementarity plays a role here or whether the Security Council acting, as it does in such a case, under Chapter VII of the UN Charter, also replaces the will of the State concerned by setting aside the domestic criminal jurisdiction of that State with regard to the crimes committed within the particular situation or by implicitly ordering it not to exercise its jurisdiction, which is thus *ipso jure* passed on to the ICC.

As the Statute does not offer a clear answer here, there has been some discussion among legal experts on the issue. It would be possible to consider that the Security Council is, indeed, empowered to do so, that is to set complementarity aside, on the basis of the same justification which allows that organ to refer a situation to the ICC where the State concerned is not a party to the ICC Statute.

The practical advantages of supporting such a position are obvious. If complementarity was dispensed with, precious time would perhaps be saved while an undoubtedly painful and difficult investigation into the legal system of the State involved and the way justice is applied by it in general and on the situation in question in particular would be avoided to the benefit of the ICC, the attribution of justice and, ultimately, to the benefit of the persons who have suffered by the situation being referred to the Court by the SC.

It could furthermore be argued that when the Security Council takes such a decisive step as a referral to the ICC – to its Prosecutor, to be more exact – it is beyond doubt that the situation is extremely serious, which in itself militates in favour of the assumption that the SC referral implies that the primary jurisdiction of the State in question – party or non-party to the Statute – is either relinquished in favour of the ICC or purely and simply set aside.

In a more general context, there is a widespread view which finds it worrying that a court is required to take a case from an international organ concerned only with security matters. Such concerns had already been expressed by many States during the preparatory negotiations for the Statute as well as during the Rome Conference. Within this line of thought there are scholars who go as far as to suggest that in their view the ICC constitutes two courts in one, that is one which operates normally in the case of State referrals or where the Prosecutor exercises his *proprio motu* powers to bring a case before the Court, and one which deals with Security Council referrals.[4] Interestingly, these writers consider that if the Security Council can stop the ICC in its tracks by making use of the possibility offered to it by article 16 of the ICC Statute, it should not be difficult to accept that the rules on complementarity are set aside in the case of Security Council referrals.

4 Fletcher, G.P. and Ohlin, J.D. (2006), 'The ICC – Two Courts in One?', in *Journal of International Criminal Justice* 4:3, 428–33.

Despite the appeal of these arguments and the advantages they present, it is difficult to find a solid foundation for this position in the Statute. Indeed, as already mentioned above, the Statute of the ICC is not particularly helpful in clarifying the matter. Article 17, which deals with issues of admissibility, does not distinguish between the provenance of referrals. Article 19, which deals with challenges to the jurisdiction of the Court, does not make such distinction either. Article 18, on the other hand, does refer to State referrals and *proprio motu* initiation of investigations by the Prosecutor but does not mention Security Council referrals. This apparent omission of Security Council referrals from the ambit of article 18 is quite puzzling. Does it mean that the ICC is not supposed to examine complementarity issues in the case of situation referrals by the Security Council because the particular State's primary jurisdiction would in such a case be set aside?[5] It is my view that no such far-reaching inference can be made from the omission in article 18, whatever the reasons which led to it. Indeed, where the Statute regulated matters of such significance, it did so with considerable clarity. This is particularly true where the Security Council is involved, for example in the situations envisaged in articles 16 and 13. In both of them the powers of the Security Council are clearly delineated so that the intention and ambit of these provisions leave no room for doubt.

From a political viewpoint, on the other hand, it should be remembered that the involvement of the Security Council in the Court's work was, as already mentioned above, among the main difficulties in the negotiating process of the ICC Statute. This involvement was finally established in a number of instances, among which the possibility of referrals through the operation of article 13(b) of the Statute, and was one of the reasons for which many developing countries preferred to stay out of the Statute.[6] Taking this into consideration, it is clear that if the powers of the Security Council in this regard were interpreted to include the power to set complementarity aside, this would meet with further mistrust by a considerable number of States. The relationship between the ICC and the Security Council has always been a difficult one and the discussions on aggression still provide ample proof of that. If, therefore, even a slight degree of preponderance were afforded the Security Council on this matter (that is, by considering that complementarity is dispensed with in the case of Security Council referrals), there would be a risk of upsetting the balance reached in the Statute with potentially far-reaching consequences. These are political considerations, of course, but they cannot be ignored. At no point should it be forgotten that the matter affects fundamentally the sovereignty of States and any doubt should therefore be resolved in favour of such sovereignty. It has already been emphasized that criminal justice is a crucial manifestation of such sovereignty and

5 A division of opinions on this issue has been also noted among the group of experts set up in 2003 for the benefit of the then future prosecutor and the staff of his office (see ICC-OTP, Informal Expert Paper, The Principle of Complementarity in Practice, 2003, 21–22 http://www.icc-cpi.int/library/organs/otp/complementarity.pdf accessed 10 September 2007).

6 Gowlland-Debbas, V. (2001), 'The role of the Security Council in the new International Criminal Court from a systemic perspective', in *Mélanges G. Abi-Saab* (The Hague: Martinus Nyhoff). The article also reproduces (at p. 636) the statement given in explanation of vote by the Indian representative following the adoption of the Statute in Rome on 17 July 1998, which is very characteristic of the stance of many developing States on the matter.

it is for this reason that the primary jurisdiction of the State yields only under very specific conditions which are carefully described in the Statute.

While the discussion on these questions was going on, the referral by the Security Council of the Darfur situation[7] gave the Prosecutor of the International Criminal Court the opportunity to make his own interpretation of the consequences of the referral by the Security Council. The importance of the Prosecutor's decision cannot be overemphasized as it sets a precedent which cannot be changed from now on[8] unless under extreme circumstances, which will have to be done with a different resolution of the Security Council on a similar matter.

The decision which the Prosecutor took is, as was expected of him and of every cautious Prosecutor who would not like to put the ICC under any risk of a controversial situation, one which does not recognize to the Security Council the power to require that the State in question – the Sudan in the particular case – relinquish or yield, in effect, its own jurisdiction in favour of that of the ICC. In his Reports to the Security Council[9] as well as in his Application to the Pre-Trial Chamber of last February, the Prosecutor does not, however, take up this matter first or on its own. He examines the overall question of admissibility of cases which he has identified among the 'universe' of cases in the Darfur situation referred to the Court by the Security Council, and within that question he finds he has to examine two parameters: first, the gravity of the case; second, the complementarity question.

On the question of gravity, the Prosecutor might have taken it for granted that the mere fact that the Security Council referred the situation to him acting on the basis of Chapter VII proves in itself that the crimes allegedly committed within that situation are grave enough for the purposes of admissibility. He does not follow that road, however. He investigates the matter and finds that, indeed, the crimes are of sufficient gravity to satisfy the threshold required for admissibility.

Then the question of complementarity arises, that is whether the Sudan has exercised or is exercising its own primary jurisdiction on the particular crimes and whether that State is willing and able to try the relevant case or cases in a legally convincing manner. The Prosecutor undertook here a fully fledged investigation to find out whether Sudan is in fact exercising or has exercised its primary jurisdiction on the matter. His office went on several occasions to Sudan, met with the competent

7 UNSC Resolution 1593 (2005).

8 Pre-trial Chamber I issued arrest warrants for two persons: Pre-trial Chamber I, 'Warrant of arrest for Ahmad Muhammad Harun' ('Ahmad Harun') (ICC-02/05-01/07-2), 1 May 2007; Pre-trial Chamber I, 'Warrant of arrest for Ali Muhammad Ali Abd-Al-Rahman' ('Ali Kushayb') (ICC-02/05-01/07-3), 1 May 2007.

9 First Report of the Prosecutor of the International Criminal Court, Mr. Luis Moreno Ocampo, to the Security Council pursuant to UNSC 1593 (2005), 29 June 2005 (available at http://www.icc-cpi.int/library/cases/ICC_Darfur_UNSC_Report_29-06-05_EN.pdf accessed 10 September 2007); Second Report, 13 December 2005 (available at http://www.icc-cpi.int/library/organs/otp/LMO_UNSC_ReportB_En.pdf accessed 10 September 2007); Third Report, 14 June 2006 (available at http://www.icc-cpi.int/library/cases/OTP_ReportUNSC_3-Darfur_English.pdf accessed 10 September 2007); Fourth Report, 14 December 2006 (available at http://www.icc-cpi.int/library/organs/otp/OTP_ReportUNSC4-Darfur_English.pdf accessed 10 September 2007).

people and investigated the legal system as well as the cases pending before the various Sudanese Courts and other judicial or investigative instances. It was after that investigation that it reached the conclusion that the requirements set already by the ICC had not been met and that therefore the Court had to go forward with the cases itself. The Prosecutor specifically referred to the requirements set by Pre-Trial Chamber I in the *Lubanga* case, which are 'that national proceedings encompass both the person and the conduct which is the subject of the case before the Court'.[10]

The Prosecutor did not therefore even discuss whether the Security Council resolution relieved him of the obligation to look into the matter of the exercise of jurisdiction by the Sudanese judicial authorities, which means that he took it for granted that complementarity was fully operational. He also placed the question within article 53(2), of which complementarity is only one matter out of a number of others and asserted his full independence by examining all the prerequisites set by that article, including, and this must be underlined, the question whether the interests of justice are served, a question which, it could be argued, the Security Council, by adopting a resolution on the matter, should have been considered to have answered. Indeed, the Prosecutor states in his Second Report[11] to the Security Council:

> In the first phase of the investigation the Office collects information relating to the universe of crimes alleged to have taken place in Darfur, as well as the groups and individuals responsible for those crimes. The Office has made good progress in this first phase.
> In the second phase of the investigation the Prosecutor will select specific cases for prosecution unless he considers, in accordance with article 53(2) of the Statute, that there is not a sufficient basis for prosecution because:
> i. there is an insufficient legal or factual basis to seek a warrant or summons under article 58;
> ii. The case is inadmissible under article 17; or
> iii. A prosecution is not in the interests of justice, taking into account all the circumstances, including the gravity of the crime, the interests of the victims and the age or infirmity of the alleged perpetrator, and his or her role in the alleged crime.

The Prosecutor therefore has made up his mind on this. He does not treat Security Council referrals in any way differently from State referrals or *proprio motu* investigations as far as complementarity is concerned. He is furthermore supported in his interpretation by the Security Council itself, since no objections or misgivings seem to have been expressed by the Council when he made his intentions known in his reports to that body.

On the basis of the considerations developed above, my conclusion is that the decision of the Prosecutor on the question of complementarity in relation to Security

10 Pre-Trial Chamber I, 'Decision on the Prosecutor's Application for a warrant of arrest, article 58' (as amended by Pre-Trial Chamber I, 'Decision Concerning Pre-Trial Chamber I's Decision of 10 February 2006 and the Incorporation of Documents into the Record of the Case against Mr. Thomas Lubanga Dyilo', ICC-01/04-01/06-8, 24 February 2006)', 10 February 2006, paragraph 31.

11 See footnote 9 above, 1–2.

Council referrals has been the right one not only from the legal but also from a political point of view. It responded adequately and with conviction to misgivings which had been expressed and which are linked to the nature of the Court and the peculiarities of its Statute as the product not only of legal expertise but also of an extremely difficult political compromise. Seen from this viewpoint, it is to be hoped that this decision will offer further arguments to those who promote the adherence of more States to the Statute of the International Criminal Court, which is still in search of universality.

Chapter 7

Inability to Investigate and Prosecute under Article 17

Edoardo Greppi

In the framework of the complementarity principle, article 17 dealing with admissibility can be considered the cornerstone of the entire Rome Statute of the International Criminal Court (ICC).[1] If we enlarge our perspective, we can see that in all the provisions of article 17, the ICC and all related issues on jurisdiction are dealt with in the light of the general principle of sovereignty.

During all the negotiation phases State interests in the field of criminal justice were taken into account and granted protection and safeguard.

Unlike the *ad hoc* Tribunals established by the Security Council acting under Chapter VII, the ICC jurisdiction was not placed in a position of primacy over State courts. Domestic jurisdiction was fully respected, leaving national tribunals their traditional competence in criminal law matters in line with sovereignty and national interest.

Moreover, the preamble to the Rome Statute (paragraph 6) recalls that it is the duty of all States to exercise jurisdiction over individuals responsible for having committed international crimes. The overall results of the Rome Conference negotiations reflect the concerns of States over the protection of national sovereignty and 'the potentially intrusive powers of international institutions'.[2]

Having established the principle that national courts were granted recognition of full jurisdiction and that the ICC would be given complementary competence, the negotiations were called to deal with the issue of the limits of the international court's jurisdiction.

The International Law Commission's 1994 Draft Statute emphasises that the ICC was 'intended to be complementary to national criminal justice systems in cases where such trial procedures may not be available or may be ineffective'. The ICC itself has the statutory power and authority to solve the problems of jurisdiction

---

1 Williams, S.A. (1999), 'Article 17. Issues of admissibility', in Triffterer, O. (ed.), *Commentary on the Rome Statute of the International Criminal Court. Observers' Notes, Article by Article* (Baden Baden: Nomos), p. 383. See Holmes, J. (1999), 'The Principle of Complementarity', in Lee R.S. (ed.), *The International Criminal Court, The Making of the Rome Statute: Issues, Negotiations, Results* (The Hague-London-Boston: Kluwer Law International), p. 41.

2 Holmes, J.T. (2002), 'Complementarity: National Courts *versus* the ICC', in Cassese, A., Gaeta, P. and Jones, J.R.W.D. (2002) (eds), *The Rome Statute of the International Criminal Court: A Commentary* (Oxford: Oxford University Press), vol. I, p. 668.

and admissibility, and there are aspects which appear of not easy interpretation. In particular, unwillingness and inability appeared to be two key concepts.

The experience of both *ad hoc* Tribunals shows that States are potentially unwilling to investigate and prosecute (it is the case of the Former Yugoslavia) or that they are unable (as in Rwanda, whose judicial system had been destroyed by the genocide, and where municipal courts were clearly in a condition of impossibility to start proceedings against the perpetrators of the crimes).

Nevertheless, even in the cases in which the primary jurisdiction of the International Tribunal was clearly desirable, it appeared important that some role were still to be recognised for national courts. Facing the large number of perpetrators and the different levels of their individual responsibility, the international community could envisage a twofold solution: a way of complementarity by the exercise of jurisdiction by both international and national tribunals. Leaving a margin to national jurisdiction appears a way to underline that the principle of primacy by the *ad hoc* tribunal does not weaken the principle of the general obligation of States to prosecute international crimes.

The Rome Conference chose the criteria of unwillingness and inability, which appeared to be a practical solution for the cases of national authorities having already started investigations or prosecutions.

The easiest cases to deal with are those in which the 'inability' is a total one. Already former Secretary General Boutros Boutros Ghali, in his Agenda for Peace, underlined that a feature of modern conflicts 'is the collapse of State institutions, especially the police and the judiciary, with resulting paralysis of governance, a breakdown of law and order'.[3]

Much more difficult are all those situations in which a State shows a certain degree of willingness to investigate or prosecute (and is therefore in principle not 'unwilling') but at a given moment is not able to go on. In these situations, the investigation started, the police authorities seemed to be 'able', but then the investigation led nowhere, since the judiciary collapsed or proved to be unable to prosecute.

The International Law Commission, in its 1994 Draft, chose the concept of 'ineffective' to qualify these situations. The ICC was intended to complement national criminal justice systems in cases where trials 'may not be available or may be ineffective'. But ineffectiveness seemed to be too subjective, like other envisaged solutions, such as 'good faith', 'diligently' or 'sufficient grounds'.

In the negotiations, there was fear that such an approach could hide the underlying thought that investigation or prosecution by the ICC would by definition be more effective than those conducted by State authorities. Even the speed of such activities could be the object of an assessment in terms of effectiveness. In other words, a comparative analysis of the time needed to investigate between one State or another and/or the ICC could lead to the conclusion that the latter would be more efficient and, therefore, preferable.

---

3 Boutros-Ghali, B. (1995), *An Agenda for Peace*, Second edition (New York: United Nations), p. 9.

The result was the choice of the word 'genuinely' as less subjective than 'reasonable' or 'sufficient'. 'Genuinely' was finally chosen as it allowed to take into account cases in which a genuine action was taken by the State, in good faith, but it proved to be insufficient, for lack of resources or weakness of structures or personnel. In general, 'the enigmatic adjective "genuinely" is left entirely to the appreciation of the Court'.[4]

The Preparatory Committee concluded to the effect that for a case to be inadmissible a State must have acted genuinely in investigating and prosecuting. The Court would not enforce jurisdiction unless the State was unable or unwilling to carry out the investigation or the prosecution. As a result, the issue of inability proved to be less controversial than that of unwillingness. The latter, as a matter of fact, has heavier implications as far as sovereignty is concerned. The negotiation was less contentious because inability is 'a more objective, fact-driven notion'.[5]

At the Rome Conference, the negotiations had to address the issue of a collapse of judicial institutions. A total collapse is not controversial. Less easy to accept is the floating concept of 'partial collapse', since it seems to be lacking objective elements. What is 'partial'? To which extent can a judicial system be considered 'unable' because the judiciary is in a state of collapse but still permits authorities to conduct investigations in good faith and with acceptable results?

The solution was a new wording, adopted in the final package presented to the Committee of the whole: 'substantial collapse'. Of course, and again, what 'substantial' means is a matter of interpretation.

Article 17(3) explains that 'the State is unable to obtain the accused or the necessary evidence and testimony or otherwise unable to carry out its proceedings' 'due to a total or substantial collapse or unavailability of its national judicial system'.

The paradigmatic case is that of Somalia, a failed State without a central government. The absence of a functioning prosecutor's office or established courts are rather objective elements. But there may also be cases of civil wars or extended natural disasters, or public disorders, which cause substantial if not total inability.

The other situation is that of a State willing to investigate or prosecute but which is unable, like Rwanda.

To decide on admissibility, the Court must consider the following factors:

a. the State is unable to obtain the accused;
b. the State is unable to obtain the necessary evidence and testimony; or
c. the State is unable to otherwise carry out its proceedings.

The first two factors are rather objective in their nature. The third one leaves a certain margin of appreciation to the Court, since that 'otherwise' seems to permit it to

4 Schabas, W. (2001), *An Introduction to the International Criminal Court* (Cambridge: Cambridge University Press), p. 67.

5 Holmes, J.T. (2002), 'Complementarity: National Courts *versus* the ICC', in Cassese, A., Gaeta, P. and Jones, J.R.W.D. (eds), *The Rome Statute of the International Criminal Court: A Commentary* (Oxford: Oxford University Press), vol. I, p. 677.

take into account unforeseen circumstances which may cause an obstacle to national proceedings.

We could take as an example a State which has obtained the accused, has the necessary evidence and plenty of witnesses, but is lacking personnel (office of the prosecutor or judges or qualified clerks) to carry on the proceedings in a genuine way (not to use the word 'effective', which could imply other consequences).

In conclusion, the ICC is entitled to affirm its jurisdiction in those cases in which 'it identifies a gap in State jurisdictions, a gap created by the lack of repression, a gap created by impunity'. This may be the result of 'a breakdown of the institutions of a State or of widespread anarchy'; but it may also be caused 'by poor administration of justice'.[6] A last situation of inability is that of the existence of legislative impediments, such as an amnesty law, or a statute of limitations, making it impossible for the national judge to start proceedings against the suspect or the accused.[7]

The Cases Referred to the ICC

A first significant case offering some interesting elements for consideration is that of the Democratic Republic of Congo. The government is not a homogeneous entity, as it consists of a number of factions with different authority and power. The President referred the situation to the ICC essentially on his own authority, while his most powerful political rivals (some of whom are likely to be the object of ICC investigations) can influence domestic policy and perspectives of judicial reform. In particular, Vice-Presidents Bemba and Ruberwa, whose interest is 'to keep national courts weak so as to avoid prosecution', largely prefer to leave the ICC outside the borders as much as possible.[8]

Quite different seems to be the case of Uganda, where inability essentially affects prosecution rather than investigations. The ICC Prosecutor justified admissibility on the grounds that the Ugandan Government was unable to prosecute because the rebels were in Sudan, and thus difficult to capture. This kind of inability, therefore, has not much to do with the one connected with the collapse of institutions or the unavailability of national judicial remedies or structures.[9]

A third important and relevant case is the one of Darfur, which concerns a State insufficiently organised to gather evidence or 'otherwise unable' to carry out its proceedings.

---

6 Benvenuti, P. (1999), 'Complementarity of the International Criminal Court to National Criminal Jurisdictions', in Lattanzi, F. and Schabas, W. (eds), *Essays on the Rome Statute of the International Criminal Court* (Ripa Fagnano Alto: Sirente), vol. I, p. 21.

7 Cassese, A. (2003), *International Criminal Law* (Oxford: Oxford University Press), p. 352.

8 Burke-White, W.W. (2005), 'Complementarity in Practice: the International Criminal Court as Part of a System of Multi-level Global Governance in the Democratic Republic of Congo', in *Leiden Journal of International Law* 18:3, 569.

9 Southwick, K. (2005) 'Investigating War in Uganda: Dilemmas for the International Criminal Court', in *Yale Journal of International Affairs* 1:1, 105.

The 'Report of the Commission of Inquiry on Darfur' provides the Security Council with some relevant elements, useful to adopt the decision to refer the situation to the ICC.

The Commission's conclusions were that there had been no genocide in Darfur, but that war crimes and crimes 'no less serious and heinous' (paragraph 642) against humanity had been committed. Perpetrators were both government officials and rebels.

As far as the complementarity issue is concerned, the key point is the one in which the Commission states that Sudan was 'unable and unwilling to prosecute and try the alleged offenders' (paragraph 568). In more detail, the Commission observed:

> The Sudanese justice system is unable *and* unwilling to address the situation in Darfur. This system has been significantly weakened during the last decade. Restrictive laws that grant broad powers to the executive particularly undermined the effectiveness of the judiciary. In fact, many of the laws in force in Sudan today contravene basic human rights standards. The Sudanese criminal laws do not adequately proscribe war crimes and crimes against humanity such as those perpetrated in Darfur, and the Criminal Procedure Code contains provisions that prevent the effective prosecution of these acts. In addition, many victims informed the Commission that they had little confidence in the impartiality of the Sudanese justice system and its ability to bring to justice the perpetrators of the serious crimes committed in Darfur (paragraph 586).

> and

> The Commission's recommendation for a Security Council referral to the ICC is based on the correct assumption that Sudanese courts are unwilling *and* unable to prosecute the numerous international crimes perpetrated in Darfur since 2003 (paragraph 609).

As a matter of fact, the Report goes far beyond this result, as it suggests several alternatives, among which we also find the possibility of adjudicating in a third-party State exercising universal jurisdiction (like Germany, Austria, Spain and Switzerland, because they have specific legislation) (paragraph 613). The universal jurisdiction solution would imply the involvement of a third-party State proving to be willing and able to genuinely undertake proceedings on an appropriate basis of jurisdiction (paragraph 616).

Before initiating criminal proceedings a State should request the territorial State (namely, the State where the crime has allegedly been perpetrated) or the State of active nationality (that is, the State of which the person suspected or indicted is a national) whether it is willing to institute proceedings against that person and hence be prepared to request his or her extradition. Only if the State or States in question refuse to seek the extradition, or are patently unable or unwilling to bring the person to justice, may the State on whose territory the person is present initiate proceedings against him or her (paragraph 614).

In the case of Darfur this condition would not need to be applied, for Sudanese courts and other judicial authorities have clearly shown that they are unable or unwilling to exercise jurisdiction over the crimes perpetrated in Darfur (paragraph 615).

The conclusion is the suggestion to refer to the ICC: 'the Sudanese justice system has unfortunately demonstrated that it is unable or unwilling to investigate and prosecute the alleged perpetrators of the war crimes and crimes against humanity committed in Darfur. It is absolutely essential that those perpetrators be brought to justice before a competent and credible international criminal court' (paragraph 627).

Where the Report recommends that the international community help strengthen the Sudanese criminal justice system (paragraph 622) and increase its independence and impartiality by training judges, prosecutors and lawyers (paragraph 624), it both affirms the conclusion that Sudan is 'unable' and offers suggestions which appear to be a sort of complement to the proposed ICC referral (paragraph 604).

In his various Reports to the Security Council, the ICC Prosecutor determined 'the existence of sufficient information to believe that there are cases that would be admissible in relation to the Darfur situation'. He also emphasized that the decision did not imply 'a determination on the Sudanese legal system as such', but was essentially 'a result of the absence of criminal proceedings' relating to the cases on which he would be likely to focus. According to the Prosecutor, 'the admissibility assessment is an on-going assessment'. In other words, only after investigations have been carried out and specific cases selected, the Office of the Prosecutor (OTP) will assess whether or not the cases have been 'the subject of a genuine national investigations or prosecutions'. Moreover, considering that a national specialised tribunal was established in June 2005, the OTP will follow its works to assess whether the national proceedings 'meet the standards of genuineness as defined by Article 17 of the Rome Statute'.[10]

In his Second Report of 13 December 2005, the ICC Prosecutor specified that 'the continuing insecurities in Darfur currently prohibit the establishment of an effective system for the protection of victims and witnesses' and that 'this represents a serious impediment to the conduct of effective investigations into the alleged crimes in Darfur by national judicial bodies'. The reference to effectiveness does not seem to be consistent with the choice made in the framework of the Rome negotiations, but it helps us to understand what the real issue is. The conclusion is that the Prosecutor will continue to follow the work of the special Sudanese Court (and the other tribunals which were added in the meantime) in order to check whether the proceedings meet the standards established in the Rome Statute.[11]

---

10 *Report of the Prosecutor of the International Criminal Court, Mr. Luis Moreno Ocampo, to the Security Council pursuant to UNSCR 1593 (2005)*, paragraph 1.2, 29 June 2005 (available at http://www.icc-cpi.int/library/cases/ICC_Darfur_UNSC_Report_29-06-05_EN.pdf accessed 10 September 2007).

11 *Second Report of the Prosecutor of the International Criminal Court, Mr. Luis Moreno Ocampo, to the UN Security Council pursuant to UNSCR 1593 (2005)*, 13 December 2005 (available at http://www.icc-cpi.int/library/organs/otp/LMO_UNSC_ReportB_En.pdf accessed 10 September 2007).

In his Fourth Report, the Prosecutor concluded that the indications given by the Sudanese Judicial Investigating Committee 'do not appear to render the case inadmissible'.[12]

In general, the ICC Prosecutor avoids openly addressing the issue of inability (and/or that of unwillingness), choosing instead to evaluate admissibility in terms of 'genuineness' and 'effectiveness' of national proceedings.

The interpretation given by both the Commission on Darfur and the ICC Prosecutor seems to interpret the wording of article 17 'unable *or* unwilling' in an extended way: that is, as 'unable *and* unwilling'.[13] As a matter of fact, the border between the two is not clearly traced. Situations like the one in Congo or the one in Darfur seem to demonstrate that such States are both unable *and* unwilling, in an interlocking manner, because of the coexistence of inability and unwillingness.

All this allows us to offer interesting reflections on the fact that a correct interpretation of complementarity should lead to a close and fruitful interaction between the ICC and State jurisdictions, aiming at solving the delicate problems connected with various forms of inability.[14]

A last point deserves to be highlighted even if not expressly mentioned by article 17. Can we consider a State lacking the legislation for the implementation aiming at the repression of serious crimes of international concern to be considered 'unable or unwilling'? Of course, this approach implies an overall and comprehensive evaluation of a national legal system as such, including its criminal code and criminal procedure. It appears reasonable that complementarity is intended to be conceived only for States complying with their international obligations, that is, having adopted an implementation legislation which enables them to investigate and prosecute the perpetrators of international crimes.

A State wishing to give solid foundations to its right to investigate and to prosecute crimes, and to avoid being considered in a potential situation of inability, should conform its legal system to the requirements of the Rome Statute, in a correct approach to the principle of complementarity.

This is clear in the German Code of Crimes against international law (26 June 2002), one of the aims of which is 'to ensure, in the light of the complementary

12 *Fourth Report of the Prosecutor of the International Criminal Court, Mr. Luis Moreno Ocampo, to the UN Security Council pursuant to UNSCR 1593 (2005)*, 14 December 2006 (available at http://www.icc-cpi.int/library/organs/otp/OTP_ReportUNSC4-Darfur_English.pdf accessed 10 September 2007).

13 In paragraphs 586 and 609 the Commission refers to Sudan as a State 'unable *and* unwilling'; in paragraph 615 'unable *or* unwilling' and in paragraph 647 concludes once again that 'the Sudanese justice system has demonstrated its inability *and* unwillingness to investigate and prosecute the perpetrators of these crimes'.

14 Delmas-Marty, M. (2006), 'Interactions between National and International Criminal Law in the Preliminary Phase of Trial at the ICC', in *Journal of International Criminal Justice* 4:1, 6.

prosecutorial competence of the International Criminal Court, that Germany is always able to prosecute crimes within the jurisdiction of the ICC'.[15]

But this would lead us to conclude that even the State which hosted the Diplomatic Conference does not represent an example to be followed, since it has not yet adopted a specific legislation!

15 www.icrc.org/ihl-nat.nsf/ (accessed 10 September 2007). See also Yang, L. (2005), 'On the Principle of Complementarity in the Rome Statute of the International Criminal Court', in *Chinese Journal of International Law* 4:1, 124.

Chapter 8

The Complementary Role of the International Criminal Court: Are there any Time-limits?

Federica Gioia[1]

1. A Neglected Area: How Important?

Since 1 July 2002, much has been said, written and researched on the International Criminal Court (ICC) and on what many regard as its most distinctive feature: the principle of complementarity, as the relationship between the Court and national jurisdictions is comprehensively referred to. The novelty and complexity of this principle largely account for the fact that scholars have focussed their attention on the principles and rules governing it, as well as on the practical aspects of its implementation and functioning. Yet, there seems to be at least one relevant aspect which, to the best of our knowledge, has so far failed to reach the limelight: the question whether the action of the Court is subject to any limitation in time, once its jurisdiction has been triggered pursuant to one of the mechanisms provided under the Statute. Otherwise stated, the temporal dimension following the triggering mechanisms of the jurisdiction of the Court appears to remain in a sort of limbo.[2] Once a referral has been filed, whether by a State or the Security Council, or the

---

1 The valuable assistance of Sévrine Knuchel in carrying out part of the underlying research is hereby gratefully acknowledged.

2 Burke-White, W.W. (2007), 'Proactive complementarity: the International Criminal Court and national Courts in the Rome System of Justice' (available at http://papers.ssrn.com/abstract=964201 accessed 30 August 2007), 25, does not go beyond the statement that 'at some point, based on resource allocation, global events, national prosecutions, and impact to date, the OTP will need to move on to a new situation' or that 'the Court could always decide to reopen a particular situation for further investigation, though that appears an unlikely scenario' (p. 25, footnote 85), without however providing any indication as to which legal rule or principle would support or justify such 'moving on' or 'reopening'. It is unclear whether O'Donohue, J. (2005), 'The 2005 Budget of the International Criminal Court: contingency, insufficient funding in key areas and the recurring question of the independence of the Prosecutor', in *Leiden Journal of International Law* 18:3, 594, implies that the submission of a situation to the Court would entail the Court being seized of that situation on a permanent basis, when listing the number of situations pending before the Court at a given point in time as its 'constant docket' (an expression appearing in official documents of the Court: see infra, footnote no. 7 and corresponding text).

Prosecutor has secured an authorisation to start a *motu proprio* investigation by the relevant Pre-Trial Chamber, several questions arise: shall the Court consider itself seized of the situation for an undetermined duration of time, or should its power to proceed with investigation and prosecution be subject to a time-limit? Is any time-frame relevant to the investigative action of the Prosecutor? Are referrals (or authorisations to proceed *motu proprio*) subject to any time-limit?

The current debate on the purported 'lengthiness' of Court proceedings makes all these questions anything but theoretical. There seem to be at least two perspectives under which they can be considered: on the one hand, in the light of human rights principles, namely from the standpoint of one or more individuals liable to be the target of the investigating and prosecuting action of the Court; on the other hand, within the broader and specific context of complementarity, namely from the standpoint of a State.

2. Reasons in Favour of the Existence of a Time-limit: From the Standpoint of the Individual(s)...

It is a matter of general knowledge that the crimes falling within the jurisdiction of the Court are not subject to a statute of limitation[3] due to their gravity. However, this does not seem to detract from the need to ensure that, once criminal action in the form of an investigation has been started, it must come to a close within a reasonable time-limit. Such need is supported by manifold considerations: first and foremost, to preserve the right to a fair trial, in particular as regards that particular facet thereof consisting in the right to be tried 'within a reasonable delay'.

The Statute appears acutely aware of this with respect to both the pre-trial and the trial phases: suffice it to mention article 61 for the pre-trial phase (mandating the Pre-Trial Chamber to hold a hearing to confirm the charges on which the Prosecutor intends to seek trial 'within a reasonable time after the person's surrender or voluntary appearance before the Court')[4] and article 64 for the trial, making it a duty for the Trial Chamber to 'ensure that a trial is fair and expeditious' as a matter of procedure; this provision finds a substantive *pendant* in article 67, listing the fact of being tried 'without undue delay' as one of the fundamental rights of the accused.

No mention is instead made of principles or rules setting forth or governing the time-frame, if any, between the moment when the jurisdiction of the Court is triggered and the moment when the person subject to the investigation is brought before the Pre-Trial Chamber for the confirmation of the charges. On the contrary, provisions concerning the action of the Prosecutor seem to suggest that no temporal

3 Article 29 of the Statute (Non-applicability of statute of limitations).

4 See also article 19(4) of the Statute, pursuant to which a challenge to the jurisdiction of the Court or the admissibility of a case shall – as a matter of principle – only take place 'prior to or at the commencement of the trial'; when brought by a State, such challenge shall be made 'at the earliest opportunity'(article 19(3) of the Statute); article 59(7) (the person arrested on the basis of an ICC warrant 'shall be delivered to the Court as soon as possible'); article 60(4) ('the Pre-Trial Chamber shall ensure that a person is not detained for an unreasonable time due to inexcusable delay by the Prosecutor').

boundaries apply to such action: in particular, article 19(10), allowing the Prosecutor to request a review of the Court's decision that a given case is inadmissible, based on new facts, and article 53(4), providing that 'the Prosecutor may, at any time, reconsider a decision whether to initiate an investigation or prosecution based on new facts or information'.[5] Along the same lines seems shaped article 16 and the Security Council's power to request the Court to defer an investigation or a prosecution by means of a resolution adopted under Chapter VII of the UN Charter; such a request lasts for a period of 12 months but can be 'renewed by the Council under the same conditions'. A proposal suggesting that the request may be extended only 'for a further period not exceeding 12 months' was specifically defeated during the preparatory works,[6] this suggesting that no time-limit applies to the Council's power to renew such requests.[7]

It comes therefore as no surprise that yearly reports submitted to the Assembly of States Parties by the Prosecutor make broad references to the number of investigations which the Office is expecting to conduct during the forthcoming years, without however addressing the issue of their completion; to reinforce this, the rather ambiguous expression 'constant docket' is being used by the Committee on Budget and Finance and the Assembly of States Parties to refer to the workload of the Court at a given point in time.[8]

It may be argued that setting a time-limit to the action of the Prosecutor preceding the request for either a warrant of arrest or a summons to appear would be unfeasible, due to the complex and manifold nature of the investigations to be carried out by the Court. Yet, this way of arguing would deliberately neglect the fact that the existence of a temporal limitation on all of the Court's organs, including the Prosecutor, may be regarded as a core aspect of the right to a fair trial, and in particular the right to be tried within a reasonable delay[9], as currently construed in legal doctrine and in

---

5 Bergsmo, M. and Kruger, P. (1999), 'Article 53', in Triffterer, O. (ed.), *Commentary on the Rome Statute of the International Criminal Court, Observers' Notes, Article by Article*' (Baden Baden: Nomos) pp. 713–14, argue that this provision 'grants the Prosecutor a discretionary power to resurrect an investigation or prosecution that he or she had previously decided had no reasonable basis or sufficient basis to proceed' and that 'the only requirement for the Prosecutor to be able to reconsider a prior decision is that new facts or information become available'. The authors also argue, on the basis of the wording of the provision, that the Prosecutor's power to reconsider also applies to positive decisions to investigate and prosecute.

6 United Nations Diplomatic Conference of Plenipotentiaries on the Establishment of an International Criminal Court, Rome, 15 June–17 July 1998, Official Records, Volume III, Reports and other documents, F. Documents of the Committee of the Whole, Document A/CONF.183/C.1/L.20 (Spain: proposal regarding article 10, 25 June 1998).

7 Della Morte, G. (2002), 'Les frontières de la compétence de la CPI – Observations critiques', in *Revue internationale de droit pénal* 73:1–2, 49: 'la période de douze mois peut être renouvelée aux mêmes conditions, et donc, le cas échéant, aussi ad libitum'.

8 ICC-ASP/2/10 (Draft programme budget for 2004 prepared by the Registrar), 25.

9 Article 54 (1) (c), of the Statute sets forth that the Prosecutor shall 'fully respect the rights of persons arising under this Statute', among which the right of accused to be tried without undue delay features prominently under article 67(1) (c).

the case-law of the various regional human rights courts, as well as national legal systems.

The most developed considerations on the right to be tried within a reasonable time are to be found in the case-law by the European Court of Human Rights sitting in Strasbourg (ECHR). Time and again the ECHR has cautioned States against the practice of delaying justice without a proper justification, by highlighting that excessive delays in the administration of justice represent 'an important danger' for the rule of law.[10]

More specifically, the Court clarified that in criminal matters the 'reasonable time' referred to in article 6(1) (of the European Convention on Human Rights) begins to run as soon as a person is 'charged'[11] or '*mise en examen*'[12] and that 'this may occur on a date prior to the case coming before the trial court, such as the date of arrest, the date when the person concerned was officially notified that he was to be prosecuted or the date when the preliminary investigations were opened';[13] the Court highlighted that in either of these procedural steps the action by the relevant investigating and prosecuting authorities has 'substantially affected' the situation of the suspect.[14] This broad approach is taken by the Court with a view to ensuring that the right to a fair trial is preserved irrespective of the label or name given to a specific procedural step in a given national system; otherwise stated, a substantive rather than a formal conception of the 'charge' is adopted by the EHCR for the purposes of article 6(1) of the European Convention on Human Rights.[15]

The views of the European Court of Human Rights are echoed in the case-law of other regional courts. The Inter-American Court of Human Rights held that the purpose of the principle of the 'reasonable time', within which every person has a right to be heard, is 'to prevent accused persons from remaining in that situation for a protracted period and to ensure that the charge is promptly disposed of'.[16]

A similar stance is taken by some human rights bodies. The Committee on Torture censored Argentina for allowing 'unlimited extension' of the period for preliminary investigations, in spite of the existence of a time-limit of four months.

---

10 ECHR, Kudla v. Poland, 26 October 2000, Grand Chamber, paragraph 148; ECHR, Bottazzi v. Italy, 28 June 1999, paragraph 22.

11 ECHR, Weil v. France, 5 February 2004, paragraph 32; ECHR, Coeme et autres c. Belgique, 22 June 2000, paragraph 133.

12 European Court of Human Rights, Djiad v. France, 29 septembre 1999, paragraph 26.

13 ECHR, Weil v. France, 5 February 2004, paragraph 32; ECHR, Coeme et autres c. Belgique, 22 June 2000, paragraph 133; ECHR, Eckle v. Germany, 15 July 1982, paragraph 73; ECHR, Ringeisen v. Austria, 16 July 1971, paragraph 110.

See also Milano, L. (2006), *Le droit à un tribunal au sens de la Convention européenne des droits de l'Homme* (Paris: Dalloz), p. 465.

14 ECHR, Weil v. France, 5 février 2004, paragraph 32; ECHR, Coeme et autres c. Belgique, 22 June 2000, paragraph 133; ECHR, Eckle v. Germany, 15 July 1982, paragraph 73.

15 ECHR, Deweer v. Belgium, 27 February 1980, paragraph 44.

16 Inter-American Court of Human Rights, Suarez v. Rosero, 12 November 1997, paragraph 70.

The committee voiced the view that the 'undue prolongation of this pre-trial stage represents a form of cruel treatment of the individual concerned, even if he is not deprived of his freedom'.[17]

The principle that the 'reasonable delay' also applies to the investigation phase is also to be found in national legal systems. Depending on whether a country of civil law tradition, rather than a common law country is at stake, different techniques are put in place to implement the principle. In civil law countries, the most favoured technique appears the setting forth of specific time-limits within which investigative acts have to be completed.

The French code of criminal procedure, for instance, sets forth the general principle that the duration of the investigation cannot exceed a reasonable delay, in the light of the gravity of the facts at stake, the complexity of the required investigations and the rights of the defence.[18] Accordingly, any individual '*mis en examen*' by the Prosecutor has the right to receive a 'provisional calendar' of the investigation and the subsequent developments; if no such calendar has been provided, after one year, or four months if no investigative act has been performed in the meantime, the person may request the *juge d'instruction* to issue a '*non-lieu ou un renvoi en jugement*'; other actions can be taken (in particular, recourse to the authority of the President of the *Chambre d'instruction* in the event of failure by the *juge d'instruction* to provide an answer). Additional guarantees are triggered after two years from the opening of the investigation; in this event, every six months the investigating judge has to issue an order providing reasons for the delay, which cannot be other than those listed in article 175-2 of the code of criminal procedure.[19]

Similar temporal thresholds are enshrined in the Italian Code of Civil Procedure[20] and are usually justified in light of the need to avoid that the procedural fate of the person investigated by the Prosecuting authorities remain indefinitely unpredictable.[21]

Common law countries construe delays in commencing or pursuing a prosecution as 'abuse of process',[22] as such warranting a stay in the proceedings.

---

17 Office of the High Commissioner for Human Rights, Concluding observations of the Committee against Torture: Argentina, 21 November 1997 (A/53/44), paragraph 68.

18 Article 175-2, alinéa 1, *Code de procédure pénale* français.

19 Article 175-1, *Code de procédure pénale* français. Merle, R. and Vitu, A. (2001), *Traité de droit criminel – Procédure pénale*, Fifth edition, Tome II (Paris: Cujas), p. 616, labels these time-limits as '*deux verrous successifs*', having been established '*afin que soit respectée l'exigence d'un "délai raisonnable" pour la conduite de l' instruction*'.

20 Article 407 Italian *Codice di Procedura Penale*: the overall duration of the preliminary investigation cannot exceed two years, even when particularly complex and serious crimes are at stake.

21 Garofoli, V. (2006), *Istituzioni di diritto processuale penale*, Second edition, (Milano: Giuffré), p. 291: 'Si vuole evitare che l'indagato permanga oltre il tempo ragionevolmente necessario in una situazione di instabilità tra il rinvio a giudizio e la chiusura del procedimento con archiviazione'.

22 House of Lords, R. v. Horseferry Road Magistrates' Court, ex parte Bennett [1994] 1 A.C. 42: 'Justices... have power to exercise control over their proceedings through the abuse of process jurisdiction. However, such power should be strictly confined to matters

In light of the above, it seems reasonable to hold that the opening of the investigation pursuant to article 18(1) of the Statute, and the ensuing notification to States by the Prosecutor, may be construed as amounting to the opening of a preliminary investigation for the purposes of the right to be tried without undue delay; a right which should be upheld by any Court, including the International Criminal Court. Such holding could not be seriously challenged by arguing that, at that stage, no individual yet has been identified by the Prosecutor as specific target of his investigative action. Indeed, national systems also provide for time-thresholds in respect of investigative activities carried out *vis-à-vis* individuals who cannot be identified.[23]

3. … and From the Standpoint of States

The foregoing remarks demonstrate *per se* the need for all stages of the action of the Court, including the investigative stage, to be subject to a time-limit, if the Court is truly to abide by 'international law and internationally recognised norms and standards' as prescribed by its Statute.[24] Moreover, failing to ensure that the investigating action of the Prosecutor be limited within a reasonable time would inevitably result in depriving of meaningful content those provisions of the Statute setting forth the right of the accused to a trial (and a pre-trial) which are both fair and expeditious. This appears even more obvious, when considered in the light of the claim that the Statute enshrines the highest available standards of guarantee in terms of fair trial in criminal matters. Additional arguments may be drawn from considerations rooted at the heart of the complementarity regime.

Apart from the provisions on the expeditiousness of the trial, a few provisions in the Statute take into account the developing in time of the action of the Court. Pursuant to article 18(5), after deferring an investigation to a State, the Prosecutor 'may request that the State concerned periodically inform the Prosecutor of the progress of its investigations and any subsequent prosecutions', to which requests the relevant State Party 'shall respond … without undue delay'. How crucial these reports are meant to be is best appreciated by considering article 18(3) according to which 'the Prosecutor's deferral to a State's investigation shall be open to review by the Prosecutor six months after the date of the referral or at any time when there has been a significant change in circumstances based on the State's unwillingness or inability genuinely to carry out the investigation'. Furthermore, article 18(6) of the Statute vests the Prosecutor with the power to seek authority from the Pre-Trial Chamber, albeit on an exceptional basis, 'to pursue necessary investigative

---

directly affecting the fairness of the trial of the particular accused … such as delay or unfair manipulation of court procedures'.

23 In the language of the Italian Code of Criminal Procedure, this is the case of '*procedimenti penali contro ignoti*' (criminal proceedings *vis-à-vis* unknown – not yet identified – persons): article 415 of the Italian code of criminal procedure subjects such investigation to a six-month time-limit, at the expiration of which the investigating magistrate has to decide whether to close the file or to request the judge for an authorisation to pursue the investigation.

24 Article 21 (1) (c) and 21(3).

steps for the purpose of preserving evidence where there is a unique opportunity to obtain important evidence or there is a significant risk that such evidence may not be subsequently available', notwithstanding the fact that the investigation has been deferred to a State.

These provisions suggest that the Statute appropriately enshrines guarantees against a State's failure to act in respect of the period *following* an initial favourable assessment of its action by the Court.[25] This seems entirely in line with the core essence of complementarity as currently identified, whereby the Court is meant to complement, rather than replace national jurisdictions whenever they fail, in the joint pursuance of a common objective, without any hierarchy or superiority vested in the Court.[26] Accordingly, a balanced vision on complementarity may require that some kind of reciprocity be built into this provision: a State also, once 'divested' of its competence pursuant to article 18(2), should be able to rely on mechanisms allowing it to return in full control of its duties in case the Court fails to act in a prompt and efficient way. At the very minimum, the State should be allowed to request the Prosecutor or, in case of non-cooperation by the latter, a Pre-Trial Chamber, to provide a report on the action taken, as well as to submit arguments supporting its claim to return in full charge of its investigating and prosecuting duties.

Neither is this an idea entirely unknown to the debate on the right to be tried within a reasonable delay. The ECHR often couples references to article 6 with references to article 13 of the European Convention, establishing the principle whereby 'everyone whose rights and freedoms as set forth in this Convention are violated shall have an effective remedy before a national authority'. Accordingly, contracting States are under an obligation to create remedies *vis-à-vis* excessive length of proceedings, although no prevailing pattern as to the specific features of such remedy can be found.[27] As to the effectiveness of such remedies, it is to be measured against their suitability 'either of preventing the alleged violation or its continuation, or of providing adequate redress for any violation that had already occurred',[28] which is tantamount to saying that the effectiveness of the remedy is to be evaluated against its suitability to expedite the determination of the charges.

---

25 Such guarantee is actually triggered even at an earlier point: article 18(2) of the Statute provides that a State has one month to respond to the Prosecutor's notification as to the existence of a reasonable basis to commence an investigation.

26 This approach has been recently taken a step forward by Burke-White, W.W. (2007), 'Proactive complementarity: the International Criminal Court and national Courts in the Rome System of Justice', 3 (available at http://papers.ssrn.com/abstract=964201 accessed 30 August 2007), who argues that the complementarity regime should be transformed 'from a limitation on the Court's power into a proactive mechanism for encouraging national prosecutions and allocating authority between the ICC and domestic courts'.

27 ECHR, Kudla v. Poland, 26 October 2000, Grand Chamber, paragraph 154.

28 ECHR, Kudla v. Poland, 26 October 2000, Grand Chamber, paragraph 158.

4. The Interpretation of the Scope of the 'Situation' as a Way to Achieve the Goals Outlined Above. The Principle of the 'Exhaustion' of a Referral

It may be argued that the inherent difficulties of investigations to be entrusted to the Court make the very notion of the Court's action being subject to a specific time-limit unfeasible. Practical obstacles, whilst existing, can however hardly justify a course of action which would be tantamount to denying one of the most critical features of the right to a fair trial. Hence the need to enquire whether, instead of a time-limit, the right to a fair trial can be fully preserved and the cooperative notion of complementarity be enhanced by alternative means. While the building into the system of mechanisms allowing a State to promptly return in full possession of its jurisdictional prerogatives may sound interesting in a perspective *de iure condendo*, the urgency of the needs highlighted above calls for alternative means which may already be invoked under the Statute as it currently stands.

The adoption of appropriately strict criteria in construing a 'situation', with a view to precisely determine its subjective, temporal and territorial boundaries, may provide a first answer. Only if and when this determination is accomplished, the action of the Court will satisfy those requirements of predictability, which should be paramount for the action of any criminal court.

Any situation submitted to the Court, whether by way of referral or as a consequence of the authorisation to a *motu proprio* investigation, should be precisely identified as to its territorial, temporal and possibly subjective boundaries as of the moment when the Prosecutor has determined that there is a reasonable basis to commence an investigation pursuant to article 18(1). Once the thus determined scope of the investigation has been covered, the referral (or authorisation) at stake should be considered as 'exhausted'; accordingly, the operation of a new, separate triggering mechanism would be required for the Court to continue or resume investigating or prosecuting in a given country crimes which fall beyond the scope of the 'first' referral.

The constitutive instruments of international criminal jurisdictions established over time seem to lend further support to the reasoning outlined so far. Mandates vested in those jurisdictions are usually characterised by specific boundaries, whether subjective, territorial or temporal.[29] Even in respect of the International

29 See for example, the following: Charter of the International Military Tribunal sitting in Nuremberg (London Charter), article 1: 'In pursuance of the Agreement signed on the 8th day of August 1945 [accessed 8 September 2007] by the Government of the United States of America, the Provisional Government of the French Republic, the Government of the United Kingdom of Great Britain and Northern Ireland and the Government of the Union of Soviet Socialist Republics, there shall be established an International Military Tribunal (hereinafter called "the Tribunal") for the just and prompt trial and punishment of the major war criminals of the European Axis'; Statute of the International Criminal Tribunal for Rwanda, article 1 (Competence of the International Tribunal for Rwanda): 'The International Tribunal for Rwanda shall have the power to prosecute persons responsible for serious violations of international humanitarian law committed in the territory of Rwanda and Rwandan citizens responsible for such violations committed in the territory of neighbouring States between 1 January 1994 and 31 December 1994, in accordance with the provisions of the present

Criminal Tribunal for the Former Yugoslavia (ICTY), the mandate of which does not indicate an expiration date,[30] at one point the need was felt to devise a 'completion strategy', which is currently being implemented. Among the reasons supporting such strategy, the need to be able to refer 'certain cases back to national courts'[31] appears of particular relevance in the perspective of complementarity. The very idea that investigating and prosecuting the most heinous crimes is, and has to remain, first and foremost a duty of a State requires *per se* that the Court be 'divested' of a situation in respect of which it has played its complementary role, whether it be because the genuine willingness and ability of that State to honour that duty have been restored or because the Court has covered the scope of a situation as referred to it.

5. Final Remarks

A negative answer to the questions outlined at the outset would result in each referral concerning a country vesting the Court with perpetual jurisdiction in respect of that country, or at least a part of it. Once a relevant amount of referrals has been secured, the Court would be seized on a permanent and world-wide basis, thus depriving of meaningful content the very mechanisms of referrals, clearly aimed at restrictively shaping the boundaries of its jurisdiction.

It is our view that the simple utterance of this implication exposes its debatable compliance not only with the right to be tried within a reasonable delay, but also with the complementarity regime, the main purpose of which is to have the Court act on a case-by-case basis, whenever a lacuna or a flaw in actions taken at the national level can be shown. Whilst the very nature of the crimes within the scope of the jurisdiction of the Court and the operational difficulties entailed thereby might make it unfeasible and ultimately inappropriate to set specific time-limits, there is a need to find alternative ways whereby both the right to a fair trial and the core essence of complementarity may be preserved. Two ways may be envisaged, one of a procedural and one of a substantive nature.

From a procedural standpoint, and in a perspective *de iure condendo*, appropriate mechanisms allowing States subject to ICC investigation to react in case of inertia or 'unjustified delay' by the Court's organs, including the Prosecutor, should be provided. As 'an unjustified delay' in the proceedings triggers the stepping in of

---

Statute'; Statute of the Special Court for Sierra Leone, article 1 (Competence of the Special Court): 'The Special Court shall… have the power to prosecute persons who bear the greatest responsibility for serious violations of international humanitarian law and Sierra Leonean law committed in the territory of Sierra Leone since 30 November 1996, including those leaders who, in committing such crimes, have threatened the establishment of and implementation of the peace process in Sierra Leone'.

30 ICTY Statute, article 1 (Competence of the International Tribunal): 'The International Tribunal shall have the power to prosecute persons responsible for serious violations of international humanitarian law committed in the territory of the Former Yugoslavia since 1991 in accordance with the provisions of the present Statute'.

31 Mundis, D.A. (2005), 'The judicial effects of the "completion strategies" on the ad hoc international tribunals', in *American Journal of International Law*, 99:1, 143.

the Court under the heading of unwillingness,[32] a truly cooperative notion of complementarity seems to require that any 'unjustified delay' on the part of the Court's organs, including the Prosecutor, result in the jurisdiction of the relevant State being fully restored.

From a substantive standpoint, no obstacles are to be found in the Statute as it currently stands in holding that situations brought before the Court should be subject to rigorous process of determination of their scope, including their temporal and territorial boundaries and that, accordingly, any action the Court would purport to take falling beyond such boundaries would be considered 'exhausted' and therefore illegitimate, unless and until covered by a separate, distinct referral.

As we tried to demonstrate, the view that the Court will be seized on a permanent basis *vis-à-vis* one or more States once and every time the investigative powers of the Prosecutor are triggered in respect of that or those States runs counter to one of the tenets of the right to a fair trial and, ultimately, defeats the very idea of complementarity as a cooperative relationship built on mutual trust between the Court and national jurisdictions. It is hard to accept that this is meant by those who, since the early days of the Court, continue to regard its 'permanency' as one of its most distinctive features.

32 Article 17 (2)(b) of the Statute.

PART III
Recent Developments on International Cooperation and National Implementation

Introductory Statement by Fausto Pocar

I would like to thank the organizers of this International Colloquium on the relationship between the ICC and national jurisdictions for having me here presiding over this round table on cooperation matters. Allow me a few words of introduction related to my experience at the ICTY.

Of course, it is a truism that international cooperation is a crucial aspect in order for international criminal jurisdictions to be able to carry out their mandate effectively. It certainly appears to be so for the ICC, during its first steps, as it has been – and continues to be – for the ad hoc Tribunals as well as for the various mixed tribunals. Experience shows, however, that despite the best efforts to foresee problems and possible solutions in advance on the theoretical level, unforeseen practical problems will always arise. This is all the more so in instances when State cooperation is at issue and an international judicial institution must be able to show its 'teeth' to achieve the goals of justice set by the international community.

In the past few years, the ICTY has indeed endeavoured to strengthen its cooperation with States, both in the region of the Former Yugoslavia and elsewhere, as well as with regional intergovernmental organizations. I would like to stress that cooperation with States by international judicial institutions may be understood as operating in different contexts.

On the one side, we have cooperation in what might be termed 'traditional' judicial matters: surrender of indicted persons, cooperation in evidence-gathering procedures, assistance in ensuring the presence of witnesses for trials and so on. In our experience at the ICTY, we had cases of States failing to arrest accused persons who, month after month, were allowed to walk free, to go on with their lives, maybe even to drink a cup of coffee at the local café each morning. These people remain at large due to the unwillingness of State officials to cooperate in good faith with the Tribunal – and I am not necessarily referring only to the State where that person is located, but also to other countries that have contacts in, and leverage on, that State. So, this type of cooperation extends to potentially any country, even outside the Balkans. As is well known, the continued failure to arrest and transfer the remaining high-level fugitives – in spite of some successes during the past year or so – remains a significant impediment to the activity of the ICTY. This impediment effectively hinders the Tribunal's ability to bring justice, as well as a sense of 'closure', to the region. It also remains a significant barrier to the timely completion of the Tribunal's mandate.

On the other side, there is another aspect to cooperation – in particular with States in the Former Yugoslavia. My message to various authorities and domestic courts in the Former Yugoslavia during the past few years has been that, when the time comes for the Tribunal to close, this may not mean that justice for the crimes perpetrated in the region will itself come to an end. When I became President of the ICTY, I started to increase cooperation with local courts in order to try and pass on all the know-how possible as a crucial part of the Tribunal's legacy. In meetings with local judges, we have made it clear that, whereas today it is us who are trying these cases, tomorrow it will be entirely up to them.

The Tribunal, for example, has worked with the Office of the High Representative to open a Special Chamber for war crimes prosecutions in the State Court of Bosnia and Herzegovina, which is now running a number of important proceedings, either referred back by us or initiated locally. In furtherance of the Tribunal's commitment to assisting trial readiness of the local courts, we have also been conducting a number of training seminars with judges and prosecutors from Croatia and Serbia. If one is to judge on the basis of all information before us, there will undoubtedly be more cases and new indictments coming up in the next decades, so all of these countries must put in place systems allowing them to deal with those cases. After all, Nuremberg did not finish with the International Military Tribunal: it was followed by the military courts of the occupying powers and, later on, by further cases dealt with in domestic, including German, courts. The contribution of the ICTY to the establishment of judicial institutions in the Former Yugoslavia able to conduct war crimes trials in accordance with international standards is a cornerstone of the Tribunal's legacy. For the Tribunal to have provided an incentive to reform the judiciaries in the Former Yugoslavia and to have acted as a catalyst for the creation of specialized war crimes courts in the region stands as important evidence of the complementary role that international institutions can fulfil.

My brief remarks, of course, only hint at cooperation issues that the ICTY has been dealing with in the past years and will continue to face until its mandate is completed. These issues, in turn, constitute only some of the aspects of the general question of cooperation between international courts or tribunals, on the one side, and domestic jurisdictions, on the other.

I am therefore pleased to give the floor to my esteemed colleagues, who are going to discuss various facets of the topic of State cooperation with the ICC. Judge Hans-Peter Kaul from the ICC will discuss international criminal cooperation as a permanent challenge for the ICC. Professor Håkan Friman will then focus on ICC arrest warrants, with specific reference to the situation of the Democratic Republic of Congo. Professor Annalisa Ciampi will examine the issue of human rights and State cooperation with the ICC, while Maria Malaguti will discuss whether any lessons can be drawn from the Nuremberg legacy in understanding the modern concept of 'complementarity'. Finally, Dr Teresa Moschetta will talk about the role of the European Union in supporting the activity of the ICC.

Judge Kaul, you have the floor.

Chapter 9

The ICC and International Criminal Cooperation – Key Aspects and Fundamental Necessities

Hans-Peter Kaul

As you are aware, this presentation will deal with 'The ICC and International Criminal Cooperation – Key Aspects and Fundamental Necessities' – and 'fundamental necessities' means practical and urgent necessities!

Let me start by making a confession. Even during the Rome Conference in 1998 and afterwards, until the entry into force of the Rome Statute in July 2002, when I continued to be the Head of the German ICC delegation, I was not fully aware how essential, how vital indeed effective criminal cooperation would be for the Court. Only since 2003, when I joined the Court as a Judge, did I become increasingly aware that the Court is totally dependent, 100% dependent, on full, effective and timely cooperation in particular from States Parties. Meanwhile, it is my considered view that the question, whether the Court is able to rely on effective and sustained cooperation, may indeed be decisive for its failure or success, at least in the longer perspective.

Also with regard to the issues of effective criminal cooperation, let me recall an experience which others also have had, time and again: the idea of an International Criminal Court, the Rome Statute and more specifically the system of criminal cooperation contained therein are, as such, no guarantee for progress or even success. Everything remains difficult, nothing falls into place by itself. Every inch of progress needs hard work, needs sustained effort. This is especially true also for the area of criminal cooperation. To ensure cooperation is a continuing task, a permanent necessity and also a permanent challenge where – as we will hear from Håkan Friman – the devil is often in the details.[1]

With this in mind, I would like to divide these remarks into two brief parts. First: let me recall some key aspects of the cooperation regime pursuant to chapter 9 of the Rome Statute which will have an impact on the work of the ICC also in the future. Second: in the light of these key aspects and limitations, what are fundamental necessities and challenges with regard to international criminal cooperation?

As cooperation is such a huge and comprehensive issue in itself, I will focus mainly on issues of cooperation necessary for investigation and prosecution activities. This means that I will generally not deal with requests for cooperation originating from

1 See Friman, H., Chapter 10 in this volume.

the Registry, general cooperation agreements concluded by the Presidency or other specific forms of cooperation concerning the protection of victims and witnesses. Likewise, I will not discuss possible agreements on relocation of witnesses or the enforcement of sentences in accordance with part 10 of the Statute. Instead, I would like to highlight some urgent, burning issues regarding effective criminal cooperation.

1. Key Aspects

When we assess the cooperation regime under the Rome Statute, we cannot fail to see that it is characterized by a decisive structural weakness: the Court does not have the competencies and means to enforce its own decisions.[2] Under the Statute, the ICC has no executive powers, no police force of its own or other executive units. It is totally dependent on full, effective, timely and predictable cooperation, in particular from States Parties. This is true especially with regard to the decisive question of the effective execution of arrest warrants and surrender of suspects to The Hague.[3] One may safely assume that this structural weakness was foreseen and planned by the founders of the ICC also in the field of criminal cooperation. With regard to the jurisdiction and admissibility regime of the Rome Statute, it was also with regard to issues of cooperation the wish of the Court's creators that States' sovereignty remain prevailing – and President Kirsch has recalled this morning some of the underlying reasons.[4]

Against this background, part 9 of the Rome Statute on international cooperation and judicial assistance seeks to ensure the functioning of the Court through the following main elements:

a. States Parties have a general obligation to cooperate fully with the Court with respect to its investigations and prosecutions (article 86).
b. States Parties shall ensure that procedures are available under national law for all forms of cooperation specified in part 9 (article 88).

---

2 For a discussion of the cooperation regime in the Rome Statute, see Kaul, H.P. and Kress, C. (1999), 'Jurisdiction and Cooperation in the Statute of the International Criminal Court: Principles and Compromises', *Yearbook of International Humanitarian Law*, 143; Mochochoko, P. (1999), 'International Cooperation and Judicial Assistance', in Lee, R.S. (ed.), in *The International Criminal Court: The Making of the Rome Statute – Issues, Negotiation, Results* (The Hague-London-Boston: Kluwer Law International), p. 305; Oosterveld, V., Perry, M. and McManus, J. (2002), 'The Cooperation of States with the International Criminal Court', in *Fordham International Law Journal* 25:3, 767; Swart, B. and Sluiter, G. (1999), 'The International Criminal Court and International Criminal Cooperation', in Von Hebel, H. et al. (eds), *Reflections on the International Criminal Court*, p. 91.

3 See Swart, B. (2002), 'Arrest and Surrender', in Cassese, A., Gaeta, P. and Jones, J.R.W.D. (eds), *The Rome Statute of the International Criminal Court: A Commentary*, (Oxford: Oxford University Press), p. 1639.

4 See Kirsch, P., Chapter 1, this volume.

c. States Parties shall consult with the Court without delay in order to resolve any problems which may impede or prevent the execution of requests (article 97).

The measures stipulated in part 9 represent the minimum and guaranteed obligations accepted by States Parties becoming Parties to the Statute. States not parties have no obligation to cooperate except when the Security Council refers a situation to the Court pursuant to article 13b and obliges non-Member States under Chapter VII of the UN Charter to cooperate with the Court (in passing, let me recall that Security Council Resolution 1593 on Darfur regrettably does not contain a general obligation for UN Member States to cooperate with the ICC).

All in all, the system of cooperation under the Rome Statute may be regarded as a compromise and as a hybrid system. It contains a mix of elements of vertical and horizontal criminal cooperation of both the supra-national and inter-state model of cooperation. While States Parties have a general obligation to fully cooperate with the Court, there remains in practice a lot of discretion, for example, if a request for cooperation is in conflict with a national 'existing fundamental legal principle of general application' or where the documents or evidence concerned relate to national security.[5] States are thus not under any strict obligation to give priority to the Court's requests for surrender or assistance. Instead, the Statute foresees consultations in cases of problems arising in the context of a cooperation request from the Court.[6]

This may suffice as a very brief summary of the overall situation regarding the cooperation regime under the Statute.

2. Fundamental Necessities

This regime as laid down in part 9 of the Statute must be seen as a reality and a fact of life which cannot be altered easily – and also not at the Review Conference in 2009. This regime therefore must be accepted by all concerned, namely the Court itself and in particular the Office of the Prosecutor, the States Parties, international organizations and NGOs. All these actors are called upon to breathe life into the cooperation system under the Statute and to exhaust its possibilities for effective, speedy, unreserved and sustained cooperation. This is in itself an ongoing task and challenge, with many related necessities. Amongst them, let me highlight in particular three fundamental necessities:

a. Firstly, the joint development of a new and innovative system of best practices of international criminal cooperation: direct, point to point, flexible, without unnecessary bureaucracy, with full use of modern information technology and a fast flow of information and supportive measures.

---

5 Article 93(3) and article 93(4) in conjunction with article 72.

6 In addition to article 97, other provisions in the Statute such as article 72 (7)(a) (1); article 89 (2) and (4); article 91 (4); article 93 (3) and (9); article 96 (3); article 99 (4); article 100 (1)(f) also contain the need for consultation between States and the Court in case of problems arising in the execution of a cooperation request.

b. Second, the gradual build-up and increasing strengthening of a solid and reliable network of efficient international cooperation based on trust and confidence between the Court and State Parties.
c. Thirdly, practical solutions for the making of arrests and the surrender of suspects to the ICC.

In general, these necessities require a new openness and a new thinking, a proactive thinking commensurate to the task to make the ICC system work. The starting point is clear: the ICC is located in The Hague, far away from situations like those in Uganda, the DRC and Darfur. It has no police force of its own, no soldiers, and no powers of enforcement. All concerned must be prepared to draw appropriate conclusions from these facts in order to overcome these handicaps.

Let us now have a brief look at the respective roles of the main actors involved and desirable forms of cooperation and division of labour among them.

With regard to the first and the second necessities, it is the responsibility of both the Court and States Parties to develop together a new system of best practices of effective criminal cooperation and to build up a solid and reliable new network of international cooperation.

2.a. The Role of the Court

The first responsibility to make the ICC system of cooperation work lies with the Court itself, in particular with the Office of the Prosecutor. The Prosecutor and his Office as the driving force of the ICC bear a special responsibility both for effective investigations as effective cooperation.[7] In this respect, let me share with you a saying which I have picked up from the young people at our Court. They say – and you can hear this quite often – 'The Office of the Prosecutor is the engine, systematic efforts for effective investigations and equally effective cooperation are the fuel for the entire Court.'

Now, what does this mean in terms of concrete criminal cooperation? The Prosecutor has a key interest in effective criminal cooperation. Part 9 of the Statute provides the legal framework for such cooperation. The Prosecutor and his Office are called upon to exhaust the potential of this legal framework for firstly, the sustained build-up of an appropriate organisational capacity for cooperation issues which is large enough, which is as efficacious as possible and secondly, the ongoing development of efficient working methods and best practices in particular with regard to cooperation. The question is: do we have this already? Has this already been achieved by the Office of the Prosecutor? Ideally, the Office of the Prosecutor should act as the intellectual driving force, as the creative mastermind for new, systematic and efficient forms of cooperation on the basis of a well-developed concept with clear goals and priorities.

7 Article 42(1), Part V, Investigation and Prosecution, and Part IX, International Cooperation and Judicial Assistance, of the Rome Statute.

2.b. The Role of States Parties

Especially in the field of cooperation, it is obvious that the Court and the Prosecutor cannot be successful without active and steadfast support from States Parties, both in word and in concrete deed. The hopes and expectations at the ICC are that States Parties will support it as responsible joint owners by engaging in unreserved and systematic cooperation in all practical fields. Whether they will do so remains, as it were, a question to end all questions.

Again, what does this mean in more concrete terms? Here is a short list of concrete areas of enhanced cooperation:

a. If not done already, States should enact implementing legislation pursuant to article 88 of the Statute that is sufficiently precise to allow for direct cooperation, without the need for additional arrangements.
b. If not done already, States should enact national legislation to ensure that they are able to investigate and prosecute crimes falling under the Statute.
c. States should support the Court's general or situational policies publicly and also in direct contacts with other States and civil societies.
d. States should provide contextual and background information and advice on interlocutors and suspects, particularly through relevant specialized government departments and agencies.
e. States should provide intelligence, satellite images, analytical support and communications – and here I would like to add an example: just imagine for a moment how it would help the Prosecutor if US satellite images taken over Darfur would be made available to him!
f. States should facilitate access to potential witnesses and their voluntary appearance before the Court.
g. States should establish fast and reliable communication channels including national focal points to ensure immediate cooperation.

In general, if States Parties are genuinely interested in further progress and lasting success of 'their Court', the logical course for them is to continuously search for ways and means of strengthening cooperation with the Court.

With regard to the third necessity for practical solutions to the decisive question, the unresolved question of serving arrest warrants and surrendering suspect criminals to the ICC, major responsibility for this rests squarely on the States Parties.

3. Arrest and Surrender – Crucial Responsibility of States Parties

It is obvious that States Parties and all forces who support the Court cannot let down the Court in respect of arrest by adopting an attitude along the lines of 'we have given you the money for the first budgets – now see for yourselves how you get the perpetrators before your Court…'.

This will not work. One must hope that this is clear to all concerned. In the Former Yugoslavia, NATO and coalition forces have made most arrests for the International

Criminal Tribunal for the Former Yugoslavia. With regard to Rwanda, most arrests have been made by neighbouring States. Likewise, States Parties and Security Council members must now find ways and means of supporting the ICC with regard to the decisive question of arrests and surrenders to The Hague. Currently there are since 2005 five arrest warrants confirmed by Pre-Trial Chamber II with regard to suspects from Uganda.[8] Furthermore, there are since 2 May 2007 two arrest warrants concerning two high-ranking Sudanese officials.[9] It remains unclear whether and when these arrest warrants will be executed. This is not good.

As the Court does not have the authority to execute arrest warrants directly on the territory of States, arrests are primarily the responsibility of relevant territorial States. Securing arrests is a complex process that may require the commitment of significant police and military resources. Above all, it requires the necessary political will. While it is mainly for the territorial State to decide on arrest actions, support by other or all States could involve:

a. Public and vocal support of the international community. Such support and pressure have been crucial to securing surrenders, both voluntary and coercive, to the ICTY, ICTR and the Special Court for Sierra Leone.
b. States should support territorial States, for example through sharing information on suspect tracking, through logistical support and specialized training for arrest operations.
c. States should investigate and eliminate networks of financial and logistical supply for perpetrators sought with arrest warrants.
d. States should create operational groups for coordinated military and diplomatic efforts to secure arrests.

While the ultimate responsibility for the execution of arrest warrants on a national territory remains with the territorial State, such State has the possibility to allow or to delegate arrest actions to third parties, such as for instance peacekeeping troops or police forces of other States. It is recognized under international law that arrest actions by such third parties are fully legitimate as long as they are consented to by the territorial State. Many arrests of suspects prosecuted by the ICTY were made on the territory of Bosnia by peacekeeping troops, with the consent of Bosnia. Another example is the attack on a hijacked Lufthansa airplane, liberation of its passengers and arrests of German terrorists by German special police at the airport of Mogadishu in 1977, for which permission had been given by President Barre of Somalia.

---

8 Pre-Trial Chamber II, 'Warrant of arrest for Joseph Kony issued on 8 July 2005 as amended on 27 September 2005' (ICC-02/04-01/05-53), 27 September 2005; Pre-Trial Chamber II, 'Warrant of arrest for Vincent Otti' (ICC-02/04-01/05-54), 8 July 2005; Pre-Trial Chamber II, 'Warrant of arrest for Raska Lukwiya' (ICC-02/04-01/05-55), 8 July 2005; Pre-Trial Chamber II, 'Warrant of arrest for Okot Odhiambo' (ICC-02/04-01/05-56), 8 July 2005; Pre-Trial Chamber II, 'Warrant of arrest for Dominic Ongwen' (ICC-02/04-01/05-57), 8 July 2005.

9 Pre-Trial Chamber I, 'Warrant of arrest for Ali Kushayb' (ICC-02/05-01/07-3-Corr), 27 April 2007; Pre-Trial Chamber I, 'Warrant of arrest for Ahmad Harun' (ICC-02/05-01/07-2-Corr), 27 April 2007.

In particular, those States Parties which regret that ICC arrest warrants are not executed and which want the ICC to more successful, should draw appropriate conclusions from these precedents established in full conformity with international law. When it becomes clear that a territorial State has difficulties in executing an ICC arrest warrant, other States or organizations could or should offer their assistance with adequate police forces. Already in 2000 the European Union took a decision[10] that Member States should be able to provide up to 5000 police officers for international missions across the range of conflict prevention and crisis management. EU Member States also approved the objective to ensure that together they would be able to identify and deploy up to 1000 police officers within 30 days. In 2003, the United Nations and the European Union agreed in a Joint UN-EU Declaration on Crisis Management to strengthen their cooperation in the area of civilian and military crisis management.[11] In 2006, the United Nations announced that the recruitment for a standing police capacity was under way.[12] Concerned States Parties and other actors should actively explore the potential of these and other instruments, with a view to bringing the decisive question of arrests actions in support of the ICC closer to a realistic solution.

All in all, there are some encouraging signs that States Parties are more and more aware of this necessity. On the other side, the list of possible and concrete support measures shown above indicates rather clearly how far we still are from satisfactory progress and solutions with regard to the decisive questions of effective arrests. Nevertheless, for a Judge of the ICC also, it is simply impossible to give up the expectation that over time concerned States will muster the necessary energy and political will to support the Court also in the crucial area of making arrests and surrenders to The Hague.

---

10 Santa Maria da Feira, Presidency Conclusions, 19 and 20 June 2000, Document 200/1/00.

11 Joint UN-EU Declaration on Crisis Management, signed by UN Secretary General Kofi Annan and President of the European Union Silvio Berlusconi, 24 September 2003 (available at http://europa-eu-un.org/articles/en/article_2768_en.htm accessed 10 September 2007).

12 Statement by Under-Secretary-General for Peacekeeping Operations Jean-Marie Guéhenno, Sixty-first General Assembly, Fourth Committee, 13th Meeting, 19 October 2006, UN Document GA/SPD/352.

Chapter 10

Cooperation with the International Criminal Court: Some Thoughts on Improvements Under the Current Regime

Håkan Friman

1. Introduction

Cooperation goes to the heart of the operations of the International Criminal Court (ICC). The Court is, like the International Criminal Tribunals for the Former Yugoslavia (ICTY) and for Rwanda (ICTR), dependent upon cooperation provided by States and other entities. The Court has no police force and lacks, in principle, independent enforcement powers on State territories. Clearly this is the Achilles' heel of the international criminal jurisdictions.

Concerns and criticisms are often raised concerning these weaknesses. In particular the cooperation regime of the ICC, which is described as horizontal rather than vertical in nature, and hence weaker than the regime for the ICTY and ICTR,[1] has been criticized. There can be no doubt that the scheme results in cumbersome procedures and delays, and even prevents investigative steps and prosecutions from taking place. A different scheme based upon enforcement of the Court's orders in accordance with pre-established conditions and procedures would be simpler and probably faster and more efficient; the inter-State cooperation instruments based upon the principle of 'mutual recognition' that are developed within the European Union, for example the European Arrest Warrant,[2] could serve as inspiration.

But this was as far a consensus solution as could be achieved at Rome and, apart from this, even more far-reaching powers and a more intrusive cooperation regime are not necessarily more effective in practice. In any case, this is what the Court has to live with for the time being; what the law ought to be in the future (*de lege ferenda*) is another matter. It is therefore of the utmost importance to provide for and

---

1 Nevertheless, the 'vertical' features, as compared to horizontal inter-State cooperation, are primarily: stricter obligations to the international jurisdictions, non-reciprocity, and the right of the requesting party (that is, the court or tribunal) unilaterally to interpret and determine the duties of cooperation: see Sluiter, G. (2002), *International Criminal Adjudication and the Collection of Evidence: Obligations of States* (Antwerpen, Oxford, New York: Intersentia), pp. 82–8. In that sense the ICC cooperation regime should also be considered 'vertical' in nature.

2 Council Framework Decision of 13 June 2002 on the European Arrest Warrant and the Surrender Procedures between Member States, OJ L190, 18 July 2002, 1–20.

to promote conditions for the most effective and efficient cooperation possible under the current regime.

On the side of the States,[3] the basic requirement is to ensure that all forms of cooperation can be provided in accordance with the terms of the Rome Statute; an often overlooked obligation is that of providing all forms of assistance, although not explicitly listed in the Statute, which are 'not prohibited by the law of the requested State'.[4] In addition, however, it is very important that the States take an inventive approach to the ways and means for providing cooperation.

As to the ICC, not only the legal framework but also practical pre-conditions for optimizing the use of the cooperation regime are required. This would include, for example, an appropriate organization, networking, the capacity to gather information and to act quickly on received information, good planning, and officials with extensive experience of international legal cooperation in criminal matters.

2. State Measures

Of course, the cooperation obligations set forth in the Rome Statute relate to all State Parties, not only to States directly relevant to the particular investigation or prosecution. Nevertheless, far too few States Parties have enacted implementing legislation for the cooperation with the ICC (or, for that matter, with the ICTY and ICTR).[5] Strong concerns regarding this failure have been expressed, for example by the African Commission on Human and Peoples' Rights,[6] but have not led to any concrete improvements.

States adhering to a 'monist' tradition may conclude that they formally meet the cooperation obligations without any additional legislation. But simply relying upon the Rome Statute with respect to judicial cooperation will inevitably create problems in practice.[7]

---

3 Although very important in practice, this paper will not address the cooperation with other entities such as peacekeeping forces.

4 Article 93(1)(l) of the Rome Statute. It should be noted, however, that the general grounds for refusal that are allowed under the Statute apply also to these measures.

5 Reportedly, in early 2006 less than 30 of the then 104 States Parties had enacted implementing legislation at all and of them only a few contained provisions on cooperation with the ICC; see Ciampi, A. (2006), 'Current and Future Scenarios for Arrest and Surrender to the ICC', in *Zeitschrift für ausländische öffentliche Recht und Völkerrecht* 66:3, 719, at 722. For a good survey of domestic ICC cooperation legislation, see Kress, C., Broomhall, B., Lattanzi, F. and Santori, V. (eds) (2005), *The Rome Statute and Domestic Legal Orders: Constitutional Issues, Cooperation and Enforcement, Volume II* (Baden-Baden: Nomos).

6 See *Resolution on Ending Impunity in Africa and on the Domestication and Implementation of the Rome Statute of the International Criminal Court,* adopted by the African Commission on Human and Peoples' Rights at its 38th Ordinary Session in Banjul, The Gambia, 21 November to 5 December 2005.

7 Directly applying the substantive criminal law provisions of the Rome Statute is more straightforward, however, and this was reportedly done, *inter alia*, in two high profile trials before the Bunia Military Court in the DRC in 2007; see MONUC, *Monthly*

States with a 'dualist' view, on the other hand, will require domestic law that reflects the international obligations, but they could choose to rely upon existing legislation on inter-State cooperation. However, the cooperation obligations *vis-à-vis* the ICC depart in some very important ways from ordinary inter-State cooperation, and thus from the regular domestic laws on mutual legal assistance in criminal matters and on extradition. Hence, regular cooperation legislation may not be suitable or sufficient, or give rise to problems when applied to the ICC. These departures include strictly limited grounds for refusal and requirements of more streamlined and quicker procedures.

Consequently, the introduction of special ICC cooperation laws is strongly to be recommended. Also States with a monistic approach are well-advised to adopt cooperation legislation.

Another important aspect, which is based on experience and could be accommodated in special legislation, is the need for a flexible approach to the applicable procedures when State authorities are acting upon a request for cooperation from the ICC. The outcome of the cooperation measures must be useful – and useable – in practice to the Court. For example, evidence collected must be admissible and procedural requirement of the ICC must be met. In this respect article 99(1) of the Rome Statute provides a tool for the Court, with corresponding obligations for States.

In order to make the ICC successful States should not only seek to meet the minimum requirements of the cooperation regime of the Statute. They should also be encouraged to be inventive and to seek to tap into modern and more efficient cooperation regimes as are being developed regionally in certain parts of the world. While the Statute represents what could be achieved in global negotiations at the time, there is nothing that prevents individual States, or regional groups, from going further in providing more efficient assistance to the Court. While it is hardly realistic to achieve global acceptance of more radical reforms to the cooperation regime, regional efforts could well be considered, for example among the members of the European Union. In that context there may also be a need to coordinate cooperation provided by the Member States and assistance provided by the intergovernmental organizations; information obtained during joint peacekeeping operations under the auspices of the ICC could be an example. An important first step in this regard is the cooperation agreement between the ICC and the European Union, concluded on 10 April 2006, which regulates, *inter alia*, the protection of confidential information.[8]

In spite of the detailed provisions of the Rome Statute, the applicable law for cooperation with the ICC may differ from one State to another. Hence, effective cooperation requires that the Court has good knowledge of the law of the requested State and frames its requests so that the most efficient result is obtained. But a common feature, today, is that the States have fashioned their implementation legislation, if any, after the rather traditional and request-based scheme which is set

---

Human Rights Assessment: February 2007, paragraphs 2–3, http://www.monuc.org/News.aspx?newsId=14119 (accessed 30 August 2007).

8 Agreement between the International Criminal Court and the European Union on Cooperation and Assistance, ICC-PRES/01-01-06 (available at http://www.icc-cpi.int/library/about/officialjournal/ICC-PRES-01-01-06_English.pdf accessed 30 August 2007).

forth in the Statute. Consequently, if the Court were to take an inventive and order-based approach when seeking assistance, most if not all States would not have the legal framework to meet the Court's demands; a reconstruction of the cooperation regime must therefore stem from the States and not from the Court.

It is worth noting, however, that a lack of legislation, in breach of the treaty obligations, is not necessarily fatal for cooperation in practice, as shown in the case of both Uganda and the Democratic Republic of the Congo (DRC). To some extent this can be compensated for by special agreements; examples are cooperation agreements entered into by the ICC Office of the Prosecutor (OTP) with the DRC[9] and with the Government of Sudan[10] (regarding the situation in Uganda). But in principle such agreements are wrong and will undermine the legal obligations under the Statute unless the terms extend the cooperation over and above what the Statute requires or regulates additional practical matters in a way that is fully compatible with the statutory framework.

3. Court Measures

3.a Arrest and Surrender

Without the appearance of the accused at the ICC no trial may take place and no verdict can be rendered; trials *in absentia* are not allowed.[11] As is well known, there are a number of outstanding, non-executed arrest warrants issued in the Uganda situation and directed against leaders of the Lord's Resistance Army (LRA).[12] The arrest warrants were initially issued under seal and, in September 2005, secretly transmitted to a few selected countries: Uganda, the DRC and Sudan.[13] The warrants were unsealed in October 2005[14] and in June 2006 so-called 'red notices' were submitted through Interpol. But the fugitives have not yet been apprehended even if

9 Judicial Cooperation Agreement, signed on 6 October 2004; see Office of the Prosecutor, *Report on the activities performed during the first three years (June 2003–June 2006)*, The Hague, 12 September 2006 (available at http://www.icc-cpi.int/library/organs/otp/OTP_3-year-report-20060914_English.pdf accessed 10 September 2007).

10 See *id.*, 11.

11 Article 63(2) of the Rome Statute. However, the confirmation of charges may be conducted also in the absence of the accused (see article 61(2) of the Statute). Regarding the background to these provisions, see Friman, H. (1999), 'Rights of Persons Suspected or Accused of a Crime', in Lee, R.S. (ed.), *The International Criminal Court: The Making of the Rome Statute – Issues, Negotiations, Results* (The Hague-London-Boston: Kluwer Law International), pp. 247–62.

12 Pre-Trial Chamber II, 'Decision on the Prosecutor's Application for Warrants of Arrest under Article 58' (ICC-02/04-01/05-1), 8 July 2005. One arrest warrant has later been withdrawn: Pre-Trial Chamber II 'Decision to Terminate Proceedings against Raska Lukwiya' (ICC-02/04-01/05-248), 11 July 2007.

13 Pre-Trial Chamber II, 'Decision on the Prosecutor's Urgent Application dated 26 September 2005' (ICC-02/04-01/05-27), 27 September 2005.

14 Pre-Trial Chamber II, 'Decision on the Prosecutor's Application for Unsealing of the Warrants of Arrest' (ICC-02/04-01/05-52), 13 October 2005.

it appears as if the whereabouts of most of them are quite well established and they have made public statements making it clear that they are very well aware of the arrest warrants. The failure to enforce the arrest warrants undermines the authority of the Court and the difficulties in executing the warrants has been highlighted as one of the major challenges facing the Court.[15]

Why are they still not arrested? The main reason is that they hide in areas where armed conflicts are still ongoing, and they are still armed and guarded by rebel soldiers. But one may reasonably ask whether there is also a lack of will to apprehend the fugitives, particularly in the light of the ongoing peace negotiations between the LRA and the Ugandan Government.

The responsible Pre-Trial Chamber has taken a close interest in the execution of the arrest warrants and has ordered the Prosecutor and the Registrar to submit progress reports and to answer specific, detailed questions.[16] It is clear that the Chamber was interested in finding out whether any refusal to execute the arrest warrants had occurred; but no such refusal has been established.[17]

Neither the ICC Prosecutor, nor any other organ of the Court, is given the power to execute a warrant of arrest directly where a State fails to comply with its obligations. No such power is explicitly laid down in the Statute and it is difficult to argue that any 'inherent power' or 'implied power' of this kind exists.[18] Consequently, the Court is completely dependent upon the cooperation of States (or other entities);[19] the territorial State is also responsible for the operational planning concerning the arrests, a process in which the ICC Prosecutor does not take part.[20]

Indeed, cooperation is needed even in relatively simple arrest operations and may involve many cooperation partners. The so far only successful arrest and surrender to the ICC, concerning Thomas Lubanga Dyilo, who was already in custody in the DRC, may serve as an example.[21] This operation required the cooperation of

15 Among others, by the Prosecutor's Report of 12 September 2006, *cit. supra*, fn. 9.

16 Pre-Trial Chamber II, 'Order to the Registrar and the Prosecutor for the submission of information on the status of the execution of the warrants of arrest in the situation in Uganda' (ICC-02/04-01/05-111), 15 September 2006; Registrar's 'Submission of information on the status of the execution of the warrants of arrest in the situation in Uganda' (ICC-02/04-01/05-118), 6 October 2006.

17 Pre-Trial Chamber II, 'Order to the Prosecutor for the submission of additional information on the status of the execution of the warrants of arrest in the situation in Uganda' (ICC-02/04-01/05-131), 30 November 2006, and Prosecutor's 'Submission of additional information on the status of the execution of the warrants of arrest in the situation in Uganda' (ICC-02/04-01/05-132), 8 December 2006.

18 See also Ciampi, *cit. supra*, fn. 5, at 724.

19 For example, the Prosecutor requested the UN peacekeeping force in the DRC (MONUC) to execute the arrest warrants concerning the LRA commanders; see Prosecutor's 'Submission of additional information on the status of the execution of the warrants of arrest in the situation in Uganda' (ICC-02/04-01/05-132), 8 December 2006, paragraphs 13–14.

20 Prosecutor's 'Submission of additional information on the status of the execution of the warrants of arrest in the situation in Uganda' (ICC-02/04-01/05-132), 8 December 2006, paragraph 11.

21 A warrant of arrest was issued under seal on 10 February 2006 (Pre-Trial Chamber I, ICC-01/04-01/06-2), and the request for arrest and surrender of Lubanga was transferred

authorities in the DRC (arrest and surrender) and in France (transport) as well as by the UN Security Council (to lift sanctions imposing a travel ban on Lubanga).[22]

So what can be done to improve the conditions for effectuating arrests?

Given that the lack of enforcement does not correspond to a lack of will by the State concerned, the Court should seek to improve the conditions for arrest and surrender. One measure would be to issue the arrest warrant under seal, as has happened in some cases, and allow subsequent determinations as to where and when the warrant should be distributed for enforcement; there may, however, be other reasons for immediately making the arrest warrant public and, thus, put the fugitive on notice.

But the ICC Pre-Trial Chambers have, so far, opted for an interpretation of the law which arguably is not particularly helpful for securing arrests. This concerns the practice adopted with respect to the transmission of arrest warrants whereby the Chamber itself makes the request through the Registry, which has been upheld in three of the situations under investigation;[23] the Prosecutor's application for leave to appeal the first decision was rejected by the Pre-Trial Chamber on procedural grounds.[24] The practice rests upon one interpretation of rule 176(2) of the Rules of Procedure and Evidence, which reads:

> The Registrar shall transmit the requests for cooperation made by the Chambers and shall receive the responses, information and documents from requested States. The Office of the Prosecutor shall transmit the requests for cooperation made by the Prosecutor and shall receive the responses, information and documents from requested States.

One must note that there is a difference between 'warrants and orders', on the one hand, and 'requests for cooperation', on the other. Undoubtedly, ICC arrest warrants may be issued only by a Chamber; primarily by the Pre-Trial Chamber but also by the Trial Chamber.[25] Moreover, and unlike the situation at the ICTY and ICTR,[26] a request to a State to arrest a suspect always requires an arrest warrant issued by a

---

to the DRC where he was in custody in domestic proceedings (but subject to an imminent release). Lubanga was surrendered on 17 March 2006.

22 See Prosecutor's Report of 12 September 2006, *cit. supra*, fn. 9, paragraph 84.

23 Pre-Trial Chamber II, 'Decision on the Prosecutor's Application for Warrants of Arrest under Article 58' (ICC-02/04-01/05-1), 8 July 2005; Pre-Trial Chamber I, 'Decision concerning Pre-Trial Chamber I's Decision of 10 February 2006 and the Incorporation of Documents into the Record of the case against Mr Thomas Lubanga Dyilo' (ICC-01/04-01/06-8), 24 February 2006, paragraphs 103–122; Pre-Trial Chamber I, 'Decision on the Prosecution Application under Article 58(7) of the Statute' (ICC-02/05-01/07-1) 27 April 2007, paragraph 135.

24 Pre-Trial Chamber II, 'Decision on Prosecutor's Application for Leave to Appeal in Part the Pre-Trial Chamber II's Decision on the Prosecutor's Application for Warrants of Arrest under Article 58' (ICC-02/04-01/05-20), 19 August 2005.

25 See articles 61(11) and 64(6)(a) of the Rome Statute.

26 Rules 40 and *40bis* of the ICTY Rules of Procedure and Evidence and the ICTR Rules of Procedure and Evidence respectively, whereby the Prosecutor may request any State to arrest a suspect or accused provisionally and thereafter seek an order by a judge for the transfer and provisional detention of the person concerned.

Chamber.[27] But the power to make requests for cooperation is not preserved for the Chambers. Quite apart from the use of the generic term 'the Court' in Part 9 of the Rome Statute dealing with cooperation, which should be understood as covering any organ of the Court, the Statute entails specific provisions on the seeking of cooperation. The Pre-Trial Chamber may do so 'at the request of a person who has been arrested or has appeared pursuant to a summons'.[28] No other requests for cooperation to be made by a Chamber are explicitly contemplated in the Statute (or the Rules of Procedure and Evidence).[29] The Prosecutor, on the contrary, is provided with a general power to '[s]eek the cooperation of any State or intergovernmental organization or arrangement'.[30]

The plain meaning of rule 176, sub-rule 2 is that requests for cooperation made by a Chamber shall be transmitted by the Registrar, while the Prosecutor shall transmit his own requests. The question then arises whether the issuing Chamber or the Prosecutor ought to transmit requests for the arrest and surrender (or, provisionally, arrest only) based upon an arrest warrant issued by the Court to States or other entities for enforcement.

The arguments for the current practice as given by the Pre-Trial Chambers do not necessarily lead to the chosen solution. In the most elaborate of the decisions on this issue, the Pre-Trial Chamber stresses its obligations with respect to the issuance of arrest warrants, interim release (by the Court as well as when handled by national courts), challenges against the arrest warrant or the admissibility of the case, and appointment of counsel for proceedings before the Court, as well as the Registrar's tasks concerning the practical arrangements for surrender of the arrested person.[31] But these functions could be fulfilled without impediment regardless of which organ makes and transmits the request to States and others.

Moreover, the Chambers have concluded that, unlike the regulation of the ICTY, no provision explicitly gives them discretion to allow transmission by the Prosecutor.[32] But the ICTY Rules of Procedure set out a full scheme for making requests and transmitting arrest warrants, which is different from rule 176, sub-rule 2 and which always involves the Registrar. As for the ICC there is not even a provision that designates the Pre-Trial Chamber to make requests for arrest and surrender (or provisional arrest), although this must be considered possible, and thus the comparison is hardly relevant.

Instead, the Chambers should leave it to the Prosecutor to deal with the enforcement of the warrants, and hence to make the request(s) for arrest and surrender; a

27 Article 58 of the Rome Statute.

28 Article 57(3)(b) of the Rome Statute. See also rule 116 of the Rules of Procedure and Evidence.

29 Nevertheless, one could also contemplate the Prosecutor requesting the Chamber to make a request for cooperation on behalf of the Court.

30 Article 54(3)(c) of the Rome Statute.

31 Pre-Trial Chamber I, 'Decision concerning Pre-Trial Chamber I's Decision of 10 February 2006 and the Incorporation of Documents into the Record of the case against Mr Thomas Lubanga Dyilo' (ICC-01/04-01/06-8), 24 February 2006, paragraphs 110–17.

32 *Ibid.*, paragraph 118. See rules 55 and 59*bis* of the ICTY Rules of Procedure and Evidence.

condition of 'specific and compelling circumstances', which one Pre-Trial Chamber has introduced without explaining any detailed reasons or the legal basis,[33] is not warranted. The Office of the Prosecutor (OTP) is in constant contact with domestic authorities and others, including different networks and other contacts. Hence, the OTP is most likely to receive information regarding the whereabouts of the fugitives. The request can be transmitted selectively and at the right moment. There may be cases of very short notice where very quick reaction is required in order to make the arrest; for example, the fugitive may be known to be in a particular airport at a certain time. In addition, the OTP may establish a special tracking unit assigned to track down the fugitives and acting on information that might be shared with the OTP under very strict confidentiality conditions. A very well-chosen and well-prepared moment could thus be sought and, depending on the time-frame, a choice between a request for arrest and surrender or for an initial request for provisional arrest could be made.

One should remember that preparing a full-fledged request for arrest and surrender (or provisional arrest) that meets all the requirements of the requested State is a quite complicated task. The OTP has got personnel with the relevant experience. Thanks to the close and continuous collaboration with national authorities, the OTP also has good knowledge of the legal requirements for the request in the country in question, a precondition for speedy enforcement when the window of opportunity to arrest arises very fast.

Of course the Pre-Trial Chambers are aware of the fact that it is the OTP that has got the information, but the Chambers are restricted to 'invite' the Prosecutor to share this information and this may not always be effective due to confidentiality or short reaction time.[34]

All this speaks in favour of letting the Prosecutor make the requests for arrest and surrender (or provisional arrest) and transmitting them after the issuance of the arrest warrant by the Chamber.

3.b Summons to Appear

The possibility to issue a 'summons to appear', as an alternative to an arrest warrant, is a novelty as far as international criminal jurisdictions are concerned.[35] The precondition for a summons is, apart from a reasonable suspicion of a crime, that the

33 Pre-Trial Chamber II, 'Decision on the Prosecutor's Application for Warrants of Arrest under Article 58' (ICC-02/04-01/05-1), 8 July 2005; although there is no explicit discretionary provision on entrusting the transmission of the request to the Prosecutor, 'the Chamber, in the exercise of its functions under the Statute, does not exclude the possibility' with respect to a particular request, but only if the Prosecutor can establish 'specific and compelling circumstances' for so doing.

34 Pre-Trial Chamber I, 'Decision concerning Pre-Trial Chamber I's Decision of 10 February 2006 and the Incorporation of Documents into the Record of the case against Mr Thomas Lubanga Dyilo' (ICC-01/04-01/06-8), 24 February 2006, paragraphs 120 and 122; See also Pre-Trial Chamber I, 'Decision on the Prosecution Application under Article 58(7) of the Statute' (ICC-02/05-01/07-1), 27 April 2007, paragraph 137.

35 Article 58(7) of the Rome Statute.

measure is 'sufficient to ensure the person's appearance'. It may be made subject to other conditions restricting liberty, but only insofar they are compatible with national law of the enforcing State. Also a summons to appear is to be issued by a Chamber.

This alternative to deprivation of liberty adds a mechanism promoting the principle of proportionality, which is to be welcomed from a human rights perspective. But when the provisions were negotiated, many delegates speculated that it would only rarely be put in operation in practice. Nonetheless, the Prosecutor has recently presented the first request for the issuance of summons to appear, rather than for arrest warrants, in the Situation of Darfur, Sudan.[36]

The key issue concerning the choice between a summons and an arrest warrant is whether the former order may 'ensure the person's appearance'. In the case at hand, the Pre-Trial Chamber found that this requirement was not met.[37] The Chamber made a quite narrow interpretation of the scope of the provision, which could be questioned as unnecessary. It stressed the question of 'voluntary appearance' as a key element for the assessment, but this is not a requirement of the provision. Although voluntary appearance would often be relevant, one could also contemplate circumstances when non-voluntary appearance can be secured based on a summons; however, this could not be achieved through 'surrender' in the meaning of the Statute since 'surrender' requires an arrest warrant.[38]

Leaving the law aside, in practice cooperation of course depends also upon non-legal factors, including political will and even opportunism. One can only speculate as to why the Prosecutor opted for summons as his first choice in this case. But summons is a softer, less confrontational instrument and could be seen as one step of a process where the pressure might be increased over time. This may prove effective in the individual case and should therefore be seriously considered. A caveat, however, is that the Prosecutor, according to the law, must convince the Chamber that the pre-conditions for the issuance of a summons are met; this was not done in this case and arrest warrants were issued instead. Nevertheless, the arrest warrants have not been enforced; on the contrary, they have been rejected by Sudan and one of the fugitives, Ahmad Harun, is reportedly still exercising government functions.[39]

4. Final Remarks

The debate continues as to whether the Rome Statute provides a sufficient framework for cooperation; some argue that it is sufficient, although depending upon the goodwill and adequate legislative framework of States,[40] while others are concerned

36 Pre-Trial Chamber I, 'Decision on the Prosecution Application under Article 58(7) of the Statute' (ICC-02/05-01/07-1), 27 April 2007.

37 *Ibid.*, paragraphs 115–24.

38 See Articles 58(5) and 89 of the Rome Statute. See also Pre-Trial Chamber I, 'Decision on the Prosecution Application under Article 58(7) of the Statute' (ICC-02/05-01/07-1), 27 April 2007, paragraph 121.

39 See 'Darfur war crimes suspect has free rein', *Los Angeles Times*, 5 August 2007.

40 Broomhall, B. (2003), *International Justice and the International Criminal Court* (Oxford: Oxford University Press), p. 159.

that the regime is too State sovereignty-oriented and leaves too many loopholes for States to delay and even thwart the Court's work.[41] Be that as it may, for the time being the Court must live with the existing cooperation regime and make the best out of it. Moreover, supportive States must make sure that the law permits efficient cooperation with the Court, preferably by introducing special legislation to that effect. States should be encouraged, individually or collectively, to seek inventive means of ensuring cooperation which provides results that are useful to the Court. Best practices should be identified[42] and States should be assisted in drafting and introducing implementing legislation.[43]

For the Court it is imperative to ensure the best possible conditions for obtaining the necessary cooperation. Knowledge, experience and networks must be utilised to the greatest extent possible. A high degree of inventiveness is required here, too. But basically successful requests depend upon seeking what the State in question can provide, both in substance and in form. Within the existing framework the practice of the Court should be geared towards solutions that promote efficiency. This paper has pointed out a few areas where a change of practice should be considered; most importantly concerning the making and transmission of requests for provisional arrest or arrest and surrender once an arrest warrant has been issued by a Chamber of the Court. Most likely, there are also other areas where improvements can be made. The cooperation regime has the potential to work efficiently in practice and we should all contribute to this goal.

41 Cassese, A. (1999), 'The Statute of the International Criminal Court: Some Preliminary Reflections', in *European Journal of International Law* 10:1, 144, 170.

42 See also Kaul, H-P. (2005), 'Construction Site for More Justice: The International Criminal Court After Two Years', in *American Journal of International Law* 99:2, 370.

43 One concrete example of such efforts is the *Report of the Commonwealth Expert Group on Implementing Legislation for the Rome Statute of the International Criminal Court,* The Commonwealth Secretariat, Criminal Law Section, Legal and Constitutional Affairs Division, September 2004 (available at http://www.thecommonwealth.org/document/35144/152517/report_of_the_commonwealth_expert_group_on_impleme.htm accessed 10 September 2007).

Chapter 11

State Cooperation with the ICC and Human Rights

Annalisa Ciampi

The issue of the relationship between State cooperation with the International Criminal Court (ICC) and the protection of human rights can be discussed under two different – and, to some extent, opposite – perspectives.

In one – more familiar and apparently quite developed – perspective, human rights *qua* the object of States Parties' obligations under relevant treaties and customary rules of international law should be taken into account as a limit to their obligation to cooperate with the Court under the ICC Statute. Under another – and different – approach, one could consider cooperation with the ICC by the States Parties as a way to enhance compliance with their obligations to respect human rights.

The first line of analysis finds a firm basis in article 21(3) of the Statute. Article 21(3) in the context of the overall framework of the Statute and the Court's case-law developed to date, however, shows that human rights are very unlikely to ever be successfully invoked before the Court in order to limit the obligation of a State Party to cooperate with the Court. The reverse is apparently true of the second perspective as to the relations between States Parties' cooperation with Court and their international human rights obligations.

1. Human Rights as a Limit to States Parties' Cooperation with the ICC

In principle, the possibility that States invoke their human rights obligations under customary norms and international treaties to which they are a party in order to limit their obligation to cooperate with the Court appears to be consistent with the Statute. This consistency is based on the following – cumulative – grounds.

First of all, the ICC is bound to respect human rights under customary international law *qua* an international subject (see article 4 of the Statute). It is not necessary here to dwell on the question as to whether – and to what extent – the Statute might validly derogate from general international law, in the light of the express provision of article 21(3) (which will be referred to as our third – and most important – point).

Second, several provisions in the Statute deal with human rights. Indeed, human rights underpin the whole Statute and every aspect of it.

Most of the rules relating to human rights involve the right to a fair trial and other cardinal principles of criminal law. These rights are either included incidentally in provisions dealing with procedure or evidence or are included in articles entirely dedicated to the rights of the accused, either during the pre-trial and investigation phases, or during the trial itself. For instance, article 54(1)(b), on the duties and powers of the prosecution with respect to investigation, provides that the Prosecutor shall '[t]ake all appropriate measures to ensure the effective investigation and prosecution of crimes within the jurisdiction of the Court, and, in doing so, respect the interests [...] of victims and witnesses'. Article 59, concerning arrest proceedings in the custodial State, provides that the State shall determine *inter alia* that '[t]he person has been arrested in accordance with the proper process' and that '[t]he person's rights have been respected' (article 59(2)(b) and (c)); under article 60 on evidence, the Court 'may rule on the relevance or admissibility of any evidence, taking into account, *inter alia*, the probative value of the evidence and any prejudice that such evidence may cause to a fair trial or to a fair evaluation of the testimony of a witness, in accordance with the Rules of Procedure and Evidence' (paragraph 4). Articles 55 and 67 respectively deal, instead, specifically with the rights of the suspect and the accused.

In addition – this is our third point – article 21(3), on the 'applicable law' provides that the interpretation and application of the Statute must be consistent with internationally recognized human rights.

Article 21 establishes a hierarchy of sources of the law to be applied by the Court. Under paragraph 1,

> The Court shall apply:
> (a) in the first place, this Statute, Elements of crimes and its Rules of Procedure and Evidence;
> (b) in the second place, where appropriate, applicable treaties and the principles and rules of international law, including the established principles of the international law of armed conflict;
> (c) failing that, general principles of law [...].

In accordance with paragraph 2:

> The Court may apply principles and rules of law as interpreted in its previous decisions.

Article 21, paragraph 3, in the relevant part, is so worded:

> The application and interpretation of law pursuant to this article must be consistent with internationally recognized human rights.

Human rights law seems to act as a higher standard, since all the other sources, including the Statute, the Rules of Procedure and Evidence and the Elements of Crimes adopted by the Assembly of States Parties, should conform to 'internationally recognized human rights'. Among the 'internationally recognized human rights' to be taken into account by the Court are human rights protected under treaties such as the UN Covenant on Civil and Political Rights as well as the European and the

American Conventions on Human Rights, most parties of which are also a party to the Rome Statute. It follows that not only the Court, both in interpreting and in applying norms, will be bound by internationally recognized human rights but – as the wording of article 21(3) suggests – the other sources of the applicable law, listed in hierarchical order, are operative only insofar as they are consistent with human rights. This sort of saving clause will be henceforth referred to as 'human rights clause'.

Fourth – and finally – the provisions of part IX of the Statute also impose an obligation to cooperate with the Court's investigations and prosecutions that does not extend beyond the point where a State's compliance with a Court's request for cooperation would breach an existing obligation under a human rights treaty to which it is a party. Indeed, a conflict with an existing human rights obligation is not likely to materialize in practice, the non-universality of the Statute of the Court and the binding nature of most (if not all) human rights rules notwithstanding. Should such a conflict arise, one could try to resolve it in the light of the guiding interpretive principle laid out in the human rights clause of article 21(3) of the Statute. Where the conflict could not be overcome through interpretation, the State should be able to avoid compliance with the Court's request without incurring a violation of the ICC Statute.

The obligation to execute a request for arrest and surrender is absolute in principle. Article 90, however, dealing with conflicting obligations, provides for an exception where the execution of the request would run counter to an international obligation to extradite the person to a third State. The same rationale could arguably be applied in relation to conflicting obligations arising under human rights treaties.

The same rationale should apply *a fortiori* in relation to a Court's request for other forms of assistance, which would require a State to violate its human rights obligations. The obligation to comply with requests for other forms of assistance is, in fact, expressly limited under article 93(3), where the execution 'is prohibited in the requested State on the basis of an existing fundamental legal principle of general application'. A State Party's obligation under a human rights treaty could indeed be considered among such fundamental legal principles.

To date, no issue of State cooperation in relation to human rights has been raised before an organ of the Court. The Court's case-law, however, is already replete with references to the general principle of interpretation set out in article 21(3) of the Statute.

For the purpose of our analysis, it is not necessary to get into the preparatory works or to inquire into all possible abstract meanings of this provision;[1] it is relevant, however, to look at the actual Court's case-law so as to verify whether, and to what

1 Article 21(3) of the Rome Statute is nothing but a forceful example of the central place human rights law occupies in the theory and practice of modern international law and of its spread to almost all fields of international law. For an in-depth analysis of this provision see Verhoeven, J. (2002), 'Article 21 of the Rome Statute and the ambiguities of applicable law', in *Netherlands Yearbook of International Law* 33:1, 3–22; McAuliffe de Guzman, M. (1999), 'Article 21', in Triffterer, O. (ed.) (1999), '*Commentary on the Rome Statute of the International Criminal Court, Observers' Notes, Article by Article* (Baden-Baden: Nomos).

extent, article 21(3), does have a practical impact on the way the Court interprets and applies the various sources of the applicable law.

Article 21(3) has been referred to, for instance, in relation to the system of disclosure and, in particular, restrictions thereof.[2] But article 21(3) has also – and most importantly – been relied upon by the Defence of Thomas Lubanga Dyilo to challenge the jurisdiction of the Court as well as to found Lubanga Dyilo's application for interim release pending trial.

Starting with the first: on 23 May 2006, the Defence challenged the jurisdiction of the Court relying on article 21(3) and the doctrine of abuse of process.[3] The challenge was declared unfounded on both grounds by the Pre-Trial Chamber (PTC) I's decision of 3 October,[4] which was subsequently confirmed on appeal by the Appeals Chamber on 14 December 2006.[5]

According to the Defence: 'Article 21(3) [...] vests the Court with the obligation to consider whether its exercise of personal jurisdiction over Thomas Lubanga Dyilo is consistent with such general principles of human rights, or whether, given the serious violations of his human rights, it would be an abuse of process to exercise personal jurisdiction over him in such circumstances'.

PTC I drew a distinction between the detention of Thomas Lubanga Dyilo prior to 14 March 2006 ('insofar as that detention was related solely to national proceedings in the DRC') and that after 14 March 2006 (when the 'execution of the Court's Cooperation Request by the DRC [Democratic Republic of the Congo] authorities was set into motion'). Any violation of Thomas Lubanga Dyilo's rights in relation to his arrest and detention prior to 14 March 2006 would have been examined by the Court 'only once it has been established that there has been concerted action between the Court and the DRC authorities'. The Chamber found no evidence to support allegations of 'concerted action' between the Prosecutor of the ICC and the DRC authorities to secure the detention of Mr. Lubanga Dyilo in order to pave the way to

---

2 The decisions of 23 and 27 May 2006 establishing the interim system of disclosure in the case of Thomas Lubanga Dyilo expressly refer to 'the general principle of interpretation set out in Art. 21 (3) of the Statute' and to the need arising therefrom that 'the relevant provisions of the Statute and the Rules, and in particular those relating to the disclosure procedure, [...] fully respect Thomas Lubanga Dyilo's right to a fair trial as enshrined in art. 14 (1) of the International Covenant on Civil Political Rights, art. 6 (1) of the European Convention on Human Rights and art. 8 of the American Convention on Human Rights'. Similarly, the Single Judge's decision establishing 'General Principles Governing Applications to restrict Disclosure' of 19 May 2006 restates the same principle in relation to the issue of non-disclosure of the identity of witnesses to the effect that its interpretation must be 'fully consistent with the jurisprudence of the ECHR [European Court of Human Rights]'. See Pre-Trial Chamber I, 'Decision Establishing General Principles Governing Applications to Restrict Disclosure pursuant to Rule 81 (2) and (4) of the Statute' (ICC-01/04-01/06-108), 19 May 2006.

3 'Requête de mise en liberté' (ICC-01/04-01/06-121), 23 May 2006.

4 Pre-Trial Chamber I, 'Decision on the Defence Challenge to the Jurisdiction of the Court pursuant to article 19(2)(a) of the Statute' (ICC-01/04/04-01/06), 3 October 2006.

5 Appeals Chamber, 'Judgment on the Appeal of Mr. Thomas Lubanga Dyilo against the Decision on the Defence Challenge to the Jurisdiction of the Court pursuant to article 19(2)(a) of the Statute of 3 October 2006' (ICC-01/04/04-01/06 (OA4)), 14 December 2006.

his subsequent unhindered arrest, in execution of the warrant of the Court that might be issued in due course. As to the doctrine of English law of abuse of process relied upon by the Defence, the Chamber considered that no issue had arisen with regard to any alleged act of torture against, or serious mistreatement of, Thomas Lubanga Dyilo by the DRC authorities prior to the transmission of the Court's cooperation request on 14 March 2006.

The Appeals Chamber held that abuse of process or gross violations of fundamental rights of the suspect or the accused are not identified as such as grounds for which the Court may refrain from embarking upon the exercise of its jurisdiction. The principle or doctrine of abuse of process does not find application under the Statute as part of the applicable law, and in particular under article 21(1) (b) and (c), nor the power to stay proceedings for abuse of process is generally required as an indispensable power of a court of law (in which case it would fall under article 21(2), of the Statute). However, the doctrine of abuse of process has a human rights dimension which falls under article 21(3). In relation to the case at hand, however, the Appeals Chamber confirmed the finding of PTC I that there was no evidence of concerted action between the Prosecutor and the DRC's authorities and no evidence of ill-treatment of Thomas Lubanga Dyilo.

The Defence requested the interim release of Thomas Lubanga Dyilo, with 'Request for Further Information regarding the Confirmation Hearing and for Appropriate Relief To Safeguard the Rights of the Defence and Thomas Lubanga Dyilo'[6] of 20 September 2006.

The Defence invoked the right to trial within a reasonable time or to release pending trial in accordance with internationally recognized human rights, consistency with which has to be ensured pursuant to article 21(3) of the Statute.

PTC I stressed that the reasonableness of the pre-trial detention cannot be assessed *in abstracto* but depends on the particular features of each case, especially in relation to the complexity of the case. It thus held that the length of Thomas Lubanga Dyilo's detention – started on 16 March 2006, the date he was surrendered to the Court – could not be considered unreasonable, taking into account 'that the case before the Court is complex, particularly because the vast majority of the evidence is abroad and that the volume of evidence supporting the prosecution is huge' and 'that the organs of the Court have acted swiftly and that at no moment were proceedings dormant'.[7] The same reasoning lies at the heart of the Appeals Chamber's confirmation of the PTC decision.[8]

Against this background, one is left with the general impression that the Court tends to find the express provisions of the Statute on human rights, in particular

6 'Request for Further Information regarding the Confirmation Hearing and for Appropriate Relief To Safeguard the Rights of the Defence and Thomas Lubanga Dyilo' (ICC-01/04-01/06-452), 20 September 2006.

7 Pre-Trial Chamber I, 'Decision on the Application for the interim release of Thomas Lubanga Dyilo' (ICC-01/04-01/06-586), 18 October 2006.

8 Appeals Chamber, 'Judgment on the Appeal of Mr. Thomas Lubanga Dyilo against the decision of Pre-Trial Chamber I entitled 'Décision sur la demande de mise en liberté provisoire de Thomas Lubanga Dyilo' (ICC-01/04-01/06 (OA 7)), 13 February 2007.

those dealing with the rights of the suspect or the accused, as adequate in order to ensure compliance with the guarantees of a fair trial under international law. Therefore, while article 21(3) of the Statute is relevant in principle, it will actually be successfully invoked in practice only in the presence of exceptional circumstances very unlikely to ever materialize. This is true whether one takes into account the rights of the accused in relation to the system of disclosure or the grounds which may hinder the jurisdiction of the Court or the reasonableness of the duration of detention prior to – and pending – trial.

This leads us to infer that there are few chances that an argument relying upon a conflicting human rights obligation that a State could make in order to avoid cooperation with the Court would succeed. Should an issue of compliance with a cooperation request by the Court ever be raised, the final decision would anyway rest with the Court, in accordance with article 119 of the Statute.[9]

2. Cooperation with the ICC as Way of Enhancing Respect for Human Rights by the States Parties

The other line of analysis outlined above on the relationship between States Parties' obligation to cooperate with the Court and human rights leads to substantially opposite results. The question as to whether the execution of a Court's request for arrest and surrender or other forms of assistance can be construed as a way to enhance respect by the executing States of its human rights obligations under international law can only be given an affirmative answer.

That State cooperation with the ICC is a means to enhance respect of human rights appears as a truism and/or self-evident. Indeed, in a broad, very general sense, the very existence of the Court fosters human rights, for the Court is entrusted with the prevention and punishment of 'the most serious crimes of concern to the international community as a whole' (preamble, paragraph 4). But this proposition is also true in a more specific – although up to date of limited scope of application – sense.

Out of the eight arrest warrants issued by the Court – five in relation to the situation of Uganda, one to the DRC and two concerning the situation in Darfur (Sudan) – only one has so far actually been executed, with the arrest in Kinshasa of Thomas Lubanga Dyilo and his transfer to the ICC, on 17 March 2006. While one of the persons sought by the Court in relation to the crimes committed in Uganda meanwile died, the other four still remain at large as do the persons named in the two arrest warrants concerning Darfur. The requests for their arrest and surrender to the Court were issued on 13 October 2005 and 2 May 2007, respectively.

One has to acknowledge that States (starting with – but not limited to – the States most directly concerned with the situations referred to the Court) by failing to execute the Court's requests for arrest and surrender, while being in a position to do so, are missing a chance to improve their human rights record. Not only do they fail to comply with their general obligation to cooperate with the Court flowing from

9 Under article 119(1) of the Statute: 'Any dispute concerning the judicial functions of the Court shall be settled by the decision of the Court.'

their ratification of the Statute (or the relevant Security Council's resolution, in the case of Sudan, which is not a party to the Rome Statute). Their lack of cooperation with the Court also amounts to a violation of their obligation to respect and ensure respect of human rights under applicable rules of international law.

As to other forms of assistance – which are also within the scope of the Court's requests for cooperation under part IX of the Statute – only one has so far been issued by the Court.

The first – and, to date, the only – request for other forms of assistance was issued by PTC I, on 31 March 2006, in the case against Thomas Lubanga Dyilo, for the purpose of identifying, tracing, freezing or seizing the properties and assets of the latter.[10] The measure was requested under article 57(3)(e), of the Statute and rule 99, sub-rule 1, of the Rules of Procedure and Evidence.[11] It is thus a protective measure aimed at 'securing the enforcement of a future reparation award' and therefore disposed of in the interests of the victims of the crimes allegedly committed by Lubanga Dyilo. As the request itself makes it clear, 'should Mr. Thomas Lubanga Dyilo be found guilty of the crimes of which he [was] accused, the said victims, by virtue of article 75 of the Statute, [would] obtain reparations for the harm they may have suffered'.

As Lubanga Dyilo's properties and assets are most probably located in the DRC, this State is in the unique position of exercising its sovereign powers over its territory in order to contribute to the effective functioning of the Court and by so doing to the enhancement of human rights protection. The rights here at stake are those of the victims seeking justice for the crimes allegedly committed against them by the accused, including in the form of reparation of their material and moral damages.

Actual compliance with the Court's first request for other forms assistance is also relevant in a further dimension, which adds itself to the perspective of a State Party's contribution to the protection of human rights under international law.

3. Cooperation with the ICC as a Way of Ensuring that Security Council's Targeted Sanctions Comply with Human Rights Law

The decision of 31 March 2006 was addressed to all States Parties to the Statute and binding upon them in accordance with part IX thereof. It restates, however, an obligation already incumbent upon all Member States of the United Nations, by

---

10 Pre-Trial Chamber I, 'Request to States Parties to the Rome Statute for the Identification, Tracing and Freezing or Seizure of the Property and Assets of Mr. Thomas Dyilo' (ICC-01/04-01/06-62), 31 March 2006.

11 According to article 57(3) (e), the PTC may: 'Where a warrant of arrest or a summons has been issued under article 58, and having due regard to the strength of the evidence and the rights of the parties concerned, as provided for in this Statute and the Rules of Procedure and Evidence, seek the cooperation of States pursuant to article 93, paragraph 1 (k), to take protective measures for the purpose of forfeiture, in particular for the ultimate benefit of victims.' Rule 99, sub-rule 1, of the Rules states that: 'The Pre-Trial Chamber, pursuant to Article 57, paragraph 3 (e), [...] may, on its own motion [...] determine whether measures should be requested.'

virtue of United Nations Security Council's resolution 1596 (1995), adopted on 18 April 2005.

Paragraph 15 of resolution 1596 (2005) mandates all States to 'immediately freeze the funds, other financial assets and economic resources which are on their territories from the date of adoption of this resolution, which are owned or controlled, directly or indirectly, by persons designated by the [Sanctions] Committee [...] or that are held by entities owned or controlled, directly or indirectly, by any persons acting on their behalf or at their direction'. Mr. Thomas Lubanga Dyilo has been included in the list of individuals and entities subject to these measures.[12] The list is administered by the Sanctions Committee instituted in accordance with paragraph 13 of the same resolution, a body which has the same composition as the Security Council and the deliberations of which are taken by *consensus*.

The obligation to cooperate with the Court has thus two legal bases: one in resolution 1596 (2005), the other in PTC I's cooperation request.

Thus the obligation to identify, trace and freeze Lubanga Dyilo's properties and assets does not only bind the States Parties to the Statute *qua* a treaty obligation, but extends to all members of the United Nations, is binding upon them under article 25 of the Charter of the United Nations and prevails over any conflicting treaty obligation by virtue of article 103 of the Charter.

But the partial overlapping between the Court's request for cooperation and the resolution of the Security Council also removes some doubts about the possible infringement of the rights of the targeted individual. The practice of the Security Council over the last 10 years in the field of targeted sanctions has given rise to deep criticism from various sectors of international society. Suffice here to recall that the *2005 World Summit Outcome Document*, adopted by the Heads of State and Government of the States member of the United Nations on 24 October 2005, 'call[ed] upon the Security Council with the support of the Secretary-General to ensure that fair and clear procedures exist for placing individuals and entities on sanctions lists and for removing them, as well as for granting humanitarian exemptions'. Very few significant changes have been made, however, over the years to the various sanctions committees' 'black-listing' procedures, which remain at all stages largely political with little, if any, attention to the rights of the individuals directly concerned.

Indeed, the first case initiated before the ICC offers a rare occasion for harmony of solutions among not only the Court and the States Parties to the Statute but also the Security Council and all States members of the United Nations. Actual interaction between the Court and the Security Council – in a way not foreseen under the Statute – is an important manifestation of the possible expansion of the Court's role in upholding the rule of law.

The ICC's request for other forms of assistance, in so far as it overlaps with the obligation arising under resolution 1596 (2005), contributes to the legitimacy

---

12 See *Security Council Sanctions Committee established under resolution 1533 (2004) concerning the Democratic Republic of the Congo's List of individuals and entities subject to the measures imposed by paragraphs 13 and 15 of Security Council resolution 1596 (2005)*, last updated on 14 December 2004, available at http://www.un.org/Docs/sc/committees/DRC/1533_list.htm. (accessed 7 September 2007).

of the latter and therefore of the Security Council's action thereunder. Before the Court, in fact, Lubanga Dyilo is a person in relation to whom not only are there 'reasonable grounds to believe that [he] committed a crime within the jurisdiction of the Court' – as required for the issuance of an arrest warrant under article 58 of the Statute – but there is also 'sufficient evidence to establish substantial grounds to believe that [he] committed each of crimes charged' (in accordance with the probatory standard for the confirmation of the charges before the trial set out by article 61(7) of the Statute).

Albeit in a very specific – and to date unique – circumstance, the ICC thus contributes to the fair and effective implementation of a decision of the Security Council acting under Chapter VII of the Charter of the United Nations.

Chapter 12

Can the Nuremberg Legacy Serve any Purpose in Understanding the Modern Concept of 'Complementarity'?

Maria Chiara Malaguti

We almost always refer to the Nuremberg legacy when dealing with international criminal law and especially with the working of international criminal courts. Despite being commonly considered as novel (in particular in opposition to the 'primacy' principle embodied in the Statutes of the two *ad hoc* Tribunals), also the roots of the legal concept of 'complementarity' can be tracked back to the Nuremberg trials. This, although a general conceptualization of principles on jurisdiction (I would better say, on allocation of competence) between relevant courts and main responsibility for the punishment of relevant crimes is in fact lacking in that context, and the meaning of such a concept as can be reconstructed from legal texts and their actual implementation in those trials, substantially differs from *strictu sensu* 'complementarity' as embodied in the Rome Statute on the International Criminal Court (ICC).

In the study on article 88 of the Rome Statute I carried out within the research project between the Universities of Trento and Salento as published in the proceedings of the Lecce workshop of 2005,[1] I had tried to prove that the duty of cooperation embodied in the Rome Statute has to be read starting from full awareness that it comes from the application of international law rules, and it is not instead – as for traditional 'horizontal cooperation' characterizing 'transnational' criminal law – the result of international comity. Since (I stated) international crimes are the product of international law, be it customary or conventional, and as such they can be prosecuted by both national and international tribunals, it is exactly in this coexistence of functions that the cooperation between ICC and States Parties – as well as between *ad hoc* Tribunals and States – is shaped and has to be understood. I thus concluded that there is room to consider the duty of cooperation in that context as a teleological principle of interpretation of the Statute, also affecting the way to interpret national implementing legislation and the States Parties' right to qualify their cooperation according to internal rules.

In these brief remarks, I would like to connect that conclusion – or better, the overall legal reasoning taking me to that ambitious conclusion – to the issue of

1 Malaguti, M.C. (ed.) (2007), *ICC and international cooperation in light of the Rome Statute* (Lecce: Argo).

'complementarity', although I shall only be able to outline a couple of considerations. Indeed, in this context the principles of 'concurrent jurisdiction' of article 9 of the International Criminal Tribunal for the Former Yugoslavia (ICTY) Statute or of 'complementarity' as per articles 1 and 17 of the ICC Statute (and paragraph 10 of its preamble), as well as the *ne bis in idem* principle (as per article 10 of the ICTY Statute and article 20 of the ICC Statute) might be differently highlighted.

Yet, this exercise may be productive by getting back to Nuremberg and from there onwards, showing that 'complementarity' has implications not only as a 'technical' tool to determine the admissibility of ICC initiation of a proceeding under article 17 (not as a matter of 'organization' as it has frequently been only seen), or as a plain declaration of primacy of domestic jurisdiction over ICC competence, but also as a general principle qualifying that 'concurrent jurisdiction' which lies in the foundations of both the Statutes of the two *ad hoc* Tribunals, on the one side, and of the ICC, on the other. Indeed, whilst this is tempered under the rules governing the *ad hoc* Tribunals by the general principle of primacy permitting the international court to ask for deferral of the case at any stage of the proceedings and without any statutorily established criterion, the recognition *in abstracto* of 'concurrent jurisdiction' differently shapes the relationship between the ICC and domestic courts, *in concreto* making the ICC's power of intervention limited to those cases where domestic courts cannot (because unwilling or unable) genuinely prosecute international criminals. The Rome Statute operates a statutory self-restraint within the ICC general jurisdiction over the 'most serious crimes of concern to the international community' to guarantee that these do not go unpunished and that their effective prosecution is ensured.

Yet, the ICC competence is not 'residual', but 'complementary' to that of States, all equally required to apply international criminal law. By way of consequence, I would not link unconditionally articles 1 and 17 of the ICC Statute, making the latter the sole implementation of article 1, or in the reverse making sense of article 17 only in relation to article 1. Of course the two are connected, as per the very same letter of article 17, but express different concepts and have different functions (article 1 establishing and contemporaneously defining the ICC, article 17 regulating the issue of admissibility of proceedings). In the first place, article 1 would exist and have a *rationale* also in the absence of article 17; in the second place, it qualifies other rules of the Statute, such as article 20 on *ne bis in idem*, or even articles from 13 to 15 on the exercise of jurisdiction. Indeed, this is also supported by the fact the Rome Statute makes no distinction between States Parties and non-State Parties with respect to complementarity, and affirms in its preamble that 'it is the duty of every State to exercise its jurisdiction over those responsible for international crimes'. In principle, the ICC would not intervene if a State not party has genuinely prosecuted a criminal, independently of any rule on admissibility or else. And this – I would assume – also when such a State has prosecuted individuals according to universal jurisdiction, so confirming that the goal of the ICC is to complement the implementation of international criminal law by States.

All of this is to outline the idea that 'complementarity' qualifies the ICC in the positive and not in the negative. This, with the consequence that it has to intervene somehow *in support* of national courts, to let the 'community concern' prevail in all those cases where the State primarily responsible for prosecution is not ensuring it; but also with the additional consequence that, if this 'systematic' reading of 'complementarity' is taken to its fullest consequences, the duties of States to cooperate with the ICC become a central part of such an integrated system of justice, based on the coexistence of concurrent roles to reach the common goal of full implementation of international law.

The Moscow Declaration and the Nuremberg Trials

It is well known that in the Moscow Conference of 1943 the Foreign Secretaries of the United States, United Kingdom and Soviet Union signed the Moscow Declaration (30 October 1943), whose final section – entitled 'Statement on Atrocities' – recognised the existence and gravity of crimes committed by German officers and members of the Nazi Party and consequently stated the firm commitment of the Allies to take those deemed to be responsible for such acts into courts. In so doing, they made a first attempt of 'complementarity', although only as a statement of principle and framing jurisdiction in a way far from the meaning of such a concept as embodied in the Rome Statute:

> At the time of granting of any armistice to any government which may be set up in Germany, those German officers and men and members of the Nazi party who have been responsible for or have taken a consenting part in the above atrocities, massacres and executions will be sent back to the countries in which their abominable deeds were done in order that they may be judged and punished according to the laws of these liberated countries and of free governments which will be erected therein. ... The above declaration is without prejudice to the case of German criminals whose offenses have no particular geographical localization and who will be punished by joint decision of the government of the Allies.

It is thus clear from the Moscow Declaration that the original intention of the Allies was to let each country judge those who were accused to be responsible for crimes committed in their territories under domestic legislation. Only crimes not bearing any link with a specific country would be judged by a special tribunal (although no reference was made regarding applicable law in such a case). Therefore, the general criterion should have been based on *territoriality*, and the establishment of a new (non-domestic?) Court subject to the existence of criminals having committed crimes on a wider base. Besides, judgement over the existence (that is, the definition) of such crimes and the measure of their punishment would be properly remitted to domestic law.

Such Declaration led to the setting up of the European Advisory Commission drafting the London Charter, which established the International Military Tribunal (IMT). Yet, the final allocation of judicial cases followed a different criterion than that of the Moscow Declaration, somehow based on the 'quality' of the criminals: as known, the *major* war criminals were judged before the IMT, whilst a second set of trials of *lesser* war criminals was conducted under Control Council Law No. 10 at the US Nuremberg Military Tribunals (NMT), in both cases applying a definition of crimes meant to be drawn from international law (as well as 'acting in the interests of all the United Nations': London Agreement). Besides, or better alongside, a number of countries decided to prosecute criminals under their domestic legislation.

According to article 6 of the London Charter, the IMT, indeed established for the trial and punishment of 'the major war criminals' of the European Axis countries, 'shall have the power to try and punish persons who, acting in the interests of the European Axis countries, whether as individuals or as members of organizations, committed any of the following crimes', these crimes being – as is well known – crimes against peace, war crimes and crimes against humanity as defined in the Charter itself. The IMT's jurisdiction was thus *general*, and by no means residually limited to those crimes which could not be localized. Articles 10 and 11 of the Charter then qualify the relationship between the jurisdiction of the IMT and that of other tribunals in case of participation to a group or organization declared criminal by the IMT:

> Article 10. In cases where a group or organization is declared criminal by the Tribunal, the competent national authority of any Signatory shall have the right to bring individual to trial for membership therein before national, military or occupation courts. In any such case the criminal nature of the group or organization is considered proved and shall not be questioned.
>
> Article 11. Any person convicted by the Tribunal may be charged before a national, military or occupation court, referred to in Article 10 of this Charter, with a crime other than of membership in a criminal group or organization and such court may, after convicting him, impose upon him punishment independent and additional to the punishment imposed by the Tribunal for participation in the criminal activities of such group or organization.

Thus, if a principle should apply, this is not one of 'complementarity' as nowadays understood, but possibly of 'concurrent jurisdiction', although no articulated jurisdiction criteria is in fact established such as one of 'primacy' as embodied in the Statutes of the *ad hoc* Tribunals. All of this despite the fact that the London Agreement, embodying the London Charter as an attachment, declares to draw from the Moscow Declaration and respect the jurisdiction principles herein embodied: 'Nothing in this Agreement shall prejudice the provisions established by the Moscow Declaration concerning the return of war criminals to the countries where they committed the crimes (article 4)', 'Nothing in this Agreement shall prejudice the jurisdiction or the powers of any national or occupation court established or to be established in any allied territory or in Germany for the trial of war criminals (article 6)'.

Although it had been initially planned to hold more IMT trials following that from 14 November 1945 to 1 October 1946, growing differences between the Allies made this impossible. Yet, Control Council Law No 10 of 20 December 1945 empowered any of the occupying authorities to try suspected war criminals in their respective occupation zone. On this basis, the US authorities proceeded to hold another 12 trials against major war criminals (the most known of them being the 'Doctors' Trial' and the 'Judges' Trial'), and others against lesser war criminals (such as the Dachau Trials, where 1,672 alleged German war criminals were tried in 489 separate proceedings, mostly involving camp officials), and so did the other Allies (the British authorities held for instance in their occupation zone the Hamburg Ravensbrück Trials, where

38 defendants stood trial in seven separate proceedings, being mainly camp leaders, camp doctors, male and female wardens, and the Belsen Trial, against 45 former SS individuals from the Bergen-Belsen and Auschwitz camps).

Control Council Law No 10 was meant to implement the Moscow Declaration, as well as the London Agreement and the London Charter 'in order to establish a uniform legal basis in Germany for the prosecution of war criminals and other similar offenders' other than those dealt with by the IMT: it is thus clear that the tribunals constituted under this law share the same jurisdiction as the IMT, although they are composed by representatives of a sole Ally and based on the relevant Ally's military procedures for proceedings. Yet, the scope of Law No 10 does not exactly coincide with that of the London Charter (Article II defines crimes against peace, war crimes and crimes against humanity in a way only partially overlapping that of the London Charter and also includes 'membership in categories of a criminal group or organization declared criminal by the International Military Tribunal') and allows each occupying authority to try anyone on its territory accused of a crime, independently of the latter's nationality, unless tried by another court. This seems to mean that all these tribunals had general jurisdiction, irrespective of where the crime was committed, although some cooperation mechanisms to allocate competences according to territoriality was provided in the Law and a partial exception was established for crimes only involving German nationals:

> Article II.2. Any person without regard to nationality or the capacity in which he acted, is deemed to have committed a crime as defined in paragraph 1 of this Article, if he was (a) a principal or (b) was an accessory to the commission of any such crime or ordered or abetted the same or (c) took a consenting part therein or (d) was connected with plans or enterprises involving its commission or (e) was a member of any organization or group connected with the commission of any such crime or (f) with reference to paragraph 1 (a) [crimes against peace] if he held a high political, civil or military (including General Staff) position in Germany or in one of its Allies, co-belligerents or satellites or held high position in the financial, industrial or economic life of any such country.
>
> Article III.1. Each occupying authority, within its Zone of Occupation, (a) shall have the right to cause persons within such Zone suspected of having committed a crime, including those charged with crime by one of the United Nations, to be arrested and shall take under control the property, real and personal, owned or controlled by the said persons, pending decisions as to its eventual disposition. … (d) shall have the right to cause all persons so arrested and charged, and not delivered to another authority as herein provided, or released, to be brought to trial before an appropriate tribunal. Such tribunal may, in the case of crimes committed by persons of German citizenship or nationality against other persons of German citizenship or nationality, or stateless persons, be a German Court, if authorised by the occupying authorities.
>
> 2. The tribunal by which persons charged with offenses hereunder shall be tried and the rules and procedure thereof shall be determined or designated by each Zone Commander for his respective Zone. Nothing herein is intended to, or shall impair or limit the Jurisdiction or power of any court or tribunal now or hereafter established in any Zone by the Commander thereof, or of the International Military Tribunal established by the London Agreement of August 8, 1945.

The NMT Trials open a wide number of interesting legal issues that unfortunately these few pages do not allow to analytically consider. Yet, some are worth mentioning for their relevance in the qualification of a modern concept of 'complementarity': Ordinance No 7 of the Military Government – Germany, United States Zone, establishes the organization and powers of military tribunals having the power to try and punish persons charged with offences recognized as crimes in Article II of Control Council Law No 10. Pursuant to such Ordinance, the US Office of Military Government for Germany issued Order No 68 of 26 October 1946, establishing Military Tribunal I, whose first case was *The United States of America against Karl Brandt et al.* (the so-called 'Doctors' Trial'). A number of medical doctors were indicted in that proceeding of conspiracy and actual execution of war crimes and crimes against humanity, and some (those proved to be members of SS) also of membership in criminal organization, as alleged violations of international Conventions, 'the laws and customs of war, the general principles of criminal law as derived from the criminal laws of all civilized nations, the internal penal laws of the countries in which such crimes were committed, and of Article II of Control Council Law No 10' (points 10 and 15 of the Indictment, bearing the same language). Within these proceedings, some defendants contested the applicability of Control Council Law No 10 to crimes against humanity committed upon Germans on the basis that these were not covered by international law, as well as expressly excluded by Article III.1 of the Law. In particular, defendants linked the relevance of behaviours judged by the NMT to the scope of the IMT and the London Agreement and Charter. In so doing, they affirmed that only 'international' crimes had to be punished, excluding those which have no effect beyond the borders of a single country and consequently would not involve the sphere of international law: 'The fact that no thought was given to punishment of crimes committed within the borders of Germany is evident from the Moscow Declaration of 30 October 1943. In this declaration crimes are mentioned exclusively which have been committed in other countries to which the accused are to be *returned*'.

The Prosecutor had instead objected that the NMT was only bound by the definitions in Law No 10, as the IMT was bound by those of the London Charter, in this way somehow conceptually separating the scope of jurisdiction of the two judicial bodies as per the definition of the relevant crimes (in line with the IMT itself, sentencing that 'the jurisdiction of the Tribunal is defined in the Agreement and Charter, and the crimes coining with the jurisdiction of the Tribunal, for which there shall be individual responsibility, are set out in Article 6.'). Indeed, the Prosecutor made the point clear that Law No 10 was part of the law in force in Germany, on the basis of the Control Council authority coming from the assumption of powers by the Allies with the Declaration of 5 June 1945: 'The Tribunals, in short, enforce both international law and German law, and in interpreting and applying Law No 10, they must view Law No 10 not only as a declaration of international law, but as an enactment of the occupying powers for the governance of and administration of justice in Germany'. In so doing, he also affirmed that, referring to the definition of crimes against humanity embodied in Law No 10 to 'any civilian population', this could not exclude German civilians: 'if Germans are deemed to be excluded, there is little or nothing left to give purpose to the concept of crimes against humanity.

War crimes include all acts listed in the definition of crimes against humanity when committed against prisoners of war and the civilian population of occupied territory. The only remaining significant groups are Germans and nationals of the satellite countries, such as Hungary or Romania. It is one of the very purposes of the concept of crimes against humanity, not only as set forth in Law No 10 but also as long recognised by international law, to reach the systematic commission of atrocities and offenses by a state against its own people.'

Of course, in all of this we are dealing with *ad hoc* tribunals established by occupying forces, somehow being a 'prosecution' of the IMT, and are consequently not directly dwelling in the general issue underlying the modern concept of 'complementarity', founded on the belief that national courts should be primarily responsible for international law crimes. Yet, the case-law of these tribunals offers a great source of inspiration for general (not only legal) discussion on the balance between the State's primary responsibility to deal with international crimes perpetrated in its territory by its people within its own system, and the role of the international community to intermediate inherent internal conflicts and consequently better guarantee 'justice', as the above claims on crimes against Germans in the Doctors' Trial help to understand. In the same vein, and even more specifically, in the case *The United States of America against Flick et al* (known as the 'Flick case') the issue of jurisdiction of NMTs *vis-à-vis* the IMT was tackled in a way that can help to generalize it within the modern concept of 'complementarity'. The Flick case was the first of the so-called industrialist cases tried in Nuremberg. The six defendants were leading officials in the Flick Concern (active in heavy industry, especially steel) or its subsidiary companies and were charged with the commission of war crimes and crimes against humanity, principally because of conduct undertaken as executives of the Flick Concern. The specific counts charged them with slave-labour, the spoliation of property in occupied France and the Soviet Union, the 'aryanization' of Jewish industrial and mining properties, beginning in the year 1936 (charged only as crimes against humanity), and membership in and (financial) support of the SS and the 'Circle of Friends of Himmler'. The reasoning of the Prosecutor in the Flick case merits being reported at some length, since this tries to draw the NMT's competence on crimes against humanity as such (that is, not when only connected with war crimes, as the IMT defined its own competence) from an 'odd' interpretation of the insertion of the words 'in execution of or in connection with any crime within the jurisdiction of the Tribunal' in the London Charter. Indeed, according to the Prosecutor these would limit the IMT jurisdiction to crimes of especially large proportions:

> In approaching this final point in our exposition, it is desirable to refer again to the International Military Tribunal's decision under the London Charter. Since the words were eliminated from Law No. 10, there is no need here to discuss at length the Tribunal's conclusion that the phrase "in execution of or in connection with any crime within the jurisdiction of the Tribunal" limits the definition of crimes against humanity to such as were connected with crimes against peace, or war crimes. Certainly it was not the only possible construction, and it seems to us far more probable that the clause in question was intended to make it clear that the definition was not meant to embrace private or occasional crimes, or local, petty persecutions, but only such wholesale campaigns of eradication as

> are condemned by civilized usage as contrary to the law of nations, and therefore "within the jurisdiction" of a Tribunal established to apply and enforce the law of nations.

From these statements, the Prosecutor then builds up an articulated theory of the role of international courts (under the bold assumption that the IMT was one) in cases of crimes against humanity, where prosecution occurs within the boundaries of a State:

> There can be no doubt, in summary, that murderous persecutions and massacres of civilian population groups were clearly established as contrary to the law of nations long before the First World War. Upon occasion, nations resorted to forceful intervention in the affairs of other countries to put a stop to such atrocities. Diplomatic or military intervention was, accordingly, the sanction traditionally applied when crimes against humanity were committed. Before passing to more recent declarations on this subject, the prosecution wishes to suggest that, in its view, unilateral sanctions of this kind today are ineffective if confined to words and dangerous if military measures are resorted to. Intervention may well have been an appropriate sanction in the nineteenth century, when the fearful resources of modern warfare were unknown, and particularly when resorted to by a strong nation in behalf of minorities persecuted by a much weaker nation. Indeed, lacking some vehicle for true collective action, interventions were probably the only possible sanction. But they are outmoded, and cannot be resorted to in these times either safely or effectively. It is, no doubt, considerations such as these which led the distinguished French member of the International Military Tribunal to look upon crimes against humanity with such a jaundiced eye. But the fact that a particular method of enforcing law and punishing crime has become outmoded does not mean that what was previously a well-recognized crime at international law is such no longer. International criminal law is merely going through a transition which municipal criminal law passed through centuries ago. If I discover that my next door neighbor is a Bluebeard who has murdered six wives, I am thoroughly justified in calling the police; but I cannot legally enter his house and visit retribution on him with my own hand. International society, too, has now reached the point where the enforcement of international criminal law must be by true collective action, through an agent – be it the United Nations, a world court, or what you will – truly representative of all civilized nations. This Tribunal is such an agent. It renders judgment under a statute enacted by the four great powers charged with the occupation of Germany. The principles set forth in this statute are derived from an international agreement entered into by the same four powers and adhered to by nineteen other nations. Although constituted by the American occupation authorities, and composed of American judges, it is, in short, an international tribunal.

It cannot go unnoticed that this same Prosecutor had plainly stated in the Doctors' Trial (and reaffirmed in the Flick case) that Law No 10 establishing the NMT was the expression of domestic law (although of the occupying forces). There seems to be room, consequently, to construe these statements to mean that the responsibility of applying what is deemed to be international criminal law equally lies on the IMT and on domestic courts.

This is confirmed – it seems – by the large number of proceedings indeed executed by domestic courts: this was for instance the case of the Romanian Trials, based on Article 14 of the Armistice Agreement, the Finnish Trials, according to Article 13 of the Moscow Armistice Treaty, the Polish Auschwitz Trials under

Polish law and finally the Frankfurt Auschwitz Trials under German law, carried out much later, between 1963 and 1965. An additional trial was held in Frankfurt in 1977, which shows the persisting relevance of the analysis of the Nuremberg Trial's implementation of 'complementarity'. In all these cases, the jurisdiction of the domestic court to judge of the international crimes was not disputed. The Nuremberg Trials thus in the first place confirm the assumption that concurrent jurisdiction is the basis for allocation of competence between international tribunals and domestic courts, and in the second place apply a 'complementary' principle only 'temporarily' reversed: the IMT did not fix pre-emptive rules on its complementarity *vis-à-vis* domestic courts, but – after the Moscow Declaration affirming the primacy of the principle that each national State should have the right to prosecute those who committed atrocities on their territories – factually applied a self-restraint criteria to only judge major criminals, leaving to other courts (the NMT or domestic courts) the main responsibility for justice in all other cases.

Can the Nuremberg Legacy thus Serve any Purpose?

Of course, a long time has passed since the Nuremberg Trials. International criminal law has evolved and international criminal tribunals have been established, so that it is clear that we cannot blindly transpose such a specific context within the general discussion on a permanent international criminal court. Besides, it cannot be forgotten that the Nuremberg Trials, with all their legal shortcomings, were an attempt not to recur to martial courts: this is the main reason why at the end priority was not given (at least for Germany and Japan) to domestic legislation (which would have in any event meant the law of the winners) in favour of a sort of international tribunal. The context was totally different from the current landscape, where we hope to be close to the reverse situation, where international criminal law can rely on States' primary assumption of responsibility to implement international principles. Yet, the various kinds of 'quasi-international', 'hybrid' or 'mixed' tribunals that are created alongside international tribunals and the frequent call for 'universal jurisdiction' by domestic courts leave the issue open on what institutional framework could better respond to 'the most serious crimes of concern to the international community'. The concrete implementation of 'concurrent jurisdiction' in Rwanda, where around 90,000 criminals had to be theoretically prosecuted by a domestic court, against a relatively small number of 'top-level leaders' being prosecuted by the International Criminal Tribunal for Rwanda (ICTR), and where a plea agreement system was implemented to contain the volume of proceedings against the risk of death penalty, that the top-level leaders would in any event not be exposed to under the ICTR Statute, raises a large number of question marks. Among them, the 'distribution of defendants' under a 'stratified-concurrent jurisdiction' – as the phenomenon has been called – namely leaving to international courts only top-level leaders and all the others to domestic courts, as also complementarity risks to lead to if we limit ourselves to a 'technical' discussion on organization, would clearly not do. The Nuremberg legacy could at least offer us the legal basis to affirm that international justice is not deemed to *limit* sovereignty of States to prosecute crimes within their own territories, but rather *enrich* the positive content of sovereignty, also entailing the faithful implementation of international criminal law. In this context only – I believe – such a concept as 'positive complementarity' as used by the ICC Office of Prosecutor in its Report on Prosecutorial Strategy of 14 September 2006 can bear a concrete legal meaning.

Chapter 13

Cooperation between the European Union and the International Criminal Court: Legal Bases and Opportunities for Implementation

Teresa Maria Moschetta

1. Introduction

The aim of this article is to analyze the cooperation between the European Union (EU) and the International Criminal Court (ICC) in the light of the objectives, competences and operative instruments set out in the European Union Treaty. It especially focusses on the European Union's international capacity, which is weakened operationally by fragmented competences and procedures.[1]

The external competences of the European Union sit alongside those of the European Community and they are defined by Common Foreign and Security Policy as well as by the Policy and Judicial Cooperation in Criminal Matters.[2] For this reason, the cooperation between the European Union and the International Criminal Court appears to be influenced by the complexity of EU external actions.

The legal basis used by the European Union to enter into the recent Agreement on Cooperation and Assistance with the International Criminal Court is outlined and the opportunities the European Union Treaty offers to establish a stronger role for the EU in support of international criminal jurisdiction are underscored.

1 Cannizzaro, E. (2003), 'Differenziazione e unitarietà nell'azione esterna dell'Unione europea', in *Il Diritto dell'Unione europea*, 765; Govaere J., Capiau J. and Vermeersch A. (2004), 'In Between Seats: The Participation of the European Union in International Organization', in *European Foreign Affairs Review* 9:2, 183.

2 Monar, J. (1997), 'The European Union's Foreign Affairs System after the Treaty of Amsterdam: a Strengthened Capacity for External Action?', in *European Legal Affairs*, 413; Dashwood, A. (1998), 'External Relations Provisions of the Amsterdam Treaty', in *Common Market Law Review* 35:5, 1039; Novi, C. (1998), 'Il Trattato di Amsterdam in tema di politica estera e di sicurezza', in *Il Diritto dell'Unione europea*, 467; Mignolli, A. (2001), 'Sul treaty making power nel secondo e terzo pilastro dell'Unione europea', in *Rivista di diritto internazionale*, 978.

2. Cooperation between the European Union and the International Criminal Court

The Rome Statute, which established the International Criminal Court, only recognizes States as legitimate members of the Court. It nevertheless allows the Court and the Prosecutor to establish relations with intergovernmental organizations by asking for information and documents and by agreeing on other forms of cooperation. Intergovernmental organizations are legal entities and as a result have a relevant role in promoting human rights and fundamental freedoms at an international level. In accordance with the Rome Statute, in order for there to be cooperation between International Criminal Court and intergovernmental organizations, agreements compatible with their competences need to be entered into.[3]

The European Union Treaty states that the European Union asserts its identity in the international arena by carrying out its Common Foreign and Security Policy (CFSP), the main objective of which is to promote and fortify democracy, the rule of law, respect for human rights and basic freedoms as well as safeguarding peace and international security. The establishment of an international criminal jurisdiction on a permanent basis seems to be an expression of these objectives.[4]

To date, the role of the European Union has been to promote the setting up of the International Criminal Court by drawing on instruments available from its own external competence. The EU has taken various initiatives to this purpose: declarations have been made by the sitting EU Presidents at the United Nations to express their support for the Rome Statute coming into effect,[5] common positions have been taken regarding the International Criminal Court as part of the Common Foreign and Security Policy so that political choices of Member States could be harmonized;[6] and the International Criminal Court has been included in political and economic discussions with third countries.[7]

---

3 Articles 87(6), 15(2), 54(3)(c) of the Rome Statute.

4 Articles 2–11 of the European Union Treaty.

5 See Statement in the Sixth Committee of the 50th United Nations General Assembly on the establishment of an International Criminal Court, New York, 30 October 1995; Statement at the United Nations Conference of Plenipotentiaries on the establishment of an International Criminal Court, held in Rome from 15 June to 17 July 1998, Rome, 17 July 1998; Statement at the 53rd Session of the United Nations General Assembly on the establishment of an International Criminal Court, New York, 21 October 1998.

6 Council Common Position 2001/443/CFSP of 11 June 2001, in OJEU L 115 of 12 June 2001, 19; Council Common Position 2002/474/CFSP of 20 June 2002, in OJEU L 164 of 22 June 2002, 1; Council Common Position 2003/444/CFSP of 16 June 2003, in OJEU L 150 of 18 June 2003, 67.

7 Council Regulation 975/1999/EC of 29 April 1999, laying down the requirements for the implementation of development cooperation operations which contribute to the general objective of developing and consolidating democracy and the rule of law and so that of respecting human rights and fundamental freedoms, in OJEU L 120 of 8 May 1999, 1; Council Regulation 976/1999/EC of 29 April 1999, laying down the requirements for the implementation of Community operations, other than those of development cooperation, which, within the framework of Community cooperation policy, contribute to the general objective of developing

Recently, the European Union and the International Criminal Court have signed an Agreement on Cooperation and Assistance to strengthen the Court's international criminal jurisdiction.[8] This agreement confirms the role played by the European Union in support of the International Criminal Court by providing a wide range of legal and political tools. Under the Agreement, the European Union undertakes to ensure the regular exchange of information and documents of mutual interest as well as to provide various facilities and services required by the Court for its purposes.[9] Besides, the cooperation between the European Union and the International Criminal Court aims to promote the dissemination of the principles, values and provisions of the Rome Statute through meetings and conferences relating to matters of interest to the Court.[10]

Various authors have viewed the Agreement on Cooperation and Assistance as the first noteworthy expression of the EU's international legal personality since it is an important political agreement within the Common Foreign and Security Policy. This view is supported by the fact that article 2 of the Agreement defines the European Union's institutions – the Council of the European Union, the Secretary General/High Representative, the General Secretariat of the Council Secretary and the Commission of the European Community – but not its Member States in their own right, as contracting parties. Therefore the European Union's institutions are under legal obligations that do not bind the EU Member States.

The International Criminal Court may make any request directly to the relevant Member State but the European Union cannot request information from the Court which originated from an individual Member State without that State's consent.[11]

---

and consolidating democracy and the rule of law and so that of respecting human rights and fundamental freedom in third countries, in OJEU of 8 May 1999, 8.

8 Agreement between the International Criminal Court and the European Union on cooperation and assistance (ICC-PRES/01-01-06), signed on 10 April 2006, entered into force on 1 May 2006 (http://www.icc-cpi.int/library/about/officialjournal/ICC-PRES-01-01-06_English.pdf accessed 31 August 2007).

9 Articles 7, 11, 14, 15 of the Agreement between the International Criminal Court and the European Union on cooperation and assistance. In particular, if the Court requests the testimony of an official or other staff of the European Union, the European Union shall take all necessary measures to enable the Court to hear that person's testimony, by waiving that person's obligation of confidentiality (article 10). Even if the person alleged to be criminally responsible enjoys any privileges and immunities according to relevant rules of international law, the European Union will waive any such privileges and immunities (article 12). On the other hand, the International Criminal Court undertakes appropriate measures of protection when the disclosure of information or documents endangers the safety or security of current or former staff of the European Union (article 18). The Agreement includes an annex regarding special ways of dealing with the communication of classified information.

10 Article 5 and 6 of the Agreement between the International Criminal Court and the European Union on cooperation and assistance.

11 Article 3, paragraph 2 of the Agreement between the International Criminal Court and the European Union quotes article 73 of the Rome Statute that states: 'if a State Party is requested by the Court to provide a document or information in its custody, possession or control, which was disclosed to it in confidence by a State, intergovernmental organization or international organization, it shall seek the consent of the originator to disclose that document

The European Union thus appears to be a different and self-governing authority that chooses not to interfere in bilateral relationships between the International Criminal Court and its States Parties.[12]

Nevertheless, such a choice could limit the European Union's international capacity and could demean its domestic and international competences. In this regard, the legal bases chosen by the European Union to set up the Agreement on Cooperation and Assistance with the International Criminal Court does not value the role that the European Union could play in supporting the exercise of international criminal jurisdiction through its competence within the Police and Judicial Cooperation in Criminal Matters.

3. The Legal Bases of the Agreement on Cooperation and Assistance

The Cooperation and Assistance Agreement was drawn up on the basis of article 24 of the Treaty of Amsterdam. The Council Decision approving the agreement also states the European Commission's competence in adopting the relevant community measures.[13] No mention is made of the European Union's competences within the Police and Judicial Cooperation in Criminal Matters although this is the domain where the European Union may play an important role by prosecuting international criminals and promoting a homogeneous conformation of the Member States' legal orders to the Rome Statute.

In this regard, it is worth remembering that the main responsibility in prosecuting international crimes falls on Member States of the Rome Statute, since the International Criminal Court jurisdiction is complementary to national criminal jurisdiction.[14] EU Member States, as parties of the Rome Statute, have to exercise their domestic jurisdiction over people who are suspected of international crimes.

In the light of more recent events, the European Union has promoted closer cooperation among national judicial authorities by adopting decisions about

---

or information. If the originator is a State Party, it shall either consent to disclosure of the information or document or undertake to resolve the issue of disclosure with the Court, subject to the provisions of article 72. If the originator is not a State Party and refuses to consent to disclosure, the requested State shall inform the Court that it is unable to provide the document or information because of a pre-existing obligation of confidentiality to the originator'.

12 Paladini, L. (2006), 'Note a margine della conclusione dell'accordo di cooperazione ed assistenza tra l'Unione europea e la Corte penale internazionale', in *Il Diritto dell'Unione europea*, 865.

13 Council Decision 313/2006/CFSP of 10 April 2006, in OJEU No L 115 of 28 April 2006, 49.

14 El Zeidy, M. (2002), 'The Principle of Complementarity: A New Machinery to Implement International Criminal Law', *Michigan Journal of International Law*, 869; Benzing, M. (2003), 'The Complementary Regime of the International Criminal Court: International Criminal Justice between State Sovereignty and the Fight against Impunity', in *Max Planck Yearbook of United Nations Law* 7, 591; Politi, M. and Gioia, F. (2006), 'The Criminal Procedure before the International Criminal Court: Main Features', in Del Vecchio, A. (ed.), *New International Tribunals and New International Proceeding* (Milano: Giuffrè Editore), 138.

operational matters. Council Decision 2002/494/JHA established a network of contact points for the exchange of information concerning people suspected of international crimes to support national authorities holding investigations.[15] Council Decision 2003/335/JHA promoted cooperation among competent authorities to prosecute international criminals, focussing on cases of people requesting a residence permit in one of the Member States who are also suspected of genocide or other international crimes. According to the Decision, the EU Member States should adopt measures to inform the competent authorities about facts leading to the suspicion that an applicant for a residence permit has committed international crimes as well as to establish closer cooperation between national law enforcement and immigration authorities.[16]

The European Union also indirectly affected the commitment of Member States with regard to exercising their judicial authority on international crimes through the Framework Decision 2002/584/JHA on the European Arrest Warrant.[17] According to this Framework Decision, crimes under the jurisdiction of International Criminal Court are not subject to the double criminality requirement to turn over a suspect. In other words, a judicial authority of any Member State is assisted in prosecuting a person suspected of international crimes who has moved into the territory of another Member State.[18]

The Framework Decision may have beneficial effects on the cooperation between EU Member States and the International Criminal Court. It does not jeopardize the commitments set forth in the Rome Statute in the case of multiple requests made by the ICC and by a Member State. The State should deliver the person requested to the International Criminal Court when the latter has declared its jurisdiction to judge the case.[19]

The Framework Decision may foster a better cooperation between EU Member States and the International Criminal Court for another reason. As highlighted, 'a Member State requested by the Court to surrender a person may, through a European

---

15 Council Decision 2002/494/JHA of 13 June 2002 setting up a European network of contact points in respect of persons responsible for genocide, crimes against humanity and war crimes, in OJEU No L 167 of 26 June 2002, 1.

16 Council Decision 2003/335/JHA of 8 May 2003, aimed at increasing cooperation between the law-enforcement authorities of the Member States in the investigation and prosecution of genocide, crimes against humanity and war crimes, in OJEU L 118 of 14 May 2003, 12.

17 Council Framework Decision 2002/584/JHA of 13 June 2002 on the European arrest warrant and the surrender procedures between Member States, in OJEU L 190 of 18 July 2002, 1.

18 Article 2, paragraph 2 of the Council Framework Decision 2002/584/JHA. For criminal acts other than those mentioned by article 2, paragraph 2, surrender may be subject to the condition that the act for which surrender is requested constitutes an offence under law of executing Member State. See Salazar, L. (2002), 'Il Commento alla Decisione quadro sul mandato di arresto europeo ed alla procedura di consegna degli Stati membri', in *Diritto penale e processo*, 1045; Damato, A. (2005), 'Il mandato d'arresto europeo e la sua attuazione nel diritto italiano', in *Il diritto dell'Unione europea*, 24.

19 Article 16(4).

arrest warrant, return a person to custody in the case, as it is likely in an area of free movement of people, that suspect has moved to the territory of another Member State'.[20] In other words, the mutual recognition of judicial decisions in the European Union streamlines cooperation with the ICC and confers effectiveness to international criminal law.

4. Is it Possible to Widen the Legal Basis for Cooperation with the International Criminal Court?

As with the example of the Framework Decision on the European Arrest Warrant, EU actions may positively affect cooperation among Member States as well as between Member States and the International Criminal Court to prosecute international crimes. In this regard, the European Union may play an important role in ensuring an average level of cooperation between the Member States and the ICC. When the International Criminal Court decides to prosecute a person suspected of international crimes, the Parties of the Rome Statute have to cooperate with the Court to ensure the effectiveness of the legal proceeding. Hence, EU Member States have to conform their legal systems to the Rome Statute so that their national courts and criminal police may aid the International Criminal Court.[21]

The European Union may foster cooperation between the Member States and the International Criminal Court and harmonize the national legal systems with the Rome Statute principles. According to article 34 of the European Union Treaty, the Council can promote agreements among the Member States and adopt common positions and framework decisions to harmonize national criminal legislations. In particular, the introduction of framework decisions may be instrumental in harmonizing cooperation tools with the International Criminal Court arranged by national legal systems since they oblige Member States as regards the aims, but they leave Member States free as regards the way the aims are reached. Framework decisions are therefore assimilable to community directives which have played an essential role in harmonizing national legislations and in building the community legal system. However, not all authors consider the legal effects of community directives to be comparable with those of framework decisions.[22]

Nonetheless, the harmonizing effect of the framework decisions could be tenable even if they are viewed as simple international acts adopted by the Member States

20 Mignolli, A. (2006), 'The European Union and the International Criminal Court', in Del Vecchio, A. (ed.), *New International Tribunals and New International Proceeding,* (Milano: Giuffrè Editore), 344.

21 According to article 88 of the Rome Statute, 'States Parties shall ensure that there are procedures available under their national law for all of the forms of cooperation which are specified under this Part'. See Oosterveld, V., Perry, M. and McManus, J. (2001), 'The Cooperation of States with the International Criminal Court', in *Fordham International Law Journal* 25:3, 767.

22 Manservisi, S. (2001), 'Articolo 34 del Trattato sull'Unione europea', in Cian, G. and Trabucchi, A. (eds) *Commentario breve ai trattati della Comunità europea e della Unione europea* (Padova: Cedam), 62.

using the intergovernmental method. The European Court of Justice has recently stated that it is compulsory for national courts to interpret respective domestic law in the light of framework decisions, according to the principle of loyal cooperation between the Member States and European Union institutions. Even though framework decisions do not produce direct legal effects, they can influence the development of national legal systems, making it compulsory for Member States to reach the requested results and set a standard level by which to interpret different national criminal legislations.[23]

The principle of conforming interpretation produces a harmonizing effect on national criminal legislation also in consideration of the European Court of Justice's competence to give preliminary rulings on the validity and interpretation of framework decisions. Although the European Union Treaty restricted the competence of the European Court of Justice to giving preliminary rulings within the third pillar, this competence tends to harmonize national criminal legislation through national courts.[24]

Adopting acts within the European Police and Judicial Cooperation in Criminal Matters could protect individuals involved in implementing the Rome Statute nationally. According to the European Union Treaty, natural and legal persons cannot challenge legal acts adopted within the European Union third pillar nor seek redress for damages. Nonetheless, the European Court of Justice can rule on the legitimacy of these acts at the instance of the Member States and the European Union's institutions.[25]

In addition, the European Court of Justice has stated that it is incumbent upon the Member States and, in particular, their courts or tribunals to interpret and apply national procedural rules governing the exercise of rights of action in a way that enables natural and legal persons to challenge before the courts the lawfulness of

---

23 Judgement of 16 June 2005, Case C – 105/03, *Criminal Proceeding against Maria Pupino,* in *European Court Reports*, p. I – 5285. See also: Opinion of Advocate General J. Kokott delivered on 11 November 2004, Case C – 105/03, *Criminal Proceedings against Maria Pupino,* in *European Court Reports*, p. I – 5285, points 25–6.

24 According to article 35 of the European Union Treaty, any Member State shall be able to accept the jurisdiction of the Court of Justice to give preliminary rulings within police and judicial cooperation in criminal matters by a declaration made at time of signature of the Treaty. See Ingravallo, I. (2000), 'La Corte di giustizia e il terzo pilastro dell'Unione europea', in *La Comunità Internazionale*, 477.

25 According to article 35, paragraph 6 of the European Union Treaty, the European Court of Justice shall have jurisdiction to review the legality of framework decisions and decisions in actions brought by a Member State or the Commission on the grounds of lack of competence, infringement of an essential procedural requirement, infringement of this Treaty or of any rule of law relating to its application, or misuse of power. According to the case law of the Court of Justice, the respect of human rights and the principle of state of law are an integral part of the community legal system (See: Judgement of 12 November 1969, Case 29/69, *Stauder*, in *European Court Reports*, 565; Judgement of 4 May 1974, Case 4/73, *Nold v. Commission,* in *European Court Reports*, 491). This case law has been codified in article 6 of the Amsterdam Treaty. Therefore, when a framework decision or a decision adopted by the European Union's institutions infringes on human rights it is to be considered unlawful since it infringes on the European Union Treaty.

any decision or other national measure relating to the drawing up of an act of the European Union or to its application to them and to seek compensation for any loss suffered.[26]

Therefore, national courts ensure protection of individuals by elaborating the same standard of legal protection at a European level through preliminary rulings.[27]

5. Conclusions

Recent European Court of Justice case law shows a trend that has engendered considerable debate and will therefore require clarifications.[28] In spite of some noteworthy criticism by scholars, the European Court of Justice case law may lay the foundations for broader legal bases by which to improve the cooperation between the European Union and the International Criminal Court, within the European Union's competences in Police and Judicial Cooperation in Criminal Matters.

The wide-ranging discussion concerning the European Union's international legal personality has stressed the importance of effective action in its external relations. The aim of the European Union should be to affirm its own identity internationally by harmonizing the foreign policy of Member States and implementing the normative instruments as set forth in the Treaty to comply with international obligations throughout the territories of its Member States.

26 Judgment of 27 February 2007, Case C – 354/04 P and C – 355/04 P, *Gestoras Pro Aministia v. European Union Council* and *Segi v. European Union Council*, not yet published in *European Court Reports*, point 56.

27 Opinion of Advocate General Paolo Mengozzi delivered on 26 October 2006, Case C – 354/04 P and C – 355/04 P, *Gestoras Pro Aministia v. European Union Council and Segi v. European Union Council*, not yet published in *European Court Reports*, point 91.

28 Nettesheim, M. (2007), 'U.N. Sanction Against Individuals – a Challenge to the Architecture of European Union Governance', in *Common Market Law Review* 44:3, 575; Peers, S. (2007), 'Salvation outside the church: judicial protection in the third pillar after the Pupino and Segi judgment', in *Common Market Law Review* 44:4, 883.

PART IV
Round Table
The ICC Relationship with National Jurisdictions: What Future?

Chapter 14

Round Table

Theodor Meron, Chair

Good morning. I welcome you all to this morning's round table on 'The ICC Relationship with National Jurisdictions: What Future?' Yesterday, we heard many interesting presentations on complementarity. I hope that we can build on those presentations today in exploring the difficult and fascinating issue before us.

I will first put forth a few questions that come to my mind with regard to this topic, and then turn you over to our distinguished panellists.

The question at the heart of today's panel is 'What Future?' – a question that leaves open many avenues for exploration. First, we must ask how the principle of complementarity will shape the future of the ICC's relationships with nations that have ratified the Rome Statute. In a 2004 statement, the Prosecutor of the ICC emphasized that the Office of the Prosecutor would take a 'positive approach to complementarity' and 'encourage national proceedings whenever possible'.[1] In making this statement, the Prosecutor might simply be making the best of the situation before him. Given that the Rome Statute clearly grants national jurisdictions the first shot at trying war suspects, the Prosecutor will be more likely to be effective if he works closely with these jurisdictions from the start. Nonetheless, I think this statement on the part of the Prosecutor reflects more than simply recognition of the realities at hand. It also reflects the ideal that countries will themselves take direct responsibility for bringing to justice suspected war criminals within their jurisdiction.

The ideal of States taking responsibility for prosecution of war crimes is a valuable one, and was essential in the negotiations of the Statute and in promoting adherence to it. In any event, international tribunals will never be able to try all the serious war crimes. The role of national courts will always be essential. But what does it mean for the ICC as an institution? Here, I think we must ask some rather hard questions. First, will there be enough work left for the ICC? Obviously, the Office of the Prosecutor will always have work, whether investigating possible crimes or supporting domestic jurisdictions in their own investigations or prosecutions. But that work must include at least some prosecutions. I congratulate the ICC for its Darfur indictments and warrants of arrest and I hope and pray that they will lead to actual trials. For without a critical mass of actual cases, the ICC Judges and Chambers will have little to do. This in turn may cause State Parties and other actors to wonder whether the ICC is worth sustaining and funding. It may also make it difficult to attract Judges of high calibre to the ICC in the future.

1 Statement of the Prosecutor to the Diplomatic Corps (12 February 2004), available at http://www.icc-cpi.int/library/organs/otp/LOM_20040212_En.pdf accessed 9 September 2007.

This concern may be overstated. Of course, the ICC will have cases where the national jurisdiction is unwilling or genuinely unable to prosecute. National jurisdictions may be unwilling where they resent the intervention of the ICC. National jurisdictions may also be unwilling to prosecute due to practical difficulties, such as other priorities for their resources. In such cases, these nations may refer matters to the ICC – as Uganda did. Finally, national jurisdictions may be genuinely unable to prosecute due to internal conflict, the danger of exacerbating domestic strife, or other reasons. Given all these possible ways for the ICC to end up with cases, then perhaps my concern raised earlier about a critical mass of work is overstated.

But I am not sure. For one thing, we face another problem of appearances. The national jurisdictions that lack the will, the resources, or the ability to prosecute war crimes suspects are likely to be overwhelmingly from developing countries. Of course, some very wealthy jurisdictions may lack the will to prosecute war crimes suspects, but there is likely to be no jurisdiction in these cases – especially since Security Council resolutions with regard to these jurisdictions are unlikely. Thus, it seems likely that most or all of the ICC's cases will come from poor States or failed States. In cases of self-referral, there is an easy answer to charges of elitist imposition. But if the ICC's docket consists entirely or almost entirely of cases from Africa, there may well be a groundswell of resentment.

One often hears suggestions that the Prosecutor should initiate cases by acting *proprio motu* and not only by accepting self-referrals or referrals of the Security Council. Given the geographically narrow confines of the areas from which self-referrals have originated, this may be an attractive idea. The question is whether the principle of complementarity would play out any differently from the cases where it was implicated in self-referrals. While in theory it would have the same force, in reality given the prospect that the Prosecutor would act *sua sponte* only in cases of major atrocities, it may be that the role of the complementarity principles in those cases would be diminished and the prospect for the successful involvement of the ICC enhanced. Nevertheless, even in the case of Darfur, the Government of Sudan is claiming that it has conducted its own investigations.

I offer these thoughts as concerns that the ICC and State Parties should face openly and honestly so as to build a safer future and a more successful institution. Pursuant to article 123, there will be a Review Conference seven years after the ratification of the Statute – thus, there will be a conference in 2009. It may be that the Conference will decide to revisit the overall statutory principle of complementarity – though I myself think that unlikely. Instead, I think it might be wise at the Conference to take up whether the ICC needs any institutional reshaping in response to the realities arising from the principle of complementarity. I will be interested to hear if my fellow panellists have any thoughts on the matter.

Now, and briefly, I wish to turn to the question of how the principle of complementarity will shape the future of the ICC's relationships with nations that have not ratified the Rome Statute. Such States' nationals may now be subject to jurisdiction where crimes are committed on the territory of a State Party. Will consideration of how the principle of complementarity has worked so far in practice encourage additional nations to ratify or accede to the Rome Statute, or at least not to oppose the ICC in the Security Council or other *fora*? On the one hand, to the extent that these nations have concerns about their own sovereignty, the experience to date has shown that the principle of complementarity does indeed exercise a powerful check on the reach of the ICC. The principle of complementarity has helped put to bed some of the phobias associated with the creation of the ICC. On the other hand, to the extent that this principle exercises too powerful a check, so that the ICC is short on work, and thus is not a major actor on the international scene, then these new nations may not deem it worth their while to join.

I hope that in the course of today's round table we can reflect on these issues and others. Our object should be to provide through frank discussion an intellectual means for making the ICC a successful and vibrant instrument for justice and against impunity.

Now, I will introduce our distinguished panellists, all of whom have worked and published widely in international law.

Ambassador Roberto Toscano is Italy's Ambassador to Iran. Over his impressive career, he has held a wide range of diplomatic and legal appointments within the Italian Government. He has also served as a visiting professor of international relations at LUISS University in Rome.

Fausto Pocar is my colleague and good friend at the International Criminal Tribunal for the Former Yugoslavia, which he leads as its President. He holds a professorship in international law at the University of Milan, and served for many years as a member, and chairperson, of the Human Rights Committee of the United Nations.

Francesco Francioni is currently a professor of international law and human rights and Director of the Law Academy at the European University Institute in Florence. He has been a visiting professor at a near-endless number of universities, including Oxford and the University of Texas.

Håkan Friman is an official in the Swedish Ministry of Justice.

Roberto Toscano:

Thank you very much, Professor. First of all let me start with a disclaimer: I am a lapsed jurist. What I mean is that I have a law degree like a lot of Italians, but I abandoned the noble legal profession in order to devote myself to the dubious science of international relations, and to the practice of international relations, actually. I have been a diplomat for about 40 years.

So, why am I interested in the International Criminal Court? I will look at this issue not from the point of view of the law, of international law. If I were to dare to do it I would certainly be challenged and cut down to size by my eminent competitors at this conference. I will try instead to look at it from the point of view of international relations. What is the meaning of this new institution for international relations as such? And to what extent can we address certain issues that are being raised by States, and in particular certain objections? Are they valid? What do they reveal and what do they tell us about the possible future of the institution? And in trying to do that, I will also try to address what the very interesting introduction by Professor Meron prompted us to focus upon.

Well, first of all I think that the International Criminal Court has been objected to on the basis of what it entails in terms of sovereignty. Sovereignty is not only the foundation of international law as we know it, but it is also a political fetish. It is also something deeply ideological and ideologized. Sovereignty is interpreted by some not as being a guiding principle of the international law but a guiding principle *away* from international law. Because there are ways of conceiving and practising sovereignty by claming exemption from any outside, let's say, interference, even when this 'interference' happens on the basis of international law. I think the International Criminal Court points in a very important, very interesting direction. States have had the tendency to operate on the basis of the slogan: 'all the international law compatible with sovereignty'.

The ICC says something else: it says 'all the sovereignty compatible with international law'. It makes a whole world of difference. And of course it is an open fight. The jury is still out on the outcome of this fight, and yet I think what we are seeing now is a step forward in this direction.

But let me address the issue of complementarity, because I think that this lies at the centre of the discussion and also of the future perspectives of this institution. Of course for the more radical proponents of an International Criminal Court complementarity is a concession, it is a compromise, it is a way of, let's say, defusing the worst and more determined objections to the work of the Court, because it says: 'Don't worry, Nation State, we will not interfere if you take care of the issue yourself'. Okay, so far so good, but I wouldn't worry too much that the Court will be out of business, will be lacking stuff to work on, because – I would say unfortunately – a lot of countries, a lot of States try to, and will try in the future, not to address from a legal point of view touchy political issues, issues having to do with conflict, especially aspects having to do with internal power struggles. We have seen many examples. And yet the very existence of the International Criminal Court has a very, very important function even independently from the actual prosecution of individual criminals.

Here I am talking about prevention. The existence of the Court is an element of deterrence in relation to the worst crimes that can be committed. Why is it a deterrent? Because it identifies the individuals who are responsible for certain acts, and it will no longer be possible to say that crimes have been committed not by individuals, but by a State or by an anonymous political power. The Court wants to know *who*, not which country, *who*. And of course the basic principle of criminal law is that criminal responsibility is personal. So I think a lot of possibilities of escaping from personal responsibility are being taken away. Therefore there is an element of deterrence, there is an element of prevention. But it is true that we have to face the very concrete issue that was raised by Professor Meron.

Isn't it true that, since some judicial systems work better than others, in the end the Court will prosecute only or mostly cases related to developing countries or 'failed States'? I think this is true. True but almost inescapable, but, on the other hand, it is also a way of encouraging progress in national legal systems and criminal law systems. Because again, this is a very powerful external pressure: I'm talking in political terms, not in legal terms.

Some have criticized the ICC because they have contrasted law and reconciliation. This is a debate that has been going on for quite a while. The objection goes this way: in many political situations, especially when major confrontations between ethnic groups or political parties have taken place, what you need is not justice but reconciliation. The case of South Africa is of course quoted. The reasoning goes like this: 'If justice is the preferred path, then the people who can be incriminated and brought to justice will fight to the end, with terrible consequences.' Therefore they will destroy society, they will not desist from their violent path, because they will be afraid of being prosecuted. Well, as a matter of fact, if you study the South African case and consider the 'Truth and Reconciliation Commission', it looks, rather than an alternative to a judicial path, more like a quasi-legal procedure, it's almost like a plea bargain, because it works in so far as there is prosecution as a looming alternative. What I'm saying is that reconciliation can also be prompted, can be favoured as an alternative in the presence of a mechanism which guarantees that if you don't follow the path of reconciliation there will be the judicial path. And this is true both on a national and on an international level. So I think that is also a very weak objection.

But again, let's go back to the problem of sovereignty. Having worked for the cause of national sovereignty for 40 years, having been throughout that period a faithful servant of the State, I cannot definitely say that this is not a valid concept. What is not valid is to interpret it as an absolute term, I would say as an idolatrous term. Because sovereignty is a regulating principle for the functioning of a system, not in total benefit of the individual subject without taking care of the functioning of the system. I always like to quote the Italian Constitution. There are two articles, one on private property, and one on private economic initiative. The Italian Constitution is not a socialist constitution: it recognizes private property and private economic activity, but it says in essence: 'Private property and private economic activity cannot be used against the common good'. Would we dare to say that sovereignty can be used against the interests of the international community as such? I would say, instead, that both attacking your neighbours and exterminating your own population do not seem to be actions that are conducive to more stability or more viability of the international system. Therefore, I think we can put the idolatrous concept of sovereignty to rest. I think, rather, I'm sure, that this important achievement represented by the International Criminal Court is a very fundamental not only legal but also political – and even cultural – step forward in this very direction. Thank you.

Theodor Meron: Thank you very much, Ambassador, for this thoughtful statement and I will now call on President Pocar.

Fausto Pocar:

Thank you, Mr Chairman. I would like to address the issue from a slightly different perspective. Before doing that, however, I would like to agree with Ambassador Toscano that complementarity, when it was adopted, may have been a concession made to States but also an expression of the recognition of a general principle, according to which primary responsibility for dealing with these matters lies with States. If we look at the development of the whole human rights field, international instruments tend to call upon States to respect and to enforce their own responsibility as well as to deal with the protection of those rights. The international community has always been aware that the protection of human rights cannot be shifted completely to the international level: it must be first of all carried out within the single States.

The concept of international criminal jurisdiction could be considered, in this respect, a step forward. While, in principle, it rests upon States to protect basic human rights and to make use of their criminal jurisdiction at the domestic level in this respect, the international community may intervene and take over if this does not happen. In principle, however, it rests with the States to deal with the matter. Now, this reasoning of course inevitably leads to the problem of States being unable to deal properly with these violations. While there are differing views on this matter, I agree with what Professor Meron said at the beginning: the Prosecutor, and not only the Prosecutor, should work with States in order to ensure their compliance with the duty incumbent upon them to deal with such cases themselves. However, nobody can deny that States and legal systems differ one from the other: while some States may be in a position to take up these types of cases, others may be unable or unwilling to do that. I would like to stress that this is not simply a matter of legal capacity: there is also a political side to it.

For example, I am not sure that only developing countries, which do not have financial and material resources to set up these types of trials, will actually be the only ones refusing to take up these cases. There may as well be developed countries that will be unwilling to try cases for various reasons, in particular political ones. However, limiting our discussion to legal reasons, a key issue is how to enhance the capacity of domestic jurisdictions to deal with these types of cases, since a failure to achieve this will effectively prevent the Court from discharging its mandate. In fact, we should not be looking only at the present situation – for the Court is indeed taking appropriate steps – but also at the time when the number of cases will be such that the Court will not be able to deal with them. Should this ever be the case, the Court will have to make a choice and let some cases out of its own jurisdiction. I actually think that the time will come when expeditiousness will require that many cases be left to domestic jurisdictions. The experience that the ICTY had in this respect is illuminating: despite having a limited geographical situation in the Balkans, one international body is not able to deal with all of the crimes potentially falling under its jurisdiction. Thus, the ICTY itself has come to apply a sort of complementarity.

The ICTY came to the complementarity from an opposite direction as the ICC. Despite the fact that the ICTY Statute is based on the principle of primacy, at a certain point in time the ICTY proposed – and the Security Council accepted – that certain cases should be referred back to domestic jurisdiction when, and to the extent that, domestic jurisdictions would be in the position to take up the cases. Thus, this is done after an assessment regarding the capacity of the national jurisdiction to try the case and on the basis of the rank of the accused, on the assumption that the domestic jurisdiction will be able to deal with low-ranking accused persons but is not generally able to deal with high-ranking accused. This type of evaluation, in my view, should be revisited, because the problem is only whether a given domestic system is able to deal with a certain case. I do not think that such an assessment can be done *a priori*; rather, I believe that it should be left to a case-by-case analysis by the Court. I would like to mention that we do not find this element in the Statute of the ICC and, therefore, the ICC will not have the issue of 'high-level' or 'low-level' cases – complementarity will work as a matter of principle and they will assess on a case-by-case basis whether one jurisdiction is able to deal with a given case. It may be too late to correct such an approach in the Statute of the ICTY.

I would like to go back to the issue of enhancing the capacity of domestic jurisdictions to try cases. The problem in this case is the entity in charge of this task or, in other words, how much responsibility for doing this should lie with the ICC. It has been mentioned that the Prosecutor should work with domestic jurisdictions, but doing this may be not enough to enhance the capacity of domestic jurisdictions to deal with cases. And, if one proposes that the primary responsibility for enhancing domestic jurisdiction should lie with the ICC, then I am rather pessimistic. I think that, in proposing this approach, we would be assigning too many responsibilities to the ICC: the ICC will not have the strength, the means, the human resources to improve the capacity of domestic jurisdictions. Instead, State Parties should probably start considering which approach will best allow the principle of complementarity to really work. If I may be allowed to refer once again to the experience of the ICTY, such an approach might mirror the one that has been followed in establishing courts of mixed jurisdiction in the countries of the Former Yugoslavia.

Complementarity will be possible, therefore, by assisting local jurisdictions through the international community's support, by inserting internationally appointed judges and staff in national jurisdiction for a defined period of time, and by providing some structures so that these courts do remain domestic jurisdictions for purposes of complementarity but are, at the same time, able to tackle cases in a proper way. In this respect, the experience of the Section for War Crimes of the State Court of Bosnia and Herzegovina, in Sarajevo, is an extremely helpful example. The Court is indeed able to deal with cases and has already done so, it must be said, more expeditiously than the ICTY. Moreover, this is happening close to the region, so there is probably an impact on the victims and their sense that justice is being done – an impact that is much more significant than that of a trial conducted far away.

This, of course, does not mean that all cases should necessarily be dealt with at that level. There may be indeed cases where it will not be possible to try cases domestically, even with the best intentions: the Taylor case in Sierra Leone shows this. In relation to the region of the Former Yugoslavia, there is not only the example of the State Court, but also the mixed panels in Kosovo. In fact, almost no case has come from Kosovo to the ICTY, because of the mixed panels that deal with cases in that area. In other words, while the principle is complementarity, it should be applied differently in different contexts. In any event, this principle should be supported by the international community or at least by the State Parties to the ICC Statute, in order to make it really work.

In conclusion, I think that, in the future, the international community should be aware that it cannot expect the ICC to perform too many tasks. However, a workable system must undoubtedly link together the ICC and the various domestic jurisdictions, *inter alia* through an effort to enhance the capacity of domestic jurisdictions. Thank you.

Francesco Francioni:

Reflections on Victims' Reparations and on Universal Jurisdiction

I have been asked by the organisers of this symposium to contribute to the round table discussion on the relationship between the ICC and national courts. I propose to deal with two issues that are closely related to the principle of complementarity: 1) access to justice for victims of international crimes and 2) universal jurisdiction.

As to the first issue, one must note at the outset that, unlike the Statute of the *ad hoc* tribunals, such as the International Criminal Tribunal for the Former Yugoslavia and the International Criminal Tribunal for Rwanda, the ICC Statute provides for the participation of the victim of international crimes in the Courts proceedings and, more importantly, for the victim's right to reparation. This is an important improvement in the organization of international criminal justice. The most tangible and lasting injury caused by international crimes – as indeed by any crime – is that caused directly to the victims; therefore there can hardly be international justice without consideration of their loss and suffering and thus of the need to provide reparation.

This important development with the statute of the ICC has been explained in authoritative commentaries[2] in terms of influence exercised by national models of victims' participation in criminal proceedings, especially the continental European models of France, Italy, Belgium, Germany and others. This explanation is only partially correct in that it tends to downplay the role of international law in bringing concern for the victims within the scope of international criminal justice. There is virtually no human rights treaty today that does not include provisions on reparation for the victims of human rights abuses. The most well-known examples are those of article 41 of the European Convention on Human Rights and article 63 of the American Convention on Human Rights, which have been the object of extensive implementation in the jurisprudence of both Courts. It would be quite illogical if there were a right to redress in human rights law and no similar right in international criminal law, which covers the most egregious violations of human rights, those which amount to international crimes. Further, the UN General Assembly, after many years of difficult elaboration within the (former) Commission of Human Rights, has finally approved the Basic Principles and Guidelines on the Right to a Remedy and Reparation for Victims of Gross Violations of Human Rights and Serious Violations of Humanitarian Law.[3] There is no precise definition of 'gross violations of human rights' and of 'serious violations of humanitarian law' in this text. But it seems safe

---

2 Jorda, C. and de Hemptinne, J. (2002), 'The status and role of the victim', in Cassese, A., Gaeta, P. and Jones, J.R.W.D. (eds), *The Rome Statute of the International Criminal Court: A Commentary* (Oxford: Oxford University Press), p. 1387 *et seq.*

3 Adopted and proclaimed by General Assembly resolution 60/147 of 16 December 2005 (A/RES/60/147, available at http://www.ohchr.org/english/law/remedy.htm accessed on 9 September 2007).

to assume that they include the very serious international crimes – war crimes, genocide, crimes against humanity – that fall within the jurisdiction of the ICC. How is the right of victims to seek reparation guaranteed in the ICC Statute and procedure and how does it interface with national law and jurisdiction? The starting point to answer these question is, obviously, article 75 of the ICC Statute. Under this provision, the ICC has broad discretionary powers in handling the issue of victims' reparation. It may award reparation on request or on its own motion when victims are absent or remote; reparation may be awarded on an individual basis or collectively; it may consist of restitution, compensation and rehabilitation, in accordance with the above-mentioned general principles on reparation adopted by the UN. The obligation to provide reparation may be placed by the Court upon the convicted person or, where appropriate, it may be discharged by way of payments made through the Trust Fund provided for in article 79 of the Statute. No obligation to pay reparation is placed upon State Parties to the ICC Statute.

The provisions of article 75 that concern relations with national jurisdictions are paragraphs 4, 5 and 6. Paragraph 4 contemplates cooperation with State Parties to the extent that the effectiveness of a reparation order is contingent upon the availability of assistance and support by the courts or other authority of a State Party. Reference is made in this respect to article 93(1) of the Statute, therefore it is clear that the relevant measure that the ICC may seek from a State Party in order to enforce a reparation award are 1) execution of searches and seizure; 2) provision of records or documents, such as bank records and documents disclosing availability of funds; 3) identification and seizure of assets to be used in order to satisfy the victim's reparation claim.

These general provisions on reparation to victims raise some delicate issues as far as the relationship between the ICC and national law and jurisdiction is concerned.

First, the ICC Statute, as already mentioned, does not empower the Court to adjudicate reparation claims against a State. However, a State may bear international responsibility for grave violations of human rights or humanitarian law, for complicity or for negligent failure to prevent the occurrence of such violations. In the domestic law of some States such responsibility may be ascertained in national judicial proceedings and may lead to the setting aside of sovereign immunity and the award of damages to the victims. This is the case in the United States, because of the combined effect of the Alien Tort Compensation Act and the current exceptions to foreign sovereign immunities under the 1976 Foreign Sovereign Immunities Act, and also in Italy, under the recent jurisprudence of the Court of Cassation, United Sections, in the *Ferrini* case.[4] In these circumstances, should the ICC take into account the availability of reparation by the relevant State in determining the nature and quantum of reparation to be provided by the convicted defendant or through the Trust Fund? No co-ordination mechanism seems to be in place to address such

4 On this case, see XIV Italian Yearbook of International law (2004), 341, with comment by Iovane, M., at 165. On the interplay between the right of access to judicial remedies and sovereign immunity, see Francioni, F. (ed.) (2007), *Access to Justice as a Human Right* (Oxford: Oxford University Press), chapters 1 and 3.

situations and it is to be hoped that the Court will include this item in the agenda for the development and adoption of 'principles relating to reparation' pursuant to article 75(1).

The second problem arises directly from the just mentioned article 75(1). This provision assigns a limited law-making function to the ICC to the extent that the Court is empowered to develop principles on reparation. The exercise of this power by the Court may lead to the creation of 'new law' and to unavoidable tensions with State Parties. This is so because such principles may be seen as productive of additional obligations for State Parties as compared to the bare text of the Statute. This would certainly be the case were the 'principles' to require additional financial obligations for State Parties to set up and finance the Fund. Besides, strains with national jurisdictions would arise if the 'principles' were to include forms of reparation not compatible with national law, such as punitive or exemplary damages, so common in the Anglo-American systems but normally unacceptable in continental European law.

At the procedural level, rule 97 of the ICC Rules of Procedure and Evidence specifies how reparation is to be assessed and provided. It contemplates individualized reparation and reparation on a collective basis. Assessment may be made with the help of expert advice provided by persons appointed by the Court to determine the scope of damage or loss. There is today ample jurisprudence showing how international courts and bodies determine the proper reparation for serious violations of human rights. However, this jurisprudence is either the result of incremental case law based on the interpretation of relevant treaties – this is the case with the European Court of Human Rights with regard to the implementation of article 41 of the European Convention – or depends on the conscious adoption of compensations parameters borrowed from existing treaty regimes. In the well-known *Letelier-Moffit* case, concerning reparation for the terrorist killing of the former Chilean ambassador in Washington and of his secretary, the *ad hoc* US-Chile Commission determined that the proper parameters for compensation of the family members of the victims had to be those provided by the inter-American system of human rights protection and more particularly the criteria developed in the jurisprudence of the American Court of Human Rights. The ICC will not be able to readily rely on existing legal parameters or on a prior and well-settled jurisprudence on reparation. This is why article 75 of the Statute commits the Court to develop principles of reparation. But how can these principles be conceived? What concept of justice should underlie these principles? In this context the relationship between the ICC and national law and jurisdictions becomes crucial. In national law reparation may fulfil different social functions and follow different approaches. One approach is that of 'compensatory justice', entailing the restoration at a minimum level of the legal equilibrium between the tort perpetrator and the victim. Another approach sees reparation as a tool of 'deterrent justice' in the sense of bringing to a higher level the cost of breaking the law, for example by punitive damages. A more complex approach is that of 'restorative justice' that takes into account the role of reparation in the wider social context to which the victim belongs. Reparation in this context should include access to the truth, which is especially important for the type of egregious violations of human rights that fall within the jurisdiction of the ICC, memorializing the suffering of the victims, rehabilitation and healing of the victims.

These very different ideas of justice remind us that assessment of the scope and extent of damage and loss is eminently a function of domestic law and that even in this delicate field of victims' reparation the principle of complementarity is bound to play a fundamental role in the functioning of the ICC. They remind also that even in the most integrated system of 'supra-national law', that of the European Community, the enforcement of reparation awards for breach of Community law is ultimately governed by domestic law. This is the lesson we learn from the follow-up of the landmark cases on liability for non-compliance with Community law obligations such as *Francovich* and *Brasserie du Pêcheur*.

This, of course, may complicate the work of the ICC. Acknowledging such reality, however, does not mean that certain common concepts and criteria cannot be drawn by the ICC from international practice and the comparative law of States Parties. Useful inspiration can be drawn from the experience of the UN Compensation Commission set up to deal with claims by the victims of the Iraq war. This experience shows that classes of similar claims can be dealt with collectively and more expeditiously than by separate treatment of individual applications; it shows the value of the role of experts and of statistical methods of determination of the award. More important, it shows also that especially in situations of armed conflict and emergency, surrounding the occurrence of grave breaches of human rights, victims can hardly be in a position to prove beyond any reasonable doubt all their loss, damage and suffering caused by the crimes perpetrated against them and that therefore a less stringent standard of proof should be required as compared to criminal liability. But the most important source of principles and criteria for reparation is the practice of international bodies and especially of human rights courts. This practice is to a large extent exemplified in the already mentioned UN Principles and Guidelines on reparation. If we follow its schematic outline, reparation can take the form of 1) restitution, 2) compensation, 3) rehabilitation, 4) satisfaction, 5) guarantee of non-repetition. The first three forms are expressly contemplated in the text of article 75(2). Restitution is clearly the least problematic: it can entail the return of property illegally taken from the victim, the restitution of cultural objects (which, besides pecuniary value, may have enormous spiritual or religious value), re-instatement in an employment position or other status that was denied to the victim as part of the commission of the international crime. Compensation may be a problematic form of reparation, given the widely divergent views on what is compensable loss and damage. Certainly, damage should cover all physical and mental harm suffered by the victim, medical and legal costs, as well as material damage in the form of loss of earning and lost opportunities. In this respect, a question may arise as to how immediate the causal link should be between the crime and the loss of opportunities. Human rights courts are not entirely on the same wavelength in these matters: the American Court of Human Rights shows a rather generous pro-victim attitude in holding compensable damage related to the inability to fulfil an entire '*projecto de vida*' (case *Tamayo v. Peru*), while the European Court of Human Rights shows a more cautious and restrictive attitude. Rehabilitation is contemplated as a necessary form of reparation in article 75(2) as well as at clause IX.21 of the 2006 UN Principles and Guidelines. It includes provision of medical assistance, legal and social services as well as psychological therapy. Satisfaction, although not mentioned in article 75(2), is also a very important component of reparation for victims of international crimes. Probably the most unbearable affront to the victims of international crimes is letting the memory of crimes slip into oblivion, irrelevance, even denial. Satisfaction, therefore, may involve having the perpetrators of a crime pay for the preservation and maintenance of records and for the dissemination of knowledge about them. This seems a very important aspect of reparation especially at a time when historical truth about atrocities is put in doubt by dubious interpretations and manipulations for political ends. Its enforcement, certainly, depends on close cooperation with the authorities of the State where the crime was committed and where satisfaction can have a social and moral function for the victim and the society at large. Finally, with regard to guarantee of non-repetition, it figures among the forms of reparation in the law of State responsibility for internationally wrongful acts and it is not clear how it can be adapted to the situation of individual criminal responsibility. Guarantee of non-repetition of crimes entails primarily a State obligation to ensure that the rule of law is upheld and that at the level of armed forces, administration, police and judicial functions another occurrence of international crimes is prevented as far as possible. However, given the statutory requirement that crimes against humanity be committed as 'part of a widespread or systematic attack directed against any civilian population' and the special relevance given by article 8 to war crimes committed as a part of a plan or on a large scale, it seems that the guarantee of non-repetition can acquire a very important moral and social function as a form of reparation for victims who may be still terrorized by the criminal assault on their lives.

Let me now examine how the principle of complementarity will work in the context of victim reparation. Article 75(6) contains the saving clause to the effect that nothing in that article 'shall be interpreted as prejudicing the rights of victims under national or international law'. This provision raises several questions. Under the principle of complementarity, a national court may try and convict a person accused of international crimes without awarding compensation or awarding just a symbolic compensation that leaves the victim unsatisfied. Could the ICC's jurisdiction be triggered in these circumstances in order to seek full compensation? Nothing in the text of article 75 indicates that the Court should deal with such cases. Further, one could argue that the individual has no independent right of activating the ICC, the main object and purpose of which is to permit the prosecution and trial of international crimes whenever inability or unwillingness of the State to prosecute may lead to impunity. On the other hand, one could argue that nothing in the text of article 75 excludes the jurisdiction of the ICC with respect to such situations; that the jurisdiction of the Court could be triggered by Prosecutor, the Security Council and even a State Party that has a legal interest in ensuring reparation to its nationals who have been the victims of international crimes perpetrated in another State Party. Further, a pro-victim solution could be favoured by taking into account that the Statute assigns a specific mandate to the Court to provide reparation to victims. I find the latter arguments more convincing and more in line with the principle of contextual interpretation laid down by article 31(1) of the Vienna Convention on the Law of Treaties.

Another question raised by article 75(6) is that once the reparation award has been made, the relative order – unless it concerns compensation through the Trust Fund – will have to be implemented in the domestic legal order of the relevant State Party. Thus the victim may seek enforcement by a national court. However, when the individual has direct access to international tribunals, as it is the case for the States adhering to the European Convention on Human Rights, the question arises whether the reparation order issued by the ICC may constitute the legal basis for seeking compensation before the European Court of Human Rights. This is certainly a novel possibility which raises interesting questions of interpretation, not only of article 75, but also of the European Convention, namely in the part in which it requires prior exhaustion of domestic remedies (article 35(1)) since proceedings before the ICC cannot be technically qualified as 'domestic remedies'.

Finally, let me briefly touch upon two questions related to universal jurisdiction. The first concerns the relationship between the ICC and States not Parties in the event of crimes which for their gravity may be subject to universal jurisdiction; the second concerns immunity from national jurisdiction.

As to the first question, it is well known that the Statute does not expressly endow the ICC with universal jurisdiction, apart from the exceptional case of crimes referred to the Court by the Security Council acting under Chapter VII of the UN Charter. This can be seen as an anachronistic concession to the old idea of State sovereignty, but it is, indeed, entirely justified in the light of the principle of complementarity of the ICC's jurisdiction. The impact of sovereignty on the ICC jurisdiction, however, has gone beyond the reasonable application of the principle of complementarity and has taken the form of claims to exempt nationals of certain non-Party States from the jurisdiction of the Court. This, of course, raises the question whether such claims should be upheld even when the national of the State not Party is accused of crimes that under international law and even when their referral to the Court is based on the obligation or the right to exercise jurisdiction. A positive answer to this question comes from the practice of the United States, which, as it is well known, has endeavoured to foreclose the exercise of the ICC jurisdiction over its nationals by concluding bilateral agreements to this effect with a good number of countries and by promoting the adoption of Security Council Resolutions sheltering from the ICC jurisdiction nationals of States which are not parties to the ICC Statute and which participate in UN peace operations. This practice is premised on a broad idea of sovereignty and on the related notion that protection of nationals under international law includes also the right to have them exempted from criminal prosecution abroad and, in this case, by an international institution of which the United States is not a member. This position is consistent with the classical international law principle of non-interference within the sovereign sphere of governmental organization of another State. To the extent that the national accused of an international crime is an organ of that State and the crime has been allegedly committed in the performance of its governmental functions, the old idea of sovereignty could still provide the rational foundation for the granting of immunity, and indeed immunity is normally provided and regulated by specific treaty provisions. However, when the national is not an organ of the State, the claim to have him or her exempted from the jurisdiction of the ICC can hardly find a basis in international law: not in a specific principle of international criminal law; nor in the law concerning the minimum standard on the treatment of aliens, which has developed as a guarantee against abuses of power and denial of justice but not against legitimate prosecution for international crimes. On the contrary, contemporary international law has developed toward the sanctioning of universal jurisdiction for some particularly grave crimes. Some grave breaches of humanitarian law, for instance under article 146 of the Geneva Convention IV on civilians, entail the obligation of each State Party to search for the alleged offenders in order to bring them before its own courts 'regardless of their nationality'. International treaty practice and judicial practice recognize that obligations to prevent and suppress gross violations of human rights and humanitarian law, such as genocide and grave breaches of the laws of war, have acquired an *erga omnes* character (see the judgment of the ICJ in the 2007 *Genocide* case and the 2004 advisory opinion on the *Wall*, which can further support the idea of a universal sphere of justice). Treaty practice and judicial practice have also come to consider certain crimes as proscribed by *jus cogens.* This is the case with torture, recognized as a violation of *jus cogens* by the European Court of Human rights (*Al-Adsani* 2001) and by the ICTY according to which 'every State is entitled to prosecute, punish or extradite individuals accused of torture' (*Furundzjia* 1998). In extradition practice, the handing over of a person to a requesting State is allowed for treaty crimes as well as for crimes under international law: in either case the national State of the alleged offender has no legal basis for objecting to the extradition to a third country simply relying on the argument of sovereignty and of its extension, by way of the nationality link, to the accused person. It may be worth recalling that, in the well known *Soering* case, Germany as a State of nationality expressed an interest in the fate of the offender, who was to be extradited from the United Kingdom to the United States, but the objection to extradition in the proceedings before the European Court of Human Rights was the possible breach of article 3 for potential exposure of the defendant to inhuman death row conditions, not his nationality. Finally, it is useful to recall that adoption of universal jurisdiction is urged as a matter of policy and law by the 2006 Basic Principles on Remedy and Reparation.

My conclusion on this point, therefore, is that, although article 12 of the ICC Statute expressly relies on the traditional criteria of territoriality and nationality for the exercise of the ICC jurisdiction, established international law practice allows the surrender and prosecution of nationals of third States who are found in the territory of a State Party to the ICC Statute and who are accused of having committed one of the crimes covered by the Statute (genocide, crimes against humanity, crimes of war). Surrender to the ICC and prosecution in such circumstances should be allowed even in the event the crime has been committed in the territory of a third State, provided that the custodial State has a valid jurisdictional title, such as the nationality of the victims of the crime (passive personality), the injury to an essential interest of the State, or universal jurisdiction because of the nature and gravity of the crime.[5]

---

5 For a contrary view, Danilenko, G.M. (2002), 'ICC Statute and Third States', in Cassese, A., Gaeta, P. and Jones, J.R.W.D. (eds), *The Rome Statute of the International Criminal Court: A Commentary* (Oxford: Oxford University Press), p. 1876, who maintains that under

What are the implications of these conclusions on the question of immunity before national jurisdiction? As we know, article 27 of the Statute provides that immunity for heads of State and public officials shall not bar the Court from exercising its jurisdiction, nor shall it in and of itself constitute a ground for reducing a sentence. Under articles 58 and 59, the Court (that is, the Pre-Trial Chamber) may at any time issue an arrest warrant and transmit it to any State Party on the territory of which the person to be arrested may be found. However, article 98 of the Statute reintroduces an element of caution and commits State Parties which are requested to comply with an arrest order by the ICC not to violate their obligations under international law. Specific mention is made of obligations relating to diplomatic immunities of a person of a third State and host States' obligations under status of forces agreements. Does this provision provide a blanket immunity for all public officials and military personnel of third States? I do not think so. First of all, reference by article 98 to the need to safeguard 'international obligations' of third States does not imply the existence of absolute obligations in the field of immunities and of status of forces. Apart from diplomatic immunities and immunities *ratione personae* of high governmental leaders in office, international law is moving toward a restrictive notion of immunity *ratione materiae.* This is evidenced by some recent landmark decisions. In the *Pinochet* case, the House of Lords held that torture cannot be considered part of governmental functions under international law and therefore it cannot be covered by functional immunity.[6] In the already mentioned *Furundzjia* case, the ICTY held that under existing customary law even heads of State and Government are criminally responsible for acts of torture. Similarly, immunities arising from status of forces agreements referred to in article 98 are not absolute. Normally they establish a regime of concurrent jurisdiction preferential criteria for the sending State. The crimes for which such agreements were designed are common crimes, not the international crimes and atrocities that fall within the ICC jurisdiction. In the end, even if a status of forces agreement were to establish absolute immunity of the sending State's military personnel, the question would arise whether the courts of a State Party to the ICC Statute should give precedence to the obligation to comply with a surrender request by the Court rather than to the obligation to grant immunity under status of forces agreements. It may be argued that at least in cases of the most serious international crimes, such as genocide, torture and other crimes involving violations of *jus cogens*, the international community's commitment to fight impunity through the joint effort of the ICC should be given priority.

To conclude, the principle of complementarity that underlies the jurisdiction of the ICC places this Court in the unique position of exercising enormous influence in the correction, strengthening and improvement of national criminal justice with

---

the Rome Statute the ICC would never have jurisdiction 'over crimes committed by national of third States on their own territory'. This entails acceptance of the paradoxical situation where a State may exercise extraterritorial criminal jurisdiction over a foreign national but in the same situation would not be able to surrender the accused to the ICC for prosecution and trial.

6 Reprinted in International Legal Materials (1999), 581.

respect to international crimes. National courts are sometimes powerless, and often inefficient in the prosecution and punishment of international crimes; they may be also hindered by compelling political considerations as the recent history of war in Former Yugoslavia has shown. In this situation the ICC has the opportunity to play a fundamental pedagogical role for national jurisdiction; its institutional character as an international organisation places it in a good position to gauge and adapt its statutory powers to this important function. That is why the method I have chosen for the interpretation of the Statute and relevant rules of international law has been inspired by the criterion of consolidating the powers of the Court rather than undermining them in the name of deference to national sovereignty and its corollaries. This method is also consistent with the mandate of the Court to fight impunity of those who commit the most serious international crimes, which is also a fundamental objective of the international community as a whole.

Håkan Friman:

Thank you very much. I would also like to pick up on the issue of positive complementarity that was raised yesterday and also this morning. This idea relates to a more cooperative approach, rather than a confrontational one, has been raised prior to this colloquium and was included in an expert paper delivered to the ICC Prosecutor some time ago. Considering how difficult state cooperation is in practice, and the fact that the ICC investigations take place in ongoing conflicts, this approach is a very reasonable one. But not unproblematic, of course.

Positive complementarity means liaising with the government which itself would often be one of the parties to the conflict. Issues of impartiality will therefore arise. There are scenarios where this would not be a problem, especially when there is a transition, but probably that will not often be the case. So, generally speaking, the States, the governments, with which cooperation would occur under the positive complementarity approach would also in one way or another be implicated in the conflict as such, and maybe also in the crimes. Hence, the approach requires a high degree of caution in practice; the ICC and its different organs must not be seen as acting one-sidedly, decisions must be clear, and measures that are taken, or perhaps not taken, should be explained. There is a need for outreach strategies. Also technical matters, such as the taking of evidence, must be handled with care. For instance, successful interviews with victims and witnesses might depend upon the absence of military or police officials from the cooperating State. The sources of information and the collection of evidence should be diversified and not stem from one side only. The Prosecutor of the ICC must also be very diligent in exercising the principle of objectivity, which is laid down explicitly in article 54 of the ICC Statute.

The first few situations that have been addressed by the ICC must be understood in the light of establishing a new institution and laying the ground for broad acceptance of its activities and existence. Both friends and foes must be taken into account. In this sense, I believe that the first years of activity of the Court, and the positive complementarity approach in particular, have been quite successful; not without its problems, but generally successful. Like Professor Schabas argued yesterday, however, the approach will have to be evaluated and such processes have indeed been initiated.

One question is whether positive complementarity actually encourages States to take responsibility by making sure that resources are available and by conducting their own investigations and prosecutions. There are some encouraging reports. For instance, war crimes prosecutions have reportedly taken place in the Democratic Republic of the Congo, in the Eastern part, in proceedings where the local court applied the substantive criminal law provisions of the ICC Statute.

Apart from the question whether positive complementarity produces domestic investigations and prosecutions or other accountability processes, one should also ask whether it leads to good cooperation – arrest and surrender, and other forms of assistance – and whether the approach contributes to a positive image and broad support for the Court and its activities in more general terms.

I believe that positive complementarity is here to stay, although with refinements as to the way in which it is being operated, and I do not see it as necessarily linked to self-referrals. Efforts to encourage domestic investigations and prosecutions could also be a component when a different trigger mechanism is applied, even in cases of a *proprio motu*-initiated ICC investigation. But of course the practical application would then be different.

Before moving into the components that the positive complementarity approach may include, I think that it is important to underline that the intention seems to be to apply the concept very early in the process. Even before an investigation has been initiated by the ICC, a dialogue may take place between the ICC and the State. Hence, it is not a precondition that the accused has been transferred to or is otherwise available at the seat of the Court, which in turn would have prompted considerations as to the requirements for allowing a transfer back of the particular accused to be tried domesticly.

Components of the positive complementarity approach are, apart from the dialogue, domestic legislation, capacity building, and legal cooperation by the Court, which is sometimes called 'reverse cooperation'. An important question is whether the Court itself or someone else should take initiatives and provide these types of support. Other actors could be individual States, groups of States, States Parties under the auspices of the Assembly, or perhaps the international community in an even broader sense.

First of all, we should avoid placing too much of a burden upon the ICC and its limited resources. But also other doubts could be raised as to whether the ICC itself should be engaged in the development of, for example, domestic legislation on cooperation or substantive criminal law. Indeed, such legislation may subsequently be subject to critical evaluation by the ICC and it would, in my opinion, be very unfortunate if the Court had held the pen when the legislation was drafted.

Capacity-building would be a more suitable task for the Court and to some extent this is already taking place. But here again the Court's resources and capacity would be very limited and the bulk of such assistance would have to be provided by others than the Court. Efforts of this kind must also fit into a broader picture and be coordinated with other initiatives, especially bilateral or multilateral development aid that is provided for improvements of the State's legal system and infrastructure.

Such coordination is much better dealt with by others than the Court. The Court is not a specialist in that sense; it has technical knowledge and legal experience, but it does not, and arguably should not, have the expertise of running such programmes.

Finally, on legal cooperation there is a non-mandatory provision in the Statute allowing the Court to assist States with respect to evidence. Moreover, it is likely, although not explicitly provided for, that the Court may transfer an accused back to the surrendering State. In addition, one may argue that there are indications, not in the Statute but in the Rules of Procedure and Evidence and also in the Regulations of the Court, that someone who has been surrendered to the Court could be re-surrendered to another State. In accordance with general inter-State practice, such a measure would require the consent of the originally surrendering State. The issue whether the Court has the power to re-surrender someone to another State, and if so the conditions for such a measure, certainly deserves a much more thorough discussion. Thank you very much.

Discussion[7]

Theodor Meron: Please, take your seats. Let me first on my own behalf and on your behalf thank once more our very distinguished panellists for the very perceptive contributions they gave this morning. And now I will open the floor for discussion and invite questions. Who has the microphone? The microphone to Mister Hans-Peter Kaul, please. Judge Kaul.

Hans-Peter Kaul: Thank you very much, Mister President. Well, let me at first thank everybody for all these thought-provoking contributions. I could ask many questions but I will ask only one, one which is maybe a little bit provocative in tone. The question is: if we look at positive complementarity, if we look at the need for strengthening domestic national criminal jurisdiction and systems, is the ICC also a development ICC? Or, if we look at the questions of reparations and collective reparations, mass reparations, is the ICC also a humanitarian agency?

Let me clarify. This view that the ICC may appear as a development agency, that is as an institution also with the task to promote the development of national criminal jurisdiction systems, has been seriously forwarded to the ICC many times, from NGOs, from scholars, from academicians; we now have heard that there is a task to strengthen national criminal systems in order to alleviate the ICC from too much burden and to reduce the gap of immunity.

So I would like simply to leave it at this: shall the ICC be given the task to contribute actively to the build-up of national criminal justices in developing countries? And here we have the remarks also from Professor Meron, that the ICC is experienced as an institution with relevance only for developing countries. So I

7 Note by the editors: this section mirrors the questions addressed to the contributors to the round table by participants in the Colloquium. We deemed it appropriate to include it in the proceedings, with a view to providing a complete picture of the debate, whilst preserving its informal nature.

leave it at that, thank you very much. If anybody feels they have an answer on this, I would be grateful for a response.

Theodor Meron: Thank you very much, Judge Kaul. Professor Schabas, is this a continuation of the same question or will you wait? Let's take both questions and then we will have the reaction of the panellists.

William Schabas: It's probably related to the issue of victims, but it is on this last point about the focus of the ICC on developing countries. Professor Meron, you raised this yourself and another panellist spoke to this matter. What I think we make is a regional distortion of the International Criminal Court, where all of its activities are now concentrated within Africa, but not all of Africa, just a narrow horizontal band within Africa; the Africans represent a large single group of States Parties (I think there are 31 of them), not-quite one third, but they have three judges out of the 18, whereas the European States have 10 Judges on the Court, don't they? I'm talking about Europe geographically not this old, cold mix between the 'two Europes', and I'm not counting either another European; Judge Kirsch belongs to that strange genus called the 'Western European and Others Group' of States.

Theodor Meron: We all know everything is a question of definition…

William Schabas: To an African it looks rather like Europeans judging black people from Central Africa and I think that has to be a concern raised before the Assembly of States Parties. And when you relate that to things like the Prosecutor's analysis on why he has not investigated in Iraq, the explanation the Prosecutor gave (which was issued I think the same week as he obtained the arrest warrant for Thomas Lubanga Dyilo) was that although there was the strong evidence that the British had killed, British soldiers were responsible for 15 or 20 killings in Iraq, whereas there were more killings in Africa; so he had to focus on Africa, but then he goes and indicts someone for recruiting child soldiers. It doesn't make a lot of sense, it seems to me, and this is an unsatisfactory explanation. Now many people say this will destroy the Court, the fact that the Prosecutor did say it was insane to go after the British at this stage; somehow we have to do a better job of addressing these regional issues and maybe the best thing that the ICC will need in the future is a European defendant.

Theodor Meron: Thank you very much. We will now – as I said – ask our panellists, Judge Pocar, President Pocar.

Fausto Pocar: Well, I think there are two related issues at stake here. One is the question of whether prosecutors should proceed in cases of alleged crimes committed by 'Western' countries in particular, as was the case of Iraq. I also believe that the ICC or, rather, the Prosecutor of the ICC, missed an opportunity in the British case, since dealing with such a situation would have provided a good possibility for clarifying the scope of article 17 of the Statute. It is true that there were indeed prosecutions in Great Britain, but what kind of prosecutions? Shouldn't the Court look into whether war crimes were committed and correctly prosecuted? The Prosecutor could start an investigation and, if appropriate, could decide not to prosecute because prosecution was already ongoing in Great Britain. At least, by proceeding in this way, it would have clarified when domestic prosecution prevents, or does not require, intervention by the Court. Probably, these people were not tried for war crimes, but for ordinary crimes. Is that sufficient? The ICC Statute is unclear on this matter, while the Statute of the ICTY is clear. In any event, it would have been a good occasion to clarify that. At least, it would have showed that the Court is taking care of the situation and is not just disregarding it.

The second issue, raised by Judge Kaul, is whether the Court should act as a sort of development agency for local judicial systems. My answer would be, at the same time, 'no' and 'yes'. Certain aspects should of course *not* be dealt with by the Court. But the Court should have the responsibility to share know-how with domestic courts and provide guidance, and this is an essential responsibility. This is especially true with respect to the application of the Statute: if domestic courts have to apply the Statute, where should they look for guidance, if not to the ICC and its case law? In a way, this is what we are doing with the State Court in Bosnia and Herzegovina. We have regular contacts in order to share experience and we are always trying, during these meetings, to communicate our know-how. So that's why I speak of 'partnership' and of 'sharing' experience. The fact is that what we want is that these courts, when dealing with similar situations do have recourse to our case law and follow more or less what we are doing, so that the same standards are applied.

The goal of the domestic court should indeed be that of applying the same standards as the international court. So, in my view, this is part of the task of the ICC; of course, as far as other aspects are concerned – training in general justice, putting in place structures … – that is obviously not something in which the Court should be directly involved in. Thank you.

Theodor Meron: Before turning to Ambassador Toscano, let me address one other aspect of the same question, the context of the question from Judge Kaul… I think that there are limits to the role to the Court, but nevertheless the role that remains for the Court I would say is extremely important, and the Court in a way has a unique role to play. And why has it a unique role? It has a unique role to play because these are the State Parties to the Statute, it has to make sure that national standards come close to the international standards in the definition of crimes which are contained in the Rome Statute.

And we take it more or less for granted that the developed countries have standards which fit. Recently, in the ICTY – and President Pocar knows to what I'm referring – I discovered that Norway, a country that is superb in terms of compliance with the new process in international law, does not have in its statutes something that defines genocide or deals with genocide.

I'm sure on very good expectations that genocide surely will not be committed in Norway, but then in terms of complementarity it is important to have those things in place. And you, the people in the institution, are the only ones who can work on that, Ambassador Toscano.

Roberto Toscano: Yes, thank you very much. Well, I'm very grateful to Professor Schabas for raising a very fundamental political point. Let's start from the issue of the ability to prosecute. Ability to prosecute can be technical, but can also be political. So, let's say: let's take one poor country in Africa, they have technical problems and political problems. And this is why they end up being the bulk of the cases in the ICC. Now, let's take the opposite spectrum of power and development, the United States: they don't seem to have technical problems, but do they have political problems in recognizing certain and prosecuting certain acts that I see in a political and security framework? Now, since this is the case, there wouldn't be any reason not to balance the attention of the ICC Court for developed countries, and especially the number one.

But what then we have to question very frankly is that political ability to prosecute on the part of the ICC, because there are certain targets that are, let's say, politically more or less off-limits. I'm not talking only on the ICC: I think that not long ago somebody raised the issue of whether some targeting of the bombing of Belgrade by NATO was improper insofar as they included civilian targets.

I don't think that was prosecuted internationally or nationally. So I think we do have a very big problem, which is a political problem; on the other hand, we shouldn't be too shocked by that, since justice has always had to deal with real existing power, also on a national level. Therefore it's a continuous struggle which doesn't mean that we don't have to pursue the developing of new institutions and to go after crimes wherever and by whomever they are committed.

Theodor Meron: Thank you very much. More comments from other participants? Professor Francioni.

Francesco Francioni: Briefly, I have just two of them. First of all, the issue raised by Judge Kaul: should we transform the Court into a humanitarian agency? That's not the question, of course. The problems I raised in my brief introduction were not aimed at transforming the Court into a humanitarian agency, but just to look at the possibility of doing justice in an area where justice is not done, and where international law is increasingly adopting the perspective of the victim rather than only the perspective of the prosecution. There are many ways of doing justice today with international law: there are truth and reconciliation commissions; there is civil liability; there is, of course, criminal prosecution.

It seems to me that it's very difficult – when you have a clear mandate as there is in the Statute – to sweep under the carpet the question of reparation, and it seems to me that there would be a very good development in the internal legal order of the International Criminal Court to develop those principles on reparation for which there is a precise mandate. I think that you do not need to have always a fantastic amount of money and of resources; we know that reparation in international law today is mostly done at interstate level, by settlement that deals with issues on war reparation and conflicts etc. We know that and there is very little role for individuals to have access except under the Alien Tort Claims Act in the United States, but this only very seldom is successful.

The possibility, however, to develop principles does not require necessarily significant funds. Think of the issue of restitution. Restitution may involve taking into account the interest in getting back the property, being able to regain the employments that have been lost; family reunification; return of cultural objects that are often the target in these types of conflicts; all these are measures of reparation that can be achieved even without having an incredible trust fund or resources for compensation. That is one of the comments I wanted to make.

Second, the issue that was briefly hinted at by Ambassador Toscano, that of non-justiciability. When you are dealing with conflicts that are very sensitive (the bombing, the television etc.), that's exactly one area in which you have a denial of justice. I don't think we can be very happy about the results of the cases where you have victims that have lost their lives simply because we targeted a civilian objective willingly, and it was a clear violation of the humanitarian law; then we do not have the proper avenue. In this sense, I don't think that the state of the jurisprudence in Strasburg is totally satisfactory, and we are facing double standards, playing with different types of control and different types of effective control over the activities or local areas which are under the control of the armed forces. So it seems to me that the Court has an opportunity here of improving international humanitarian law, where of course the status of the victims should be the centre of the objective for our concerns in doing justice.

Theodor Meron: If I may just – thank you so much Professor Francioni – I think that one point to remember, looking broadly at the matter of criminal justice, is that the Security Council in establishing that Tribunal did not really provide us with the means to give any compensation whatsoever, we have no ability to deal with that issue, that is, the Security Council places the higher premium on ending impunity than on satisfying the victims in that respect. Would you like to add something to this, Professor?

Håkan Friman: Just a few short comments. I would yet again like to underline the importance of explaining decisions and, at times, the reasons for not taking measures. This is particularly important when the timing of events, as in the example given by Professor Schabas, turns out to be very unfortunate. As to the functions of the ICC, I do believe that most of the assistance that is needed for States which are experiencing or recently have experienced violent conflicts would go far beyond what the ICC could provide. But at the same time there are competence, experiences and knowledge within the ICC that should definitely be shared within the context of that type of assistance.

My addition to all this is that we should bear in mind the general idea of complementarity; the potential of complementarity so to speak. This principle may lead to, and has indeed led to, a debate concerning international criminal law and to the introduction of domestic legislation. Furthermore, the hope is that States will combat impunity in a more effective way and to a larger extent than has been done in the past. And of course if that is what we see as the potential of the concept as such, then certainly we should welcome measures and approaches that will contribute to enhancing that potential. Thank you very much.

Theodor Meron: Thank you very much, are there more questions? Comments? Yes?

Annalisa Ciampi: Thank you. I'd like to make two comments. First one, the issue of the role of the Court to enhance States' capacity of prosecuting international crimes. Of course, I agree that there is no other way but to agree that the Court can't play a fundamental role, but I think there is a problem with the Court, which is not only a problem of resources of course. It is a problem of legal basis as well. Professor Schabas used yesterday the words of 'diluted cooperation'. There is a lot of cooperation, a lot of activity going on by the Office of the Prosecutor with the countries it is investigating, which is not a formal cooperation and on which there are no formal checks nor records. In this informal diluted cooperation there is also a lot of assistance that the Prosecutor is giving to the Democratic Republic of the Congo, for instance. I see a problem here and I had several discussions with OTP officials around the following question: what about if someone is coming to you and says 'what is the legal basis for your office to spend so many resources on this?' We don't even know how many resources, we don't know how many men are working on this, how much energy is given to this; however, while on one hand I'm not too keen on having more checks on the Prosecutor, I think there is even too much, my real concern is that the Court is devoting 80% – that's my guess from the reading of the documents which are published on the website – 80% of its resources on doing checks and balances of what is being done and who's checking whom. So I think we have enough checks. I see really many choices which are made and would have to be made by the Prosecutor if the Prosecutor would be more into this activities giving assistance to developing countries: which countries? to what extent? in what manner? Many choices and selection of priorities, so many sensitive legal and political questions.

Then I would also comment on the issue of reparation. Maybe I do have an answer for the first procedure question that was raised by Professor Francioni, and also the question raised by Judge Kaul, about reparations by the Court. There is a choice which has already been made and that is in the regulations of the Trust Fund for the victims. The Trust Fund for the victims adopted its regulations (that is, the Assembly of the State Parties adopted them) during the fourth assembly in December 2005.

According to those regulations, the Trust Fund will be able to award the reparations to victims irrespective of the convictions by the Court. This is a revolution. I don't know why we are not so well aware of this possibility by the Court, the Court in general through the Trust Fund. It is already expressly provided that the board directors would have among these activities the activity of selecting victims, especially when we have a case of mass victims, as I suspect to be the cases in relation to most crimes. Thank you.

Theodor Meron: Thank you. I would like to refer the first question, which is very interesting, to one of the ICC judges here because they know it best. Judge Kaul or Judge Politi, regarding the proportion of the resources of the ICC which is now directed to… Judge Kaul? or Judge Politi?

Mauro Politi: Well. The question of resources for … people have told me that the ICC now has the resources that will now be given to the International Criminal Tribunal for technical assistance. We have the rules, but we don't have basically the resources, the resources can come only from the Trust Fund.

Theodor Meron: But for the compensation on the investments in generating domestic jurisdiction…

Mauro Politi: Also for that there is some money for the Prosecutor to use, but I'm afraid that there is not enough money to do what should be done or can be done. The resources of the ICC are limited. I think they should be used for and concentrated more on effective investigation and prosecution at this stage.

The question of victims, this is the crucial issue that we are facing, at the ICC. And this brings me also to address briefly the question of compensation of victims, which is linked to the participation of victims, which is the other problem. We talk about compensating victims when we have to first address the problem: *Who is the victim? Who has the right to be compensated?* And the question of participation of victims is very crucial in this moment of the activity of the ICC. I don't want to get into the interpretation of the Statute but the issue whether we have to recognize the right to participate to victims of the situation and not only to the victim of the case is the object of the current jurisprudence on this point. I cannot go beyond this because I'm dealing precisely with this issue, right now. What is crucial for the ICC now, is not to devote a lot of resources to aspects that are not the core aspects of its activity.

Investigation and prosecution: I don't want to diminish the importance of victims' participation and compensation, I just told Francesco Francioni that he has touched upon a very delicate and sensitive issue: article 75 and the principles on compensation. Who's going to do that? Not to speak about of what kind of principles we are discussing about, substantive principles or procedural principles. But now everybody is saying 'you don't have enough cases' and everybody is concerned about that. Sometimes representatives of States, even ambassadors, they come to me and they say 'you know, wouldn't it be easy to convince States to grant you 80 million Euros, when you have only one case before you', and those are the representatives of the same States who don't move one inch of their fingers to allow the arrest warrants issued by the Pre-Trial Chamber to be executed.

So there is really something that we have to face without diversions into aspects that are peripheral with respect to the activity of the Court. And it's not up to me to talk about the prosecutorial policy and especially in the absence of representatives of the Office of the Prosecutor (although we do have a former representative of the Office of the Prosecutor here[8]). I wouldn't dare to criticize anybody here, but I think that the Prosecutor, especially the Prosecutor, should concentrate his activities and resources in investigating, prosecuting and bringing cases before the Court. Then after that, it would be a problem of cooperation from States and from international organizations, which is crucial.

8 Håkan Friman (note by the editors).

The last point: I'm not pessimistic about the future of the ICC. It's a phase in which the ICC is starting really to operate, and like other institutions and tribunals of this kind we need a little bit more time I think, to really set a good pace. In other words, I want to say that the problems that we are discussing here are linked to the common desire of seeing the ICC, I would say, as a 'vibrant institution'. I agree with this expression used by Theodor Meron, but the ICC is already vibrant. It is not the ICC of three years ago sitting down and studying what to do in the future; we are acting, at least most of us; obviously the Trial Chamber is not convened yet, but the Pre-Trial Chambers and Appeal Chamber are working very very hard; it is already a vibrant institution. We have to make it even more vibrant, even more effective, but we need the impulse from those who are there to investigate, to prosecute and they should concentrate their activity and resources on that. I hope that I said something which makes some sense.

Theodor Meron: That was extremely helpful, Judge Politi. I believe that Judge Kaul…

Hans-Peter Kaul: Well, I'm extremely grateful to Professor Ciampi because she has pointed out two issues which need really further consideration. The first one, and I would like to endorse 100% what Judge Politi has just said: the Court, and in particular the Prosecutor, has to focus on its co-mandate to investigate and to prosecute, and this is the message which I tried to convey also yesterday when I spoke about the necessity that the Prosecutor acts really as the engine of the Court in all possible senses.

And now, with regard to resources and manpower. Maybe it's of interest to you (I do not have all the actual figures but it will give you a flavour of what we are talking about): for the three conflict areas and situations which are currently under consideration, the investigation division may now comprise more or less 100 investigators. My view is that it is much too little. The cooperation and jurisdiction and complementarity division may now comprise 20 to 25 staff. Imagine cooperation with the entire world. Is this enough? Yesterday I spoke about an appropriate organizational capacity and Professor Theodor Meron said 'do we need some institutional reshaping?' Well, we certainly have to make the organization fit for its genuine tasks, and this is what is maybe not yet perfect.

With regard to the somewhat remarkable decisions of the Assembly of States Parties, that the Trust Fund can award a collective and individual preparation, irrespective of a decision of the competent Trial Chamber, this is unfortunately a brilliant example of the system of the State Parties. And we are simply the subjects and the subordinates of this system. There's a lot of discussion among ourselves, on how to deal with this complex situation, but we probably will have to face also in the future the situation in many areas: State Parties – well, the owners of the Court – may take decisions which are disputable, and they do not take action, especially in the field of cooperation, where it would be absolutely necessary. I'm grateful for the opportunity to speak this out so clearly.

Theodor Meron: Thank you very much, Judge Kaul. More comments or questions? Do I see Judge Ferrari Bravo? No… my presidential intuition suggested that maybe Professor Pierre-Marie Dupuy would say something?

Pierre-Marie Dupuy: Thank you very much. I'd like just to add some remarks to what Francesco Francioni rightly said above about the issue of universal jurisdiction. I don't want to get into the detail but there are issues here… one such issue upon which we spoke a little bit yesterday morning is whether one should interpret the Statute as inciting the State Parties to develop their national legislation in order to admit universal jurisdiction as far as war crimes are concerned. Now, if we look at the current trend, we know that since the initial Belgian legislation that was modified in a much more restrictive way (though there are new cases coming out, especially in Spain and Australia), there is still the tendency to precondition the use of universal jurisdiction and to say that universal jurisdiction should only be referred to or used when the territorial State did not begin with prosecution.

Now, another issue is whether one could, as it has been submitted by some scholars, go even further and say that universal jurisdiction would be conditioned by the abstention of the ICC itself, which in some way would be what has been called 'reverse complementarity'. So I would like to have a view of the three judges or some of the judges.

Theodor Meron: Thank you very much, Professor Dupuy. Comments on the comment?

Håkan Friman: Thank you. I have a comment not on the last point, but rather to the comment before that, by Judge Politi, if I may.

I would of course not disagree with the core task being investigation and prosecution, or the necessity of doing so as effectively as ever possible. But I think it's important to realize that investigations and prosecutions in the present circumstances must be seen in their proper context. There is no direct access to any territory. The immediately available information is often conflicting and must be tested. The actual referral and other communications which initiate the process may be unspecific or prejudicial. Hence, the Prosecutor's Office is extremely dependent upon other external sources in order to conduct investigations and later a prosecution.

In short, good cooperation is very, very important already in the investigative stage. And even at the stage before the commencement of a formal investigation. Concerning the DRC and Uganda, both countries have no laws explicitly allowing them to cooperate with the ICC. Yet cooperation takes place in practice. In the case of the DRC, the government has no control over the territory in the part of the country where most of the investigation takes place. Therefore others, like the peacekeepers of MONUC, will have to be involved for all practical purposes. In Sudan the mandate rests upon the Security Council resolution that we discussed yesterday, and with respect to cooperation the resolution leaves quite a lot to wish for.

Against these realities it is easier to say 'investigate and prosecute' than to actually do it, and it must be understood that the various actions are taking place, and should be assessed, within this broader context. Thank you.

Theodor Meron: Thank you very much. In a few moments we will bring this panel to an end but I would like to say how much I appreciated the emphasis by Judge Politi on these remarks, that is on the core function of the ICC, which is investigations and prosecutions. This is why the international community created the ICC; the ICC must rise to the standards, to this challenge, by having enough people; enough on the focus of everything else is also important, but that is the core. Just one second, Ambassador Toscano. President Pocar, the question has been raised as to the budget available to the ICC in terms of promoting rule of law and domestic jurisdictions. I think that the ICTY did quite a lot in order to encourage structures in the Balkans for establishing the rule of law and combat impunity. Could you tell us something about this?

Fausto Pocar: Well, this is relatively easy, in a way. In fact, except for some inevitable implications for the budget, which related to the activity of people working at the Tribunal – legal officers – that are paid on the budget, for the majority of such activities – the training, the meetings, the necessary documentation and so on – all these expenses were paid extra-budget: on the basis of voluntary contributions by the European Union. The European Union, in our case, has a clear interest in promoting and enhancing the capacity of the judiciaries of the countries in the Balkans, which might be, even in the long run, prospective Member States of the Union itself. And, even if in the end they never become members, the Union is nonetheless interested in their stabilization and in the promotion of the rule of law. All this has therefore been paid outside our regular budget, which is devoted essentially to prosecuting and trying cases.

Theodor Meron: Thank you very much, President Pocar. Ambassador Toscano I believe that you wanted to make a comment.

Roberto Toscano: Yes, I think that the issue of universal jurisdiction is a very crucial one. Jurists here will have been able to assess the relationship of universal jurisdiction and the ICC much better than I. Nevertheless, from a political point of view I think that if our goal is to reduce the possibility of impunity, in no way should we think that the ICC supersedes universal jurisdiction. Let's keep that tool as an alternative tool perhaps, although I don't know how it should be regulated *vis-à-vis* the ICC. But when I talk about genocide, torture, grave offences against humanitarian law, universal jurisdiction is something that we should preserve. As I said, jurists will have to tell me how to relate that to the existence of the ICC. But in no way I think we should say 'now we have the ICC, universal jurisdiction can be put to rest'.

Theodor Meron: Thank you, Ambassador Toscano. This comment was of the kind of generality that grants itself the nature of concluding comment on this panel and I think that we will now declare ourselves *functus officio*, and I suggest that we should now here give the floor to Professor Condorelli, for his closing remarks.

Chapter 15

Closing Remarks

Luigi Condorelli

Je suis très reconnaissant à mon vieil ami Mauro Politi de l'honneur qu'il me fait en m'invitant, non seulement à participer à cette importante rencontre qui confirme et consolide de la plus éclatante des façons la belle tradition des Colloques de Trento dédiés à la justice pénale internationale, mais aussi à tirer cette fois-ci encore des conclusions générales. Je vais tenter d'être à la hauteur de la confiance qu'il a en moi en essayant de présenter quelques réflexions inspirées par le stimulant débat auquel ont participé tant d'experts reconnus.

Il me semble important de commencer par deux remarques d'ensemble ayant une portée méthodologique.

Par la première j'entends attirer l'attention sur une observation faite tant par William Schabas que par Mauro Politi au sujet du rôle qu'il convient d'accorder (ou, si vous préférez, qu'il convient de maintenir) aux travaux préparatoires du Statut de Rome, s'agissant d'interpréter correctement telle ou telle de ses dispositions et de résoudre l'un ou l'autre des innombrables problèmes juridiques auxquels on est confronté maintenant que la Cour est mise sur pied et fait ses premiers pas. J'exprime ce point par des mots nets: il est grand temps de – pour ainsi dire – ranger les travaux préparatoires à leur place, en leur faisant jouer le rôle mineur et secondaire qui leur appartient à fin d'interprétation, d'après les principes pertinents de droit international général tels que consacrés aux articles 31 et 32 de la Convention de Vienne sur le droit des traités. Comme chacun le sait, on ne doit recourir aux travaux préparatoires (et aux circonstances existant à l'époque de la conclusion) qu'en tant que moyen 'complémentaire' d'interprétation, sans prétendre d'en faire l'un des outils principaux à privilégier! Or, il me semble que ce n'est pas vraiment comme cela que les choses se passent actuellement : le souvenir des clivages, des tensions, des dures batailles et des compromis difficiles ayant caractérisé la négociation du Statut de la Cour Pènale Internationale (CPI) est encore trop vif et trop présent dans les esprits, ceci d'autant plus que la plupart des protagonistes du débat actuel ne sont finalement (je devrais dire plutôt: n'êtes finalement) que des 'anciens combattants' de Rome, dont les attitudes sont souvent par trop influencées par le passé, au lieu d'être – pour ainsi dire – tournées vers l'avenir.

Je ne prétends pas, bien entendu, qu'il faille oublier les travaux préparatoires. Je dis que il faut désormais absolument privilégier le texte et son interprétation objective à la lumière de l'objet et du but du Statut; il faut mettre en valeur les virtualités de celui-ci, ses ouvertures, les possibilités qu'il offre pour ce qui est de l'analyse et de la solution des problèmes, en ayant à l'esprit les besoins auxquels doit répondre la justice pénale internationale dans le cadre de la lutte contre l'impunité.

Il faut en particulier, me semble-t-il, cesser de se laisser influencer par ce qui a été l'une des composantes, et pas des moindres, de l'atmosphère qui enveloppait les travaux préparatoires, à savoir le sentiment de méfiance à l'égard d'une cour pénale internationale risquant d'être trop active, trop entreprenante et trop indépendante comme l'ont été les Tribunaux Pénaux Internationaux *ad hoc*, et plus spécialement le Tribunal Pénal International pour l'Ex-Yougoslavie (TPIY). En somme, je recommande vivement que l'on abandonne une fois pour toute ce que j'aime appeler le 'reflex anti-Cassese', qui a tellement influencé les débat lors de la conférence de Rome et précédemment, et qui a amené une partie substantielle de la communauté internationale a se battre pour ligoter la Cour, en la serrant de toutes parts par des filets de contraintes, d'entraves et d'empêchements afin de la rendre docile et sans dents, incapable de trop dérager ceux qui comptent.

La négociation maintenant c'est fini et classé! Le affrontements qui s'y sont déroulés entre les divers partis ont abouti, de compromis en compromis, au Statut de Rome; celui-ci il faut le lire maintenant tel qu'il est, sans remettre sur le nez les lunettes du négociateur, mais en en valorisant le sens objectif à la lumière – j'y insiste – de son objet et de son but. Il faut donc, dans l'interprétation du Statut, exploiter à fond le sens des mots qui le composent et en combler les lacunes en ayant toujours à l'esprit qu'il faut travailler (comme le souhaitait Ted Meron) au succès d'une Cour Pénale Internationale qui soit réellement capable de fonctionner et de combattre efficacement l'impunité par rapport aux crimes les plus graves qui affectent la communauté internationale dans son ensemble en menaçant la paix, la sécurité et le bien-être de tous.

C'était ma première observation générale. La deuxième, la voici: plusieurs orateurs ont fait référence à un mot, à mon avis plutôt malheureux, du procureur, faisant valoir que, finalement, si la Cour ne fait rien, cela veut dire que tout va bien. Si la Cour ne travaille pas, cela veut dire que les Etats font ce qu'il doivent et donc ils permettent à la Cour de croiser les bras et regarder un globe terrestre paisible dans lequel chaque Etat fait pleinement la justice chez lui. La boutade est grossière, évidemment, puisque c'est le contraire qui est vrai: une Cour inactive signifierait que le Statut a essuyé un échec retentissant! Seul un nouveau docteur Pangloss pourrait vraiment croire que, si la CPI ne poursuit aucun criminel, cela veut dire que nous vivons dans le meilleur des mondes possibles: un monde dans lequel il ne reste aucun crime grave à soumettre à la répression internationale. Cela serait à peu près comme si l'on pensait que, quand la police n'attrape personne, c'est qu'il n'y a ni de voleurs, ni d'assassins, ni d'autres meurtriers qui se promènent...

En réalité, n'importe quel Candide voit que la CPI est là, les Tribunaux Pénaux Internationaux sont là, et malgré cela, dans les domaines de compétence de ces instances judiciaires, les malheurs, les horreurs, les méfaits affreux continuent d'avoir lieu et ne sont nullement stoppés par la peur du juge. Comment oublier la tragédie de Srebrenica, un génocide perpétré sous les yeux du TPIY? L'idée fondamentale qui a animé historiquement la bataille en faveur de la création des tribunaux pénaux internationaux, suivant laquelle l'existence même de ces tribunaux jouerait un rôle préventif essentiel, pêche malheureusement d'ingénuité, comme nous le montrent tant de tragiques expériences à l'instar de celle de Srebrenica, sans oublier celles des droits internes. En somme, les faits démontrent impitoyablement que bien souvent l'existence des juges n'œuvre pas vraiment comme le moyen de prévention efficace dont nous parlait l'ambassadeur Toscano. L'épouvantail, pour redoutable qu'il puisse apparaître, ne suffit pas, même s'il peut aider. Pour répondre aux besoins du monde, il faut des mécanismes de répression pénale internationale bien outillés, prêts à l'action, rapidement déclenchables et efficaces. C'est à leur mise en place qu'il nous faut travailler tous.

Sur la base de ces prémisses, je voudrais en venir maintenant aux deux thèmes centraux dont nous avons discuté hier et aujourd'hui, c'est-à-dire la complémentarité d'une part et la coopération de l'autre, outils essentiels pour le fonctionnement de la Cour.

Le point de départ pour en discuter est le rappel d'une notion de base: la CPI est appelée à intervenir en réprimant les crimes internationaux seulement lorsque cette répression ne peut être réalisée convenablement au niveau interne, et ce à cause du fait que les Etats ne s'acquittent pas de leur 'devoir' en la matière (celui, rappelée par le 6ème considérant du Préambule, d'exercer leur juridiction pénale sur les responsables de ces crimes: le Président Kirsch a beaucoup insisté à juste titre sur son importance) pour incapacité ou manque de volonté. En somme, le Statut organise une sorte de division du travail entre les juges internes et internationaux, en confiant à ces derniers la haute mission de parer à l'impunité engendrée par la défaillance des premiers.

Or, il me semble, quant à moi, tout à fait évident qu'une telle division du travail présuppose, pour pouvoir fonctionner correctement, que les principes juridiques à appliquer pour évaluer si il y a crime ou non soient les mêmes pour tous. Autrement dit, il faut que les crimes soient définis de manière identique aux deux niveaux. Comme on le voit, je suis en train de prendre nettement position sur la question, qui est revenue à plusieurs reprises pendant nos débats, de savoir si le Statut, même s'il ne le dit pas expressément, implique ou non l'obligation pour tous les Etats d'armer leur droit pénal interne de façon qu'il lui soit conforme. Pour moi, il n'y a pas de doute que la réponse doit être positive : c'est la notion même de complémentarité qui l'impose.

Dans cette logique, il convient me semble-t-il de valoriser à fond le concept encré dans le Statut d'après lequel – pour utiliser les mots de Pierre-Marie Dupuy – la CPI est appelée à jouer le rôle de '*sanctioning power of the unwillingness or inability of States*'. Autrement dit, l'article 17 demande à la CPI d'être non seulement le juge des individus qui commettent des crimes, mais aussi le juge des Etats qui ne s'acquittent pas de leur devoir de répression pour quelque raison que ce soit. Or, l'article 17 se prête parfaitement à ce que la Cour puisse juger qu'un Etat ne se dotant pas d'un droit interne conforme au droit international en matière de crimes manifeste par là son incapacité (ou '*inability*') pour ce qui est de la répression de ces mêmes crimes, avec toutes les conséquences que le Statut en tire.

J'avoue que je suis heureux d'avoir entendu ici plusieurs intervenants mettre en évidence que le fait que le droit interne d'un Etat ne soit pas rendu conforme au statut peut être jugé comme un indice de '*inability*' de cet Etat: ce point de vue a été exprimé, par exemple, par les professeurs Ferrari Bravo et Greppi. C'est ce que j'avais soutenu il y a déjà longtemps, dans le premier commentaire du Statut de Rome que j'avais publié en 1999 dans la *Revue générale de droit international public.*[1] A l'époque cette idée pouvait paraître saugrenue, et je suis content de voir que aujourd'hui elle commence à être accepté largement. A la base du jugement de la Cour constatant l' '*inability*' ou l' '*unwillingness*' d'un Etat il peut donc y avoir, non seulement la vérification d'un manque de volonté politique de réprimer ou de la défaillance du système judiciaire interne, mais aussi le constat d'une carence grave quant à la mise en œuvre du droit international pénal en droit interne.

Il y a encore une chose à ajouter, toujours dans la même clé d'analyse, qui est d'exploiter au maximum toutes les ouvertures du Statut. On vient de voir que le mécanisme de l'article 17 pourrait permettre à la Cour de surveiller et de sanctionner les Etats qui – comme l'Italie, d'ailleurs, ainsi que M. Braguglia nous l'a expliqué – ne prennent pas au sérieux leur obligation de conformer leur ordre juridique interne au Statut de Rome. Il s'agirait de toute façon – il convient de le souligner – d'une surveillance au cas par cas, c'est-à-dire relative à une situation donnée, par rapport à laquelle la Cour serait amenée à juger de la recevabilité ou non du cas d'espèce. Je me demande cependant, et je vous demande: est-ce qu'on ne pourrait pas concevoir que la Cour fasse davantage pour contribuer à la réalisation d'une pleine correspondance entre droits internes et droit international dans ce domaine? Personnellement, je pense que oui. Il suffirait pour cela qu'elle ait l'hardiesse d'utiliser convenablement toutes les possibilités et tous les moyens que le Statut lui accorde implicitement.

Je crois utile de me référer ici aux articles sur la coopération des Etats, qui mettent en exergue (comme le fait l'article 86) l'obligation générale de ceux-ci de coopérer pleinement avec la Cour, en insistant ensuite sur la notion d'après laquelle (article 87, 1er alinéa) '*the Court shall have the authority to make request to state parties for coopération*'. La Cour est donc habilitée à demander aux Etats parties une pleine coopération pour tout ce qui est utile à fin qu'elle puisse exercer correctement ses fonctions dans le domaine de l'investigation et de la poursuite. Et bien, voilà des dispositions susceptibles d'interprétations courageuses! Pourquoi la Cour, peut-être quand elle sera mieux assise, plus sûre d'elle même, ne pourrait pas envisager d'utiliser les demandes de coopération pour exiger que les Etats s'acquittent de l'obligation d'harmoniser leur droit interne avec le droit international pénal? Et pourquoi ne pas avoir recours le cas échéant, contre l'Etat défaillant, au paragraphe 7 de l'article 87, établissant que, si un Etat partie ne fait pas ce que la Cour lui demande en matière de coopération, en l'empêchant ainsi d'exercer correctement ses fonctions, '*the Court may make a finding to that effect*' et ensuite soumettre l'affaire à l'Assemblée des Etats Parties? En somme, la Cour pourrait adopter une constatation à caractère – évidemment – judiciaire établissant que l'Etat en question a engagé sa responsabilité internationale pour violation de ses obligations statutaires du fait de ne pas avoir pris les mesures requises de lui au titre de la coopération pour organiser son droit interne comme le Statut l'impose, faisant ainsi obstacle à ce que la complémentarité puisse correctement fonctionner.

Je n'oublierai pas de conforter les remarques que je viens de soumettre en me référant à une observation à mon sens importante venant de Francesco Francioni.

1 Condorelli, L. (1999), 'La Cour pénale internationale: un pas de géant (pourvu qu'il soit accompli)', in *Revue Générale de Droit International Public*, 1999, 7.

D'après l'article 4 du Statut, la CPI est un sujet international jouissant de la personnalité juridique et pouvant donc être assimilé à une organisation internationale. Il s'ensuit que les fonctions et pouvoirs qu'elle a à exercer ne sont pas seulement ceux explicitement listés dans le Statut, mais aussi les pouvoirs et compétences pouvant être qualifiés d'implicites, c'est-à-dire qui sont nécessaires pour remplir la mission qui lui est confiée, et ce même si le traité constitutif ne les indique pas *apertis verbis*. Les années à venir amèneront assurément la Cour à utiliser cette notion pour faire face aux nouveau besoins qui apparaîtront au fur et à mesure: d'ailleurs ce que le Président Pocar nous présentait, lorsqu'il discutait des arrangements adoptés par le TPIY et par le Tribunal Pénal International pour le Rwanda (en dehors de toute disposition explicite des Statuts respectifs) en matière de répartition du travail répressif entre juge pénal international et juges nationaux, est bien une preuve éclatante du rôle que le principe relatif aux pouvoirs implicites est en mesure de jouer concernant la justice pénale internationale (et la complémentarité en particulier) .

Evidement, ce ne sont là que des exemples, pour ce qui est des possibilités d'adopter des interprétations dynamiques et courageuses du Statut. Je voudrais maintenant en citer un autre, relatif à un thème important qui a été discuté à plusieurs reprises (notamment par Francesco Francioni) même si il touche moins directement la question de la complémentarité : celui de la réparation en faveur des victimes.

On sait que le Statut a introduit en son article 75 ce principe novateur d'après lequel la CPI a compétence pour déterminer les dommages et préjudices causés par le crime aux victimes et pour en ordonner la réparation à la charge du coupable (voire, le cas échéant, du Fond de garantie), alors qu'il incombe aux Etats de mettre à exécution les décisions internationales pertinentes. Or l'article 75 est extrêmement sommaire et – c'est bien connu – laisse dans le brouillard le plus épais beaucoup de questions importantes dont le règlement est pourtant indispensable afin de rendre opérationnel ledit principe.

L'article débute cependant par une phrase qui a fait l'objet de divers commentaires, et qu'il convient de citer '*The Court shall establish principles relating to reparation in respect of victims... including restitution compensation and rehabilitation*'. Qu'est-ce que cela peut bien vouloir dire que '*the Court shall estabilish principles...*'? Doit-elle identifier et appliquer par une méthode prétorienne les principes pertinents au cas par cas, c'est-à-dire lors du règlement de chaque situation donnée? Ou bien peut-elle déterminer au préalable ces principes par une décision de caractère général, à savoir par un acte relevant de ce qu'on appelle couramment l' '*international legislation*', pour en faire ensuite application *in casu*? Pour moi, la deuxième voie est parfaitement utilisable et la Cour pourrait fort bien s'y engager! On sait d'ailleurs qu'il existe pas mal d'organisations internationales dont certains organes sont dotés par le traité constitutif d'un pouvoir de *law making*. Un tel pouvoir n'a pas été octroyé à la CPI pour ce qui est de son règlement (à la différence des tribunaux pénaux internationaux *ad hoc*), mais une interprétation dynamique (et nullement hérétique) du Statut peut permettre d'en découvrir l'existence concernant l'ensemble des principes relatifs à la protection des victimes. En somme, demain, lorsque la Cour sera bien assise dans sa fonction, elle pourra sans doute exploiter – ce qui n'apparaît peut-être pas possible maintenant – ce véritable pouvoir législatif que le Statut lui accorde (ou, si l'on préfère, que le Statut peut être interprété comme lui accordant).

Il va de soi, cependant, que pour que la Cour puisse explorer tous les chemins que le Statut lui ouvre et faire plein usage de tous ses pouvoirs (explicites ou implicites), il faut qu'elle soit mise en mesure d'agir, c'est-à-dire qu'elle ait des affaires sur son rôle. Autrement dit, il faut que, face aux crimes internationaux qui continuent malheureusement d'être perpétrés, ceux à qui est accordée la faculté de la saisir fassent effectivement usage de celle-ci. D'après le Statut, nous le savons bien, les titulaires d'une telle faculté sont les Etats parties, le Conseil de sécurité et le procureur. Et nous savons aussi – nous en avons débattu très abondamment – que pour l'heure les quelques affaires dont la CPI est saisie lui ont été soumises à l'initiative d'Etats et du Conseil de sécurité. Quelques commentaires s'imposent à ce sujet.

Giorgio Gaja nous a entretenus sur cette forme inattendue et bâtarde qu'a pris *in concreto* le *referral* par les Etats Parties, à savoir le *self-referral*, et sur les problèmes délicats qui se posent à ce sujet. Les solutions qu'il préconise (en particulier l'idée d'après laquelle l'Etat ayant souverainement décidé de déclencher la procédure par un *self-referral* ne saurait prétendre ensuite qu'il a le loisir de la bloquer en invoquant la cause d'irrecevabilité de l'article 19(2) b) me semblent parfaitement fondées et en harmonie avec les principes herméneutiques sur lesquels j'ai insisté. Je souligne à ce sujet la juste remarque, de Ted Meron et d'autres, insistant sur le fait que le *self-referral* est sans aucun doute mieux que rien: en attendant qu'il y ait de vraies saisines par des Etats soucieux de ce qui se passe auprès d'autres Etats, au lieu de ces saisines tordues venant de gouvernants intentionnés à régler leurs comptes avec les *leaders* qui étaient au pouvoir avant eux, il est tout de même important que la CPI soit mise en branle plutôt qu'elle reste au chômage.

Mais y a-t-il des raisons d'être optimiste quant à l'avenir des 'vraies' saisines par des Etats parties? Peut-on vraiment nourrir de sérieux espoirs, quant au succès de ce mécanisme? Est-ce que nous n'avons pas par hasard assez d'expériences en droit international, pour ce qui est des domaines attenant au droit international humanitaire et aux droits de l'homme, montrant que les Etats se gardent bien le plus souvent d'attaquer un autre Etat pour l'amener devant une cour, devant un juge international, ou même devant un comité de contrôle quel qu'il soit ? Est-ce que nous ne savons pas bien que dans ces domaines les divers systèmes habilitant les Etats à accuser d'autres Etats de violations se sont traduits, en bonne substance et à quelques nuances près, par de véritables échecs, tant au niveau universel qu'à celui régional? Le fait est que, quand ces possibilités existent, les Etats n'en font usage que fort rarement, que ce soit pour ne pas apparaître hostiles voire carrément ennemis, pour manque d'intérêt sérieux en faveur les droits de l'homme de gens lointaines, voire pour éviter le danger d'être attaqués à leur tour par ricochet (chacun sachant bien qu'il y a des cadavres dans ses propres armoires…). Il est vrai que dans le cas du Statut de Rome les accusations portées par l'Etat auteur du *referral* devraient être conçues comme signalant à la CPI des crimes d'individus, et ne seraient donc pas dirigées directement contre un Etat. Ceci cependant n'est qu'apparence: d'une part parce que les *core crimes* dont s'occupe le Statut relèvent normalement de la 'criminalité systémique', c'est-à-dire qu'ils sont à peu près inconcevables sans l'implication de hauts responsables de l'Etat territorial; d'autre part parce que l'Etat en question se voit reprocher au minimum, soit d'être incapable de mettre en place une répression efficace, soit de s'y refuser.

Il faut être réalistes: il n'y a pas vraiment beaucoup à espérer, de ce côté-là ! Pour confirmer ces sombres prévisions, permettez-moi de citer une expérience personnelle certes minime mais parlante. J'ai été, pendant des longues années, membre de la Commission Internationale humanitaire d'établissements des faits (CIHEF) prévue par le Premier Protocole de 1977 additionnel aux quatre Conventions de Genève de 1949. Cette commission existe depuis une quinzaine d'années et est ouverte aux fort nombreux Etats qui l'ont acceptée, lesquels pourraient donc obtenir des enquêtes impartiales sur la conduite d'autres Etats qu'ils accuseraient de violations dudit Protocole. Or, chacun sait que d'infractions graves du droit international humanitaire dont la CIHEF aurait pu s'occuper il y en a eu entre-temps des masses; toutefois, jamais personne ne l'a saisie, elle n'a jamais été utilisée. Il peut être intéressant de savoir que, pendant que j'y siégeais, seulement à deux moments donnés il est apparu qu'on y était presque, qu'on allait bientôt avoir des affaires. Dans le premier cas (je ne peux évidemment pas donner de noms) un gouvernement voulait demander à la commission d'enquêter sur les entorses au protocole additionnel commises par le précédent gouvernement du même pays. Dans l'autre, l'Etat concerné souhaitait que l'on procède à la vérification du respect des règles humanitaires dans le conflit interne sévissant sur son territoire. Ces intentions n'ont finalement pas abouti, mais il est sans doute intéressant pour nous ici de constater que les seuls deux cas dans lesquels la CIHEF a été sur le point de se mettre au travail auraient été ni plus ni moins que des cas de... *self-referrals*!

Si il n'y a pas beaucoup d'espoirs à nourrir pour ce qui est de la saisine de la CPI par des Etats, que faut-il penser alors de la saisine par le Conseil de Sécurité? L'épisode singulier de la Résolution 1593 (2005) concernant le Darfour mérite une ou deux considération .

Certes, la Résolution 1593 (2005) a une grande qualité: celle d'exister, contrairement à toutes les prévisions pessimistes de la veille qui prenaient en compte l'opposition farouche à la CPI de certains membres permanents du Conseil de sécurité, et d'un en particulier. On pourrait alors se dire que ce qui est arrivé une fois arrivera sans doute de nouveau demain. Il faut cependant se demander si cela est vraiment souhaitable.

Le Juge Kaul a cité certains aspects fort douteux de la Résolution citée; de notre côté, Annalisa Ciampi et moi, dans une étude publiée au *Journal of International Criminal Justice*,[2] avons dressé une liste complète (à laquelle je fais renvoi, n'ayant pas le temps de la reprendre maintenant en détail) des entorses graves que la Résolution assène non seulement au Statut de Rome, mais également à la Charte des Nations Unies. En somme, le prix qui a été payé pour obtenir le *nihil obstat* des Etats-Unis m'apparaît vraiment exorbitant : tellement exorbitant que je me demande si il faut vraiment souhaiter que l'on continue à l'avenir à 'saucissonner' le Statut, en

2 Condorelli, L. and Ciampi, A. (2005), 'Comments on the Security Council Referral of the Situation in Darfur to the ICC', in *Journal of International Criminal Justice* 3:3, 590.

le défigurant de la sorte, afin d'obtenir de nouvelles saisines de la CPI par le Conseil de sécurité.

Je ne quitterai pas le dossier relatif à la saisine de la Cour par le Conseil sans dire un mot du débat fort intéressant qui a opposé Phani Dascalopoulou–Livada et Ted Meron. La première est convaincue que le déclanchement de la procédure par le Conseil ne saurait apporter la moindre dérogation aux dispositions du Statut sur la complémentarité, en particulier à celles demandant à la Cour d'apprécier en toute indépendance si oui ou non l'Etat concerné est en train et en mesure de s'acquitter de ses obligations en matière de répression (ce qui implique alors la possibilité que la Cour décide que l'affaire est irrecevable). Le second pense que la décision pertinente du Conseil jouit de toute façon de la primauté qui découle de l'article 103 de la Charte : autrement dit, si le Conseil – agissant en vertu du Chapitre VII – a considéré qu'aux fins du maintien et du rétablissement de la paix la répression internationale s'impose en l'espèce (l'appareil répressif de Etat ne méritant à son avis aucune confiance), la Cour ne saurait s'arroger le pouvoir de le contredire.

A vrai dire l'article 103, qui porte sur la primauté pour les Etats des obligations découlant de la Charte sur celles 'en vertu de tout autre accord international', ne saurait être invoqué directement concernant la CPI, celle-ci n'étant pas un Etat membre, mais une 'institution permanente' laquelle, qui plus est, ne fait pas partie de l'appareil organique des Nations Unies. Certes, la Cour a été conçue comme nécessairement reliée à l'O.N.U. par le biais d'un accord, et celui-ci (qui est de 2004) l'oblige bien à respecter la Charte. Mais à leur tour les Nations Unies ont réciproquement souscrit par le même accord la clause (article 2, paragraphe 3) relative à l'obligation de respecter le Statut de Rome! Or, celui-ci prévoit un régime unitaire de la recevabilité, sans faire la moindre distinction entre les divers types de saisine. Le Conseil de sécurité n'a donc pas le pouvoir d'apporter des dérogations au Statut (ou tout au moins s'est engagé à ne pas essayer de le faire) et doit respecter l'indépendance de la CPI, y compris pour ce qui est de l'appréciation de la recevabilité d'un affaire référée à elle par lui. Il va de soi, cependant, qu'en tout état de cause le point de vue exprimé par le Conseil et ses fondements factuels pèseront en l'espèce de tout leur poids sur la Cour et, en principe, emporteront sa conviction quant à la recevabilité.

Que reste-t-il alors, comme autre possibilité de saisine? Mesdames et messieurs, nous le savons bien, il reste, d'après le Statut, celle par le procureur *proprio motu*. Le rôle du procureur est certes central même en cas de déclanchement de la procédure par les Etats et par le Conseil de sécurité; cependant, les remarques précédentes font apparaître – on l'a vu – de sombres présages quant à l'avenir du fonctionnement de la Cour, si il faut attendre que le Conseil ou les Etats se mettent en action. Il s'ensuit que la réalisation des espoirs de voir demain la Cour se retrousser les manches pour faire activement et en continuité son métier dépend carrément du procureur. Il faut donc absolument que celui-ci prenne très au sérieux les fonctions que lui confie l'article 15, sachant que le succès ou l'échec de la Cour sont tributaires finalement dans une bien large mesure de l'usage énergique qu'il saura en faire.

Je n'ai pas besoin de rappeler que l'inclusion dans le Statut de Rome de la possibilité de saisine de la Cour par le procureur agissant *proprio motu* a été le fruit d'une négociation acharnée, menée sous une extraordinaire pression de l'opinion publique internationale. Il est vital, pour l'avenir de la lutte contre l'impunité, que ce fruit précieux soit mis en valeur. N'ayant pas les responsabilités importantes qui pèsent sur certains d'entre vous, je m'autorise à faire usage d'un langage peu châtié, et encore moins diplomatique, pour me et vous demander si il n'est pas justifié de penser ceci: les prudences paroxystiques et les atermoiements exacerbés qui semblent caractériser la conduite du procureur, concernant la mise en œuvre de l'article 15, sont en train de saper l'élément du Statut de Rome qui est de loin le plus essentiel pour le futur de la Cour.

Je terminerai par quelques mots rapides en matière de complémentarité, concernant toutefois non pas les rapports entre les juges nationaux et la CPI, mais entre la CPI et la Cour Internationale de Justice (CIJ). Ce n'est pas le thème de notre rencontre, mais il est impossible de ne pas y toucher étant donné que nous sommes à deux mois et quelques jours de l'arrêt du 26 février dernier en l'affaire Bosnie Herzégovine contre Serbie, portant sur la responsabilité d'Etat pour génocide.[3] Ce n'est pas par hasard si, par exemple, Philippe Kirsch et Maria Chiara Malaguti s'y sont référés, en faisant allusion à la différence des mandats respectifs! C'est d'autant plus justifié qu'il y a dans cet arrêt un élément d'un grand intérêt (très préoccupant au demeurant) relatif à l'universalité de juridiction en matière de crimes internationaux, sujet qui a été discuté ici spécialement dans la table ronde finale. Je me borne – je tiens à le signaler – à quelques remarques périphériques, étant soumis à une obligation de discrétion liée au fait d'avoir été l'un des conseils de la Bosnie.

On sait que, parmi les demandes de la Bosnie, il y avait celle faisant valoir que la Serbie avait violé et continuait de violer son obligation de répression du crime de génocide, du fait de ne pas avoir mis en place une répression appropriée contre les auteurs du crime se promenant sur son territoire et de ne pas collaborer suffisamment avec le TPIY, notamment en remettant dans les mains de celui-ci le bourreau de Srebrenica, le général Mladic. Or, la Cour a bien jugé que le demandeur avait raison, mais la seule violation retenue est celle concernant la remise de Ratko Mladic au TPIY. La lettre étriqué de la Convention de 1948, en effet, est décisive pour la Cour: c'est l'Etat sur le territoire duquel le génocide a été perpétré qui a seul l'obligation de répression. Il s'ensuit que, comme le génocide de Srebrenica a eu lieu en territoire bosniaque, la Serbie aurait eu le droit de se considérer parfaitement respectueuse de la Convention de 1948 en laissant librement circuler chez elle le criminel, si ce n'est que cette convention oblige les Etats parties à collaborer avec un futur (et éventuel) tribunal pénal international compétent. Voilà une manière bien pressée, superficielle et irréfléchie de condamner les tentatives nombreuses d'interpréter de façon évolutive les principes pertinents de la Convention de 1948, en tenant compte de tous les développements postérieurs en matière d'universalité de juridiction pour les crimes internationaux les plus graves! Mais alors, si l'universalité n'est pas à retenir pour le 'crime des crimes', que faut-il penser pour les autres?

---

3 Affaire relative à l'application de la Convention pour la Prévention et la répression du crime de génocide (Bosnie-Herzegovine C. Serbie-et-Montenegro), arrêt du 26 février 2007.

Dernière remarque, positive cette fois-ci. La CIJ, pour décider si oui ou non la Serbie était responsable de violations de la Convention de 1948, s'est très largement appuyé sur la documentation et la jurisprudence du TPIY. Comme l'observe Pierre-Marie Dupuy dans un article qui sortira très prochainement à la *Revue générale de droit international public* (et que j'ai eu le plaisir de lire en avant-première) la Cour esquisse en effet une sorte de division du travail entre elle-même, quand elle est appelée à régler un contentieux de la responsabilité d'Etat en matière de génocide, et le TPIY, puisque les vérifications des faits, les analyses concrètes, les preuves qui ont été soumises à ce tribunal peuvent être utilisés par la CIJ sans besoin de les recueillir et vérifier à nouveau ; et les décisions du TPIY également, bien sûr. En somme, les mandats en matière de génocide du juge pénal international, d'une part, et de la CIJ, d'autre part, ont beau être différents, puisqu'ils doivent juger de la responsabilité pénale individuelle l'un et de la responsabilité internationale de l'Etat l'autre; il n'empêche que les deux mandats se recoupent sous plusieurs aspects, qu'on ne peut analyser ici en détail. Et ces recoupages, tels qu'on les perçoit au travers de la lecture de l'arrêt cité, amènent à deux notations finales.

La première est que on n'arrive pas à imaginer comment la CIJ aurait pu s'y prendre, pour juger de la responsabilité internationale de la Serbie pour génocide, si elle n'avait pas pu profiter de tout l'immense travail du TPIY sur la même matière, quoique recueilli à des fins de vérification de la responsabilité pénale d'individus : aurait-elle dû prendre des années et des années pour examiner des milliers de témoins, des wagons de papiers, pour mener des enquêtes systématiques de médecine légale sur place, etc. etc.? Ou aurait-elle dû s'avouer impuissante et pas outillée, s'agissant de recueillir et vérifier tous les éléments de fait nécessaires pour y appuyer ses analyses juridiques?

La seconde est que l'expérience vécue concernant les affaires relatives au génocide en Bosnie, et la division du travail qui s'est imposée entre juge international 'inter-étatique' et juge international pénal, pourraient se répéter à l'avenir, tout au moins en matière de génocide (mais non seulement), cette fois-ci entre CIJ et CPI. De surcroît, tous les crimes soumis à la compétence de la CPI étant, ainsi qu'on l'a souligné, de caractère 'systémique' (c'est-à-dire mettant presque inévitablement en cause la responsabilité internationale de l'Etat en même temps que la responsabilité pénale d'individus), il y a de quoi se mettre à rêver de mécanismes futurs appelant les deux juges à exercer leurs compétences respectives de façon coordonnée… Mais il s'agit, c'est évident, d'un futur lointain, sinon carrément utopique!

Index

For Product Safety Concerns and Information please contact our EU representative GPSR@taylorandfrancis.com
Taylor & Francis Verlag GmbH, Kaufingerstraße 24, 80331 München, Germany

www.ingramcontent.com/pod-product-compliance
Ingram Content Group UK Ltd.
Pitfield, Milton Keynes, MK11 3LW, UK
UKHW022125190926
475702UK00013B/1651
9781138254190